Author: Dr. Jake Tayler Jacobs

In loving memory to Connie Wright
TABLE OF CONTENTS

PRIVATE BANKING BLUEPRINT MASTERCLASS INTRODUCTION

- KINGDOM BANKING INTRODUCTION

KINGDOM BLUEPRINT

CH 1-Setting up your Kingdom Blueprint	**PG 5**
CH 2-Know Your Enemy (Find your Stage of Financial Cancer)	**PG 23**

KINGDOM MANAGEMENT SERIES

CH 3- Management over Ownership: Control, Alt, Delete	**PG 44**
CH 4- Why would I settle for less? Legacy Management	**PG 56**

FINDING THE MONEY: WHAT'S IN YOUR WALLET?

CH 5- The Evolution of Money: Value, Wealth and Income	**PG 63**
CH 6- Finding the Money Part 2: Income, Wealth, and Budgeting	**PG 81**
CH 7- Finding the Money Part 3: Balancing your Kingdom Budget	**PG 95**

BECOMING THE BANKER

CH 8- It's a Financing Game: The mind of a Banker: Choose your side	
CH 9- Two Types of Insurance Banks	**PG 102**

WELCOME TO KINDGDOM BANKING

CH 10- The Power in Owning my Debt	**PG 127**
CH 11- IT'S A FINANCING WORLD PART 1	**PG 133**
CH 12- IT'S A FINANCING WORLD PART 2	**PG 136**
CH 13- The Power of the Banking Game: Switch the Power in your Favor	**PG 138**
CH 14-DON'T ROB THE BANK (Why paying yourself back is important)	**PG 142**
CH 15- I AM THE BANK (Snow balling debt)	**PG 152**
CH 16- THE LAST CALL (Business, Real Estate and Lending)	**PG 161**

CREATOR & FOUNDER – Dr. JAKE TAYLER JACOBS

Jake has been educating families and college students on the topic of financial literacy since 2012. Though he was passionate about teaching on the topics of legacy building and financial freedom Jake never thought in a million years he would build a business in the financial industry especially since he went to school to be a PE Teacher. Clearly, God had other plans for him, because Jake's break in the entrepreneurial world came in 2016 when he built his financial firm on 7 napkins in a local Applebee's.

Since then, the company has evolved to a brokerage vastly growing to having clients to 17+ states and counting. He and his team of superheroes are building one of the most impactful minority-owned financial firms in the country and are dead set on helping as minorities create their own banking system. Seeing a huge disparity and misrepresentation of diversity in the financial services industry, Jake has made it his mission to change the face of the industry by having an organization that is reflective of the communities they serve.

Jake is also the author of a phenomenal financial awareness book: "We are Sick: Surviving Financial Cancer" a phenomenal financial transformation book! Jake's passion for transforming and developing the lives of anyone searching for purpose is second to none. He feels it's his calling to help as many people become truly free; free of financial struggles, free of negative peer pressure, free from self-doubt and worry and most importantly free from living a life of underachieving.

Jake created the ABS FINANCIAL INSTITUTE to continue his teaching legacy by helping families become successful. Jake has a passion for helping anyone and this platform proves just that! ABS helps more minorities become more profitable and less dependent on traditional financial teaching. His work has touched the lives of entertainers, business leaders, youth, and future college grads. He believes that the millennials will impact this world like never before.

Jake is a loving son, brother, devoted husband, and father. He wants to use his platform to not only impact people around the world but be the biggest hero in his family's eyes. Poverty knows his family all too well and he is on a mission to single-handedly propel his family to prosperity and financial peace. Jake lives in Dallas, Texas with his wife AJ and their daughter Tayler.

Welcome to PBB MASTERCLASS!

Just a little bit of about our company, **ABS** stands for **Assets Before Splurging,** and the reason why our company is named **Assets Before Splurging** is because a lot of us have a false understanding when it comes to achieving the goals that we want to achieve, driving the cars that we want to drive, getting the homes that we know that we are not ready for, or maybe getting real estate or properties that we are not properly engaged with or spending money on clothes or food. We find ourselves literally spending the very capital that can help us build assets that can change our life. So, **Assets Before Splurging** is more of a movement, more of a culture shaker to help people understand, **"IT's no longer cool to not have your stuff together, and not have $10K saved!**

"IT IS NOT COOL NO MORE!"

We want to get to the point of when people are out driving a Mercedes Benz and they are driving around telling us what they do and how much they make and all that stuff, it should be to a point of where someone would reply with "Oh that's cool but, what does your savings account look like? What assets do you have? We want to be to that point of where we are no longer impressed with material things because material things are what you are supposed to have when it comes to the cream of the crop. You are supposed to have the nice things, the nice clothes, and the quality stuff, WHEN YOU ARE READY FOR IT!

You are supposed to walk around with bling on – these are things you are supposed to have when your assets are locked in first. Examine a cash reserve, your assets, your savings before you start spending and splurging on unnecessary things. Your assets should be locked in first. Do not be overly impressed because someone is driving a Benz or Bentley, do not be impressed with nice fashionable clothes, IF you have the mind of building assets, you will know if a person is really "balling". That is the mindset of Assets Before Splurging that we must have in order for us to be in certain situations and have the success that we want.

As students and our "client cousins" going through these courses, we want you to change your mindset to Assets Before Splurging. Stop eating your wealth away, stop drinking and smoking your wealth away. Stop dating your wealth away, stop cheating your wealth away, it costs to do these things! Stop allowing other people to tell you that they can control your assets, and your capital better than you, - that is the whole point of Assets Before Splurging. Have the mindset that you can control your assets. There is no King and Queen that runs a true domain or Kingdom, that doesn't have control over their currency. If you are a true King or Queen, you need to make sure that you control your currency. Stop giving it to these financial advisors that do not take the advice they are giving you. Stop giving it to these people that have no understandings about how money really works. Stop taking advice from traditional America, conventional wisdom, and start asking deeper questions, and if you do not know about an investment and you are not sure on it, - save your money, dump it in your policy!

ABS Presents: Private Banking Blueprint

(HOW TO BECOME YOUR OWN BANK, Introduction)

Welcome to Master Class. I am your host **Jake Tayler Jacobs, *MR BE THE BANK*** and in this segment of Master Class we will be discussing how to become financially independent and debt free and in order to do that you have to understand one thing, that this is only going to work when you are ready for it to work.

Just a little bit about me, our headquarters is stationed out of Grand Prairie Texas, which is a smaller city outside of Dallas Texas. I have been teaching financial literacy for seven years, and we wrote a book entitled, "We Are Sick: Surviving Financial Cancer," where we statistically and scientifically prove how financial stress can actually and literally kill you, and we will discuss that during this segment.

To give you a little bit more about me, I am five years licensed in this industry, and we are currently now in 24 states with over 200 registered licensed brokers within our company. We are debt free and we are black owned and we are proud to say that we have never used a bank's dollars to grow the company that we are proud to boast about. So, that's what we want to talk to you about, which is how you can do the same thing for your family and how you can take control of your finances as well as your future.

There are three things we will learn during this segment:

       ✓ **We want to teach you how to insure your financial future**

       ✓ **We want to show you the real rules to the money game**

       ✓ **We want to help you become free from any financial bondage that you are in.**

The very first thing I want you to look at, and if you are able to take notes during this module, write down the word:

INTELLIGENCE

A lot of us believe that intelligence alone is all you need in order to be successful. We think that intelligence is the ability to acquire information. We think that intelligence is getting a degree. We think that intelligence is reading a book. We think that intelligence is having somebody coach you and teach you. But all that is only one portion of the full definition of intelligence.

Intelligence is the ability to acquire and apply knowledge and skills.

What's to acquire? It means to consume or retain something and to come into possession of something. So if intelligence is the ability to acquire information and apply that new information, then that is the full definition of intelligence. And if we cannot do that – then guess what? It's going to be hard for us to progress and it's going to be hard for you to be successful if you only think that success and intelligence is simply acquiring information. We have a lot of people that do that right? We have a lot people who boasts their degrees. We got a lot of people who boasts how many books they read. We got a lot of people who boasts their certifications. We got a lot of people who boasts that they're extremely informationally intelligent and they always have a comeback for anything that you say.

But the Bible says that a poor man's wisdom is despised and his words are not heard. Which means that if somebody is poor and they have all the right information in order for them to **"quote on quote"** succeed, and they have not applied it into their life, that lets you know either they don't know what they are talking about or the information is wrong or you shouldn't be listening to them. **Do you agree?**

If they have all the information and all the success tactics and are saying they are successful and I do not see that happening in your life, there is a problem. Either the information is wrong or the person is a little slow, or I shouldn't be talking or listening to you because you can't apply that information. **Is that safe to say?**

What does currency mean to you? Currency means money. One of the biggest things that we have to understand when we talk about currency – it's one of the only things that we consider money. Money is something that controls our entire livelihood but when we think about that – we do not think about how it affects our day to day living. Most of us have no idea of what currency is.

First write down the word currency and draw a line in the middle:

Money is supposed to "RUN CONSISTENTLY" like water.

When you are thinking about it running consistently and when it comes to money and when it comes to the things that we want to achieve in life, and we have to know that in life our money has to be always moving. Your money is supposed to be moving like the water system.

When you think about the water system, how does the water system move? It's always moving, it's current, it's always flowing. When you think about water, it goes from precipitation, it falls off and has puddles, it's in oceans, lakes, streams, and it evaporates and turns into clouds and back to rain. So when you think about water, our entire eco-system is supposed to flow the exact same way. The water in the eco-system is supposed to be always flowing, moving, and going.

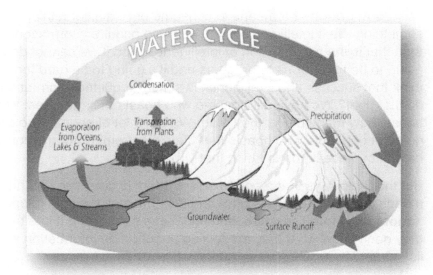

If you think about the blood inside of your body – if your blood stops, what happens to you? You die, right? If water were to ever stop, what happens to the eco-system? It dies right? Think about the dead sea, nothing alive lives in the dead sea. Why? Because the water doesn't go, it doesn't leave, it just sits. So if you think about anything that you want to accomplish when it comes to finances, you understand that currency is supposed to always be flowing, always be moving, and always supposed to be going. And if it stops, it is not in your best benefit and guess what? It is actually working against you.

As one of our brokers always says, when the heat of life heats up water, it evaporates. But the problem is that the water in most cases in our life with that currency never comes back with the heat of life.

What is the heat of life?

- ✓ The heat of life is bills coming up out of the blue.
- ✓ The heat of life is when your car stops.
- ✓ The heat of life is when you got to make some sort of unexpected payment.
- ✓ The heat of life is daycare bills and rent.

When it comes to that car payment, how to eat, where to go, all these things heat up are pools of water where our banking system is and it literally evaporates out of our bank account. And it rains into everyone else's bank account and it never comes back to us.

How many of us can admit that we're living paycheck to paycheck?

How many of us can admit that our water (our currency) is raining into someone else's bank account?

What is raining into someone else's account?

Raining into someone else's account is when your money is going to:

You see your money is going into everybody's bank account and it's hard for us to flow back. How many of us are having that problem where that money is evaporating and it is raining into somebody else's bank account and it is not coming back to you?

Your money is going to:

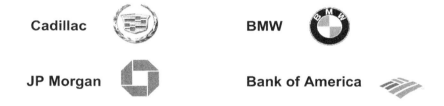

Your money is going to all of these things and it is not coming back to you as fast as it is leaving you. How many of us can admit that? These are all of the things that are messing up our eco-system. There are four entities that are stealing your money.

- The first entity stealing your money is You.
- The second entity stealing your money is the Bank.
- The third entity stealing your money is the Government.
- The last entity stealing your money is Wall Street.

These are what I call the **four horsemen** and these are the four thieves that we are going to be talking about.

Let's start with talking about "YOU."

What we all have to understand is financial cancer is killing us. I wrote a book entitled *"We Are Sick: Surviving Financial Cancer"*. *Where I **statistically** and **scientifically** prove how financial stress is the number one cause of death in black America.*

Let me prove it to you:

Reference: CDC.gov

According to the **cdc.gov** - the number one cause of death is heart disease in black and brown America.

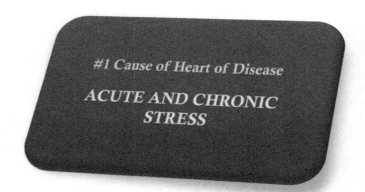

Now, let's talk about acute stress:

- Acute Stress is **short-term stress**.
- So examples of acute stress would be any stress you suffer from for a short period of time like a traffic jam, an argument with your spouse, an unkind criticism from your boss or someone breaking into your house when you aren't there.
- **The body is good at handling acute episodes of stress.**

- We are **designed to recover quickly** from short-term stress.
- That's actually how experts define **resilience**: how quickly you recover from an acute episode of stress. Your blood pressure, heart rate, breathing rate and levels of muscle tension may skyrocket for a short while, but for most people, these markers of stress quickly revert back to their normal (pre-stressful event) levels.

Now let's talk about chronic stress:

- Chronic stress is **Long-term stress**.
- However if you are a bus driver, cop or a regular worker and you get stuck in numerous traffic jams *every day*, or if you are in a bad relationship and you argue with your spouse *constantly*, or you work for a *toxic boss*, or you live in a high crime neighborhood and break-ins are relatively common, all the examples of *acute stress* I cited above can potentially transform into examples of **chronic stress.**

- The body ISN'T so good at handling chronic stress. Over time, chronic stress gradually increases our resting heart rate, blood pressure, breathing rate and levels of muscle tension so the body has to work even harder when it's at rest to keep you functioning normally.

- In other words, chronic stress creates a new normal inside your body. And this new normal can eventually lead to a host of health problems including heart disease, diabetes, chronic pain, high blood pressure and depression.

#1 Cause of ACUTE and CHRONIC STRESS

FINANCIAL HOPELESSNESS

- **76% of Americans live paycheck to paycheck**
- **Most marriages end in divorce because of financial stress.**
- **Most arguments are derived from financial stress.**

So we know this feeling and to be financially hopeless is to feel like:

- **you're never not going to pay debt**
- **you're never not going to have to pay your student loans**
- **you're never not going to have some type of car finance**
- **you're always going to have a mortgage**
- **you're always going to have these financial troubles**

How many can say we have known or thought about some sort of financial debt and said, "That is just the way it is always going to be." How many can admit to that? Be honest with yourself, is there something pertaining to financial woes that are always around you such as financial hopelessness?

Debt is literally us signing away and deciding to be somebody's slave. We are literally signing a seven-year indentured servant plan, or a ten-year indentured servant plan and when you think about it, every single day, who is the first person you think about paying? You think about serving whoever gave you that Master Card. Just think about serving that very entity that gave you that master card. So you are swiping Master's card alright. You may be swiping somebody else's money and it's causing us to put ourselves in financial straits that you have no business being in.

9

So Let's Recap:

- **Heart disease IS THE #1 CAUSE OF DEATH IN BLACK AMERICA**
- **Acute and Chronic Stress IS THE #1 CAUSE OF Heart Disease**
- **Financial Hopelessness IS THE #1 CAUSE OF Acute and Chronic Stress**
- **DEBT aka FINANCIAL CANCER IS THE #1 CAUSE OF FINANCIAL HOPELESSNESS**

✓ Are you sick and tired of having this same thing happen generation after generation?

✓ Are you ready for a solution?

✓ As you can see I just proved my theory of the number one cause of death in Black America. Is it safe to say per hypothesis that it is not the foods that we eat but it's the information financially that we digest that cause us to be in these situations to have this heart disease? So when I tell you guys that Financial Cancer is the #1 **cause of death in Black America – I'm serious.**

So let me tell you that I am 100% against debt. There is no such thing as good debt and do not let anyone tell you that. I will prove it.

Here is what debt does – debt seems small, but what happens with debt just like cancer, IT GROWS!

It begins to metastasize everywhere in our lives! It begins to metastasize in our emotions! It begins to metastasize in our relationships! It begins to metastasize in our sleeping!

You can't sleep, you toss and you turn, you are anxious and you have anxiety, you are having sleepless nights and you are literally losing your mind and years of your life because of this. So to believe that debt is a good thing is like you believing that cancer is good for your body!

Let's move on….

They tell us that the reason we are supposed to borrow from the bank is because you want to leverage other people's money. When you do not have money, you go and borrow money from the bank. That's what they tell us. When you do not have the funds what do they tell you to do? **Just borrow it!**

What has your mother told you? What has your granny and everyone said? You got to have good credit. Because when you got good credit, **"Master"** is going to take care of you forever! Isn't that what they have told you?

So let's talk a bit more about leveraging. Because most of us believe that we do not have enough money. When we talk about life time income, the average American makes $1.5M over their life time. (This is for the average black and brown American)

Do you know where the majority of our money goes? $1,082,577 of that $1.5M it literally goes to debt and interest payments. So there is no wonder why we only have $162K at retirement. Because we literally gave $1,082,577 away to JP Morgan. Did you know that these banking institutions were created by families? So we gave our money to JP Morgan, we gave it to Chase Bank, we gave it to Bank of America – and there is no question why we are dealing with what we are dealing with financially. The average American in general buys seven cars in their lifetime. That is over $105K that we spend on car debt. The average American gets two homes in their lifetime – your starter home with a little family or no family if you want to own a home. And then a home to be able to appease all of your family. That is the average of $350K just to purchase two homes.

So when you think about the interest of what we would've paid over time, all this debt would've been $425K on average. That is on INTEREST PAYMENTS ALONE!

So no wonder in all the books you got, no wonder all the financial advisors, no wonder entrepreneurial magazines, Forbes Magazines, and all these other magazines they keep telling you to borrow. Why? Because America was built and the Federal Reserve runs America. So they need us to borrow and lend and borrow and lend. So no wonder you have all these publications that push the narrative of borrowing because they know you are going to give 1000% of your money away only to look back at your life at ages between 65 and 70 and say where did my money go? You know what happens next? Your kids begin to adopt the same mentality. Which is what? It causes us to be in the same situation that our family has been in for years and decades to come. It's called the new age slavery.

Let's look at this example. There is one thing on each side that I want you to pay attention to:

WHY MOST FAMILIES STRUGGLE?	WHY FEW FAMILIES ACTUALLY SUCCEED!
1. Procrastination.	1. Proactively Working.
2. Instant Gratification.	2. Future Planning.
3. Living Beyond Your Means.	3. Creating Surplus Income.
4. Make Decisions Based on Emotions.	4. Make Decisions Based on Facts, Research & logic.
5. Easily Influenced.	5. Stick to the plan.
6. Access To The Wrong Information.	6. Access To The Right Information.
	ABSBROKERS

Why Most Families Struggle? It say **#4** but it should be **#1** which is: Most families struggle because they make decisions based on emotions. Why? Because it feels good. It felt right. Let me tell you something. IF it is from God, you would not be in debt to have it! If it were truly a gift from God – he would not put you in debt so that you can have it! Being in debt is being slaved to it or something. So stop saying God gifted you with stuff.

- **That mortgage is a debt! That isn't from God.**
- **That car is a debt! That isn't from God.**
- **That credit card is a debt! That isn't from God.**

So stop saying God blessed you with these things as it is causing a contradiction even to yourself because when you find yourself in financial straits and you can't find your way out as there is a reason why because God was never in that debt.

The reason why families succeed is because they make decisions based on Facts, Research, and logic. What gets us into situations is we say that we deserve this house or I deserve this car, or I deserve these shoes, and I worked hard for this. But you want to go in debt to get it. How does this move your family forward? These are things that we got to assess! That's why we are able to see that the number one reason why we can't get ahead financially is because of the person that looks back at us in that mirror!

The second thief is the Bank

Let me tell you how smooth the bank is – they are so smooth that they get you to give all your money to them and sit it with them and they have the audacity to tell you that we are only going to give you .01% for your money. And because we signed off on a contract, they give us .1% to use our own money! Then they go and make 6% to 28% on the money that we gave them to fund their business.

TRADITIONAL BANK, JUST A POOL OF LEVERAGED MONEY

IF I told you that I would hold your money for you, and you found out I was making 6 to 28% on your money and I was only giving you .1% -

Would you keep giving your money to me?

It's funny that everyone says no, but we do it every single day.

Can the banks survive without our money?

IF the answer is no, we have to understand that they can't survive without our money. However they have created a society where we feel like we need them. When in actuality they need us.

Let's look at a mortgage.

How many of us were taught that buying a home was a good investment?

I am about to prove to you how buying a home is one of the worst investments ever created and propaganda to us by a bank.

As you can see in the illustration the right, this is a $200K home and with this home, you're getting an APR interest rating of 4% charged to you on this $200K home.

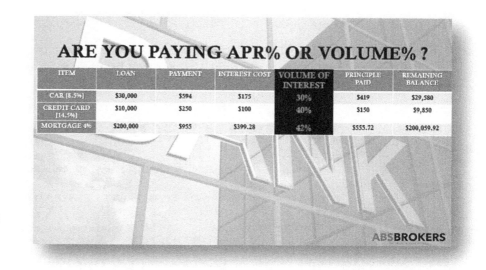

The average percentage for black and brown Americans is around 3.99% so we just rounded up to 4%. The monthly payment would have been $955 a month.

So let's do some quick math:

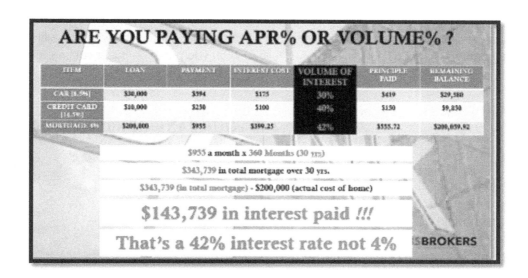

$955 a month (mortgage) for a 30-year term is $343,739 that you paid for a $200K home. That's $143,739 in interest that you paid on a home! You paid over 42% in interest – NOT 4% that they marketed to you!

That's a scam!

Let me say it again!

I'm telling you if you do $143,739 and divide that into the cost of the home, which is $343,739 you will realize that you actually paid 42% for that home in interest and not 4%

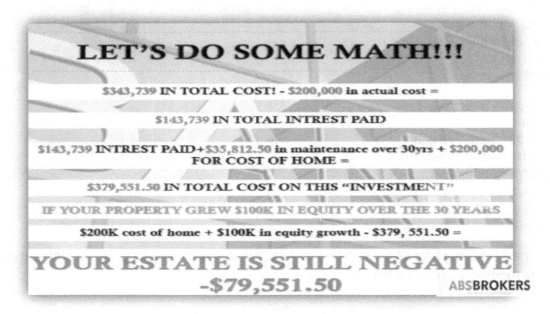

Isn't the purpose of an investment to turn a profit? We are going to see if this actual example of an investment turns a profit. So you paid $379K for this home. Let's say this $200K home borrowed $100K worth of equity. Equity is "quote on quote" the value being put on the home because of the market. If you subtract the $200k value of the home plus the $100K equity minus what you actually paid for the full cost of the home – you're still negative -$79,551.50 of what you put in on this investment.

How is this a good investment?

Now watch this – the only way you can get this equity out of the house is if you borrow against it, such as refi the home, and you are now in debt to the bank **again**. Or you sell your home, and the odds of someone spending 30 years in a home, only to sell the home is slim to none. It's not a good investment, you went to the bank to get one home and you ended up purchasing two.

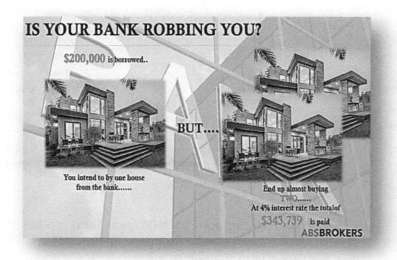

I'm trying to break your theology.

I'm trying to break what you consider to be common knowledge. That was the second thief. The third thief – who we all know is the Government and we know the government takes our money.

So let's look at the dollar: WHERE DOES MONEY GO?

So when we look at the dollar and realize that 34.5% of our money goes to Bank and Finance Charges, debts, and interest.

36% of your money goes to government and taxes. Some of you may say that taxes do not hit me like that and I would like to say that you are lying.

You got food tax, liquor tax, medicinal taxes, and gas tax. If you live in a city that has tolls – you have toll taxes. There is tax everywhere. You also have shopping tax and sales tax. Everything that you can imagine has some type of tax on it. So you will end up paying 36% of your money going to government and state taxes and then they force you to live on 29.5% of your money. How crazy is that? So before it is all said and done, you are literally living off 29%
And your crazy financial advisor tells you that if you save 5% to 10% **out of that** 29% you will be financially healthy when you retire.

I am going to show you how you can reduce in these two areas:

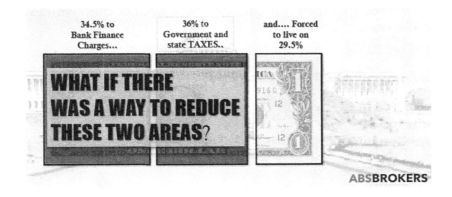

But first I have to show you this last thief. This next is so **cold** that we give our money to them willingly without ever questioning where our money is going.

It's called investment funds, **401K's**, hedge funds, and mutual funds. Most of us that do the **401K** do not know that the money is in the market. For the most part, those of us that are doing the **401K** we do not know where our money is going. You have no idea what companies these **401K's** and mutual funds use; what they invest in and if they go against what you believe. Most of us just give our money to **401K's** and mutual funds and you have no idea who is managing your funds other than the company name. You don't know the history, and we don't know the person. If I were to tell you to let me manage your money and take it out of your account and don't worry about who's managing it and how it's being managed, and where we are investing our money. Just give me your money. Now if I were to ask and say it like that, would you just give me your money? You didn't know who I was, you didn't know what my habits in my life were. I could be someone that doesn't do right with money but I have a management fund that literally manages your funds. And I am charging you 2% plus 25% capital gains and transactional fees that don't have to be shown to you and when I ask you where is your money with your **401K**? The majority of us do not even know how much is in our **401K** nor how much we put in there. And that is exactly how they like you to be – **BLIND!!**

Because when you are blind to it, you do not know you are being screwed! And they just tell you to keep investing, it's going to turn around. If you know the rules to the game and you know that they will not find out the rules to the game – more than likely you're not going to tell anybody the rules if they are not going to do the research on their own? Because you are rigged to win. So why we are funding these funds without asking real questions because we are scared to sound dumb. They're literally funding their kids, kids, kids, college fund, and if they lose all of the money in the fund, and if they legally turn a profit, they will not go to jail for it. While they have jets, Lamborghinis, and children in private school, our kids are in public school and barely making it and getting taught backwards information – and we are just funding away. And we are just singing away that tomorrow it will be better! Putting it off that you will research tomorrow. But this is what we deal with and we got to get to the point of we are tired of being mishandled, abused, and misused.

We have got to get to a point of where we stop allowing people to misuse us because we are scared of sounding dumb. I would rather you store and stash your money to where you become researched in something – remember I told you successful families only move on research, facts and logic. We don't move on emotions. And they know if they can control our emotions, they can control our paychecks.

I am about to teach you a new reserve. This reserves is so cold that it _kills_ the banks.

 Find A New Pool of Money that gives you the best of both worlds that work like both the Bank and Wallstreet

- ✓ **This pool has been used over 200 years**
- ✓ **Tax-Favored by IRS CODE** 7702, 101(a), 72(c), **TAMRA, TEFRA, & DEFRA**
- ✓ **Guaranteed 4% and safe**
- ✓ **No Stock Market Danger**
- ✓ **Liquid and Convenient**
- ✓ **You control 100%**

Your money can grow tax free; you can access it tax free, and your family can access it tax free when you leave this earth. You control it 100% and you call all the shots. People try to guess wealth, but the truth is there is no guessing. They try to make it sound difficult, and it's not difficult at all. And I am about to prove to you with just one instrument inside your portfolio – you can guarantee wealth for yourself as well as legacies to come.

First let me explain something. Traditional wisdom has taught us to put our money where? The bank right? That's what traditional wisdom has taught us. We've come to the point that we realize that maybe putting our money and keeping our reserve, is not a good place for the bank Where is another place they tell us to put our cash reserves or store money? Stock market right? So they say put your money in the banks and put your savings in the stock market. Right? So let's see if these very entities that tell us where to put our money, are actually putting their money where they are telling us to put ours. I don't take advice from millionaires and billionaires; I look at what the banks are doing and I mimic them because the banks are controlling society. Let's see if the banks actually do what they tell us to do. The banks are the one that fund these financial institutions. The banks are the ones who fund college educations and finance programs. The banks are the ones who fund text books. The banks are the ones who fund Forbes Magazine, Huffington Post and many other entities. So why would I take advice from someone who is getting funding from the bank? I need to be getting advice from the bank entity itself. I want to see what the bank is doing!

When you hear banks say they are backed by the FDIC – and you think the bank has insurance! Did you know that the FDIC is funded by the taxpayers?
So the very people who back up and insure the banks, are actually tax payers – us!

And because it's backed by us the taxpayers, they have to show the assets and liabilities to us the tax payers.

Did you know that?

So let's look up these same institutions so you can see how they operate but first choose a bank that you want to research, because I want to show you that they have taken the handcuffs off but they still have us enslaved.

Let's see where the banks put their money.

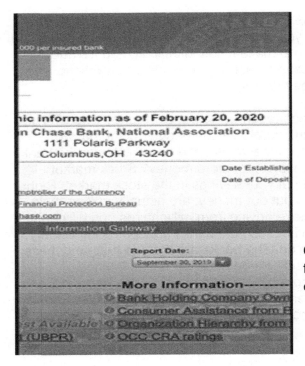

We are going to take a look at Chase Bank. The illustration shows this was a recent search as of 2/20/2020 for Chase Bank, National Association.

On this next illustration below, remember we have to add **three zeros**. Take a look at **line 28** which is common stock.

28	Common stock	2,028,000	1,785,000
29	Surplus	110,292,000	99,147,000
30	Undivided profits	132,818,000	114,166,000

So if we add three zeros and look at the entire line 28, we will see – they put over **$2 Billion dollars** into common stock. So as you can see they tell us to place all of our money into stocks? **Let's see if the banks do the same thing.**

Remember, the Bible says out of all thy getting, get an understanding. So let's get an understanding, **$2 Billion dollars** seems like a lot if you do not have anything to compare it to.

Let's compare it to a line:

*Remember to add three zeros

Line 41 – Life Insurance Assets $11.5 Billion Dollars in cash reserve

41 Life insurance assets	11,570,000

Now they put **$2 Billion** in stocks, but **$11 Billion** in cash reserves. That is six times more in life insurance than they do in the stock market. But they tell us to put ten times of our money in stocks! Ten times of our money in the stocks if we want to get rich and to focus on that.

Isn't that what they tell us?

Why are they putting so much money in life insurance? Why would they store so much money in life insurance? *That doesn't make sense.*

I'm teaching you how to become the bank, but to become the bank, you got to mimic the bank! Let's take a look at this article written by a Caucasian lady – Mary L Heen, **"Ending Jim Crow Life Insurance Rates"** This article is going to give us evidence of why we don't know insurance works this way. In the article we will look at paragraph 19:

➢ Were you taught that life insurance only works if you die?

Insurance companies provided slaveholders coverage for damage to or death of their slaves at rates substantially higher than for white lives and imposed certain coverage restrictions, including confining policy amounts to two-thirds of actual value, and covering only a limited term of years.[44] Although emancipation ended the slavery-era

[38] DREW GILPIN FAUST, THIS REPUBLIC OF SUFFERING: DEATH AND THE AMERICAN CIVIL WAR 251 (2008)
[39] *Id.* (quoting COHEN, *supra* note 1, at 205).
[40] *Id.*
[41] COHEN, *supra* note 1, at 213.
[42] *Id.* at 212–13. The preceding five censuses "had gradually departed from the Constitution's bare requirement to count the total population, first by creating, then by progressively refining, categories based on age, sex, and color." *Id.* at 176–77; *see also* MARGO J. ANDERSON, THE AMERICAN CENSUS: A SOCIAL HISTORY (1988). The historical roots of a quantification, Cohen argues, reveal how the "concerns of the moment led to a reformulation, along numerical lines," of a subject about which people were formerly "content to be imprecise." COHEN, *supra* note 1, at 207. What people chose to measure "reveals not only what was important to them but what they wanted to understand and, often, what they wanted to control." *Id.* at 206.

So Jake, you are saying, "That slaveowners had life insurance on us? They didn't put that in the history books." Yes but you are missing the best part – it not only says coverage for the death but for the damaged too! They told us that life insurance only works best if we die.

Now what's damage?

✓ **Heart Attack**   ✓ **Stroke**   ✓ **Cancer**   ✓ **Renal Failure**   ✓ **Dismemberment of Body**

Following the Civil War, race-based practices first emerged in a specialized form of life insurance marketed to low-income working people. Beginning in the 1870s, newly formed American life insurance companies, including Prudential, Metropolitan Life, and John Hancock,[55] known later as the "Big Three,"[56] sold small individual policies to a growing market of low-income wage earners.[57] This type of life insurance, called "industrial" or "burial" insurance, provided protection against the financial burden of a last illness and burial for the "industrious" classes.[58]

Although rates and benefits varied by age, they did not vary, at least initially, by race of the insured, and were typically issued with fewer restrictions than other forms of life insurance.[59] Policies covered poor workers and their families, including newly emancipated slaves, women, industrial workers, and their children.[60] Industrial insurance agents typically sold policies door-to-door in an assigned geographical area or "debit,"

[1] KELLER, *supra* note 47, at 2–11 (describing the reasons for the growth of the American life insurance enterprise from in the 1840s through the Civil War); *see also* SHEPARD B. CLOUGH, A CENTURY OF AMERICAN LIFE INSURANCE: A HISTORY OF THE MUTUAL LIFE INSURANCE COMPANY OF NEW YORK, 1843–943, at 4–16 (1946).
[2] KELLER, *supra* note 47, at 194; *see also* discussion *supra* at note 22.

As a teacher by education and certification, and what I have learned by providing research or new breaking information – not only do you have to provide the research, but you have to provide supporting research *for the research* to prove your point. The reason why banks use insurance is because they trust insurance more than they do their own bank accounts. The banking institutions actually control the stock markets, and they don't even trust their own system.

Let's see why……

In Google search type in: what is bank owned life insurance?

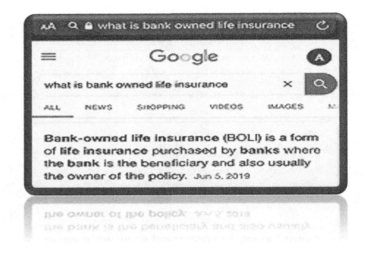

Let's take another look at this using a search with Investopedia:

Now look at the sentence that says, **"such an insurance is used as a tax-shelter for the financial institutions"**

In order for something to be a shelter, it has to protect something from something. It has to be a protection of these outside things that can potentially hurt it! Whatever the something is, it must be so airtight and so secure that nothing can break through.

Remember, successful families move on facts, research, and logic. So ask yourself this question using logic: **Is this something that needs protection from taxes? What is this something that needs to be protected from taxes?** MONEY!

That's why the banks store money inside the insurance reserves. Because they know that the money would do a lot better inside a reserve than it would sitting inside of their own bank accounts, or in the stock market that they created!

The next portion to examine states, **"which leverages out it's tax-free savings provisions as funding mechanisms for employee benefits"**

So Jake, you are saying when anybody stores their money inside of the insurance policies – the money grows tax free? And it's tax free to access it? Money can be inside of a shelter and it can grow tax free and we can access it tax free while protecting it from taxes? YES!

If it is properly designed. That's why you can't go to your old insurance agent and say I learned something!

Because if they knew this something, they would have taught you. They are unable to teach and show you something that they have no clue about!

But if they knew it and did not teach you, then that is the person, but if they learned and it and try to teach you to become their client, *simply; you need to be working with ABS because that's what we do all day every day!*

So Jake is this really something that is crazy? No! Because if any of us went to a shelter aren't the beds free? Isn't food at the shelter free? Everything inside of the shelter is free.

So is saving your money inside of the tax shelter of insurance. That's why they do it and guess what? You can do it too!

Is it making money? Yes, not only is it making money but is **guaranteed** money!

We have to first redefine what insurance is because we all thought it was a scam – because we didn't know what it was.

Insurance is *a protection from financial loss. It is a form of risk management, primarily used to hedge against the risk of a contingent of uncertain loss.*

The fact that the banks place seven, eight, even eighteen times in insurance than they do in stock markets, lets you know what? That they know the market is a risk.

Just like the Bank, just like Wall Street, and just like the Government, your insurance policy has to get monthly deposits into its system in order for it to work. That is no different than any other system. The insurance company has to grow your money and give you a guaranteed 4% on your reserve.

❖ **Does your bank give you a guaranteed 4%?**

See if you can compare this bank to bank –

❖ **Does your bank share profits with you?**

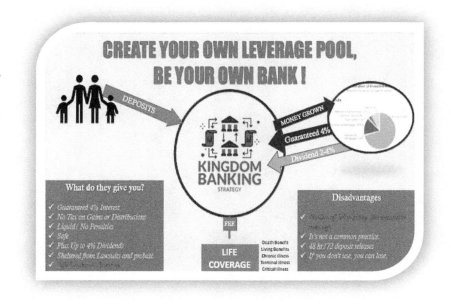

The answer is no. Well inside this insurance reserve, if you store your cash inside *the* insurance reserve, not only do they give you a guaranteed 4% but they share the profits of the insurance company with you. Typically around 2% to 4% profits. So that's 4% to 8% of interest that you can get on your cash reserve just by storing your money there.

If you go through any type of lawsuit, child support, or any type of probate, **will your bank be able to have you protected from those things?**

> **No bank can protect you from lawsuit or probate. If you keep your money inside insurance reserves it also protects you from probate, child support, or lawsuits, the money in your cash reserve inside your insurance policy cannot be touched. It's safe and its liquid!**

Jake can I access this policy? Yes! If it is properly structured right, you will be able to access the money you put in this reserve in 31 days. Not when you retire, and not at age 65, with a penalty.

❖ **Do you think your bank will give your beneficiary three to sometimes ten times more if you die other than what's in your account?**

❖ **Will your bank give three to ten times more that you put into your family if you die tax free?**

Let me give you an example - and notice that I said **guaranteed**. The illustration shows the guaranteed on left side which is 4% plus the dividend side on the right.

		Guaranteed Value			Non-guaranteed.		
Age	End of Year	Contract Premium + Riders	Cash Value	Death Benefit	Contract Premium + Riders	Cash from - Policy	= Cash Outlay
32	1	24,000	11,991	1,238,168	24,000	0	24,000

Let's look at **20 years**. There is a client of ABS that puts in $2K a month into his insurance bank. We call this an insurance bank, and he makes around $80K a year, although not a rich person, he understood the concept and didn't question it. So he put $480K into his bank in 20 years.

46	15	24,000	357,437	2,004,346	24,000
47	16	24,000	389,758	2,046,878	24,000
48	17	24,000	422,760	2,088,054	24,000
49	18	24,000	457,639	2,127,911	24,000
50	19	24,000	493,249	2,166,487	24,000
51	20	24,000	530,763	2,203,818	24,000
		480,000			480,000

With your regular traditional personal bank – if you put $480K in, will they guarantee that you will have $530K in 20 years? Will your bank give you guaranteed growth? And notice something, it also says $2.2M – that's his death benefit.

Now when he dies, *because we all die*, his family will be able to get $2.2M – he only put in $480K in his reserve, **but his family will get** $2,203,818! Will your bank give you $2.2M when you only put in $480K? This illustration does not show your bank sharing dividends with you, this is only what they guarantee.

Now look at this illustration. This person put in the same $480K over 20 years, but the difference is the additions of $96K …. that $96,436 is the profits that the insurance company shares with the policyholder. We already know that the banks do not share any profits with us.

This person put $480K inside their insurance bank and with dividends of $641K that they can use at will.

24,000	0	24,000	9,273	442,205	2,209,562
24,000	0	24,000	10,376	487,319	2,284,791
24,000	0	24,000	11,534	535,876	2,361,495
24,000	0	24,000	12,795	586,892	2,439,728
24,000	0	24,000	14,127	641,661	2,519,610
480,000	0	480,000	96,436		

So how does it work?

You put $500K into your policy and 60% to 70% of your money stays in your cash reserve. Because of laws it has to be according to tax law, or they will consider it an investment account and you lose your shelter. Because you are buying insurance, you have to buy a certain amount of insurance that validates why you are putting money in the reserve. So typically its about 30% of your money pays for the actual policy, and the other money stays in your cash reserve inside of the policy. So the 30% pays for your death benefit, or if you got sick and the other 60 -70% stays in the cash reserve.

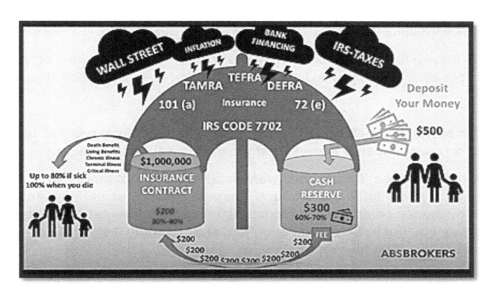

That means you put $500 in, $300 stays in your cash reserve. So what happens every month? Your cash reserve fills up and you get a guaranteed 4% plus 2% to 4% on top of that. And that's not even the part on banking.

Now we are going to see how to use this cash reserve as a bank, and I am bashing and disproving conventional wisdom. We are taught that when you do not have money, you need to have good what? Credit. So this is the backwards information that we believe. Let's say you borrow money to purchase a car only to spend years paying it back. And then what happens? After you have paid it back after all these years – what do you do with the car? You trade it in, right? You trade the car in because you are back at **zero** and you have to do what again? You have to take out another loan. So they have created a perpetuating system to where you will need them for life.

So you have paid this money over time for all these years, only to end back at $0

Not only did you pay interest to the bank, you also lost interest that you could've made if your money were in an environment where it could grow. Do you see how backwards that is! And we say that this is a system that God blessed us! What's the next best thing? Pay for it in cash.

You spent all these years saving your money and you pay for it in cash for a depreciating asset only to end back at $0 – then you do it again, trade the car in – *only to end back at zero*.

> **That's better than getting into debt because you are not paying all that interest. But you are still losing interest that the money could be earning.**
>
> **How? It's because if the money were in an account that pays you 6% interest and you literally liquidated the account, you paid cash for something, and those years that the money could have been getting compound interest are now gone. Because you got to start back over, and start building it again, to do the same perpetuating thing all over again.**

In the system that we teach you, we are teaching you how to grow your money and save it in the reserve. Guess what? When you die **because we all do**, your family can't get that property you own, and they can't get the car because they have to sell it to pay back debt and they end up back at zero. And when you die because you only keep cash because you don't have any life insurance – so your family will only get what's in your savings in cash, and you are in a losing situation all over again. The system is only a scam if you know the rules to play.

The system I am about to teach you, is in the rules of money and wealth – you will be able to grow your money and borrow from it, make the purchases that you want and pay yourself back without ever losing the momentum or integrity of your dollar.

❖ **Would you love to have your money in a system where you can borrow from it and it never takes you back to zero?**

❖ **If you have your money in a regular traditional bank account and you have $100K in this bank account and if you wanted to borrow $50K – what would you be left with? You would be left with $50K**

I am about to show you how to put your money in insurance and the cash reserve and you can have the $100K in there, but when you borrow $50K – you will still have $100K.

What we have to understand is just like any banking institution, just like any business, you have to capitalize your money system first and you have to put money into it and you have to get the system ready for you. And with anything, it takes money to get it going, and if currency is supposed to be moving, and currency is an example of energy, you got to put your energy into this system so it can start working for you.

In this illustration, the person has $100K in their cash reserve and they want access to $50K and the insurance company is going to verify if they have the $50K in their account, as well as the death benefit.

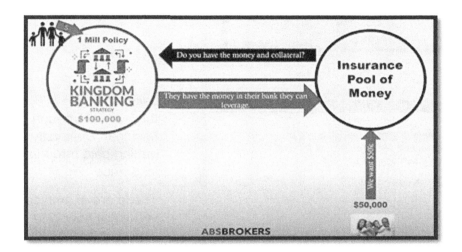

And if they do, the insurance company is going to give them $50K of their money and will not touch your $50K. What they will do to your $50K is they will place a lien on your money.

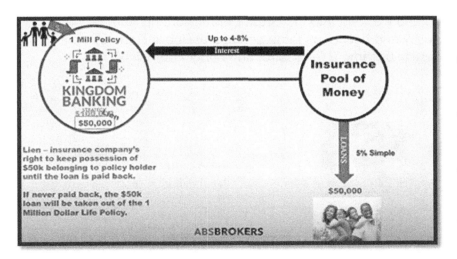

What is a lien?

The insurance company's right to keep possession of $50K belonging to the policy holder until the loan is paid back.

- You are still getting interest on the full $100K even if you borrow $50K

5

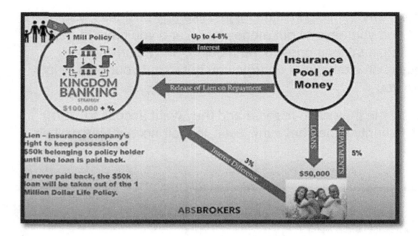

So when you repay back the loan, they release the lien on your money and you have access to the full $400K again, plus all the interest that you would've gotten the entire way.

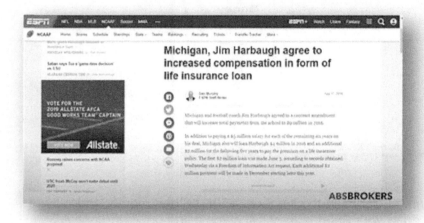

Jake, who else is doing this? Jim Harbaugh of Michigan University is getting paid through insurance.

These are examples to let you know how long they have been doing this.

Claude Boettcher –

In 1929, when the stock market crashed and we went into the Great Depression, he literally borrowed money out of his insurance policy and bought up large portions of Public companies and when the market grew again, he literally became a Billionaire, and bought up half of Colorado. All from insurance!

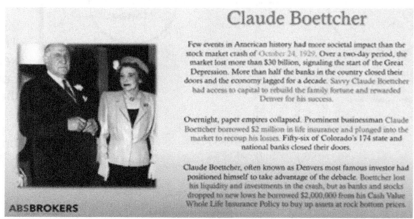

Ray Kroc – Franchised McDonalds and got his entire business up and running using insurance.

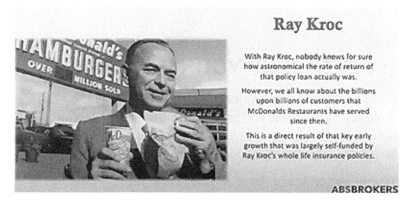

Here are a few more examples of how more people used their insurance policies to fund businesses.

FOLLOW THOSE BEFORE YOU

- Walt Disney borrowed from his life insurance in 1953 to help fund Disneyland, his first theme park, when no banker would lend him the money.

- Following the 1929 stock market crash, famous retailer J. C. Penney borrowed from his life insurance policies to help meet the company payroll. Had he not had ready access to capital, the company probably would have been forced to close its doors, adding even more people to the unemployment line.

- The Pampered Chef used her life insurance loan for initial capitalization

- In 2002, Doris Christopher sold her kitchen tool company, the Pampered Chef to Warren Buffett for a reported $900 million. Seven years earlier, she launched the company with a life insurance policy loan.

- Foster Farms was founded in 1939 when Max and Verda Foster borrowed $1,000 against their life insurance policy to buy an 80-acre farm near Modesto, CA.

- Senator John McCain secured initial campaign financing for his presidential bid by using his life insurance policy as collateral.

ABSBROKERS

You have just been given proof of other people and Billionaires who adopted this system and won with it. Now Lets learn how to fully become the bank!!!

CHAPTER 1: SETTING UP YOUR KINGDOM BLUEPRINT

Today we are going to be setting up your Kingdom BLUEPRINT and it is very important that you all know how I (Jake / Instructor) rock and roll and I am more so concerned about developing the entire version of yourself because that's how we get to the point so you can become financially stable and financially independent.

YOU will get to the Banking portion I promise you... But first we are going to re-educate you on money, but the very first thing you have to do is set up your Kingdom Blueprint.

One of the very first thing I want you to understand is that when it comes to having success in business, in marriage, in relationships, in family, in life, in spirituality, you have to have a destination of where you are going.

Siri or the person behind maps does not work unless you put in the destination! Siri can't course correct you until she knows where you are going. I can't help you get to where you want to go if you do not know where you want to go. If you say hey Jake, " I want to be wealthy, wealthy!" But you cannot be wealthy unless you know exactly where you want to go. IF you are in an airport and you tell the stewardess that you want to go somewhere, they will ask, "Sir or Ma'am, where are you going?" Your response, "The sky is the limit." They will look at you like you are crazy and say sir, or ma'am, you either pick a destination, or you have to go stage left, because somebody else knows exactly where they want to go."

You have to know that once you pick a destination, there is a price that comes with it. I can travel in the back of the plane, I can allow the airline company to choose my seat and I be by a screaming baby the whole time that makes the flight not as bearable or not as pleasant, or I could ride coach, I could ride on Spirit Airlines. I could ride first class, I can ride business class, or I could ride on a jet, but I am still going on the same destination, however the more comfortable the seat, the higher the price you got to pay.

The more comfortable you want your experience, the higher the price you got to pay, more money you got to put on the table. Which means you got to get good at managing your resources so that you can have the quality of life! That's what you want! You want to make sure that if you are going to live this life on earth, you want the best of the best and it comes with a price and one of those price tags are we got to understand where we are going, what it is going to take for me to get there and how do I want to get there. Do I want to get there on a plane or in a van? Do I want to ride a bike, or do I want to walk? A lot of us feel like we are not getting anywhere because you don't know exactly where you want to go. Which is why we have to set up our Kingdom Blueprint so that we can determine where we want to go.

Everyone right now is either on a computer in a house, in a car, in an apartment or in a building right now. All of the things I just named, had to be created on a blueprint first. You would never trust an architect that does not have it written down first, drawn out first, with a model of it first. Is that not true?

Is it true that you must have a blueprint first before you can actually go and create something. You should have it written down and made plain and the measurements have to be done exactly right. So, when it comes to trying to obtain financial excellence to get to a specific destination; and I'm sorry brothers and sisters and cousins, it is not at a million dollars, that is not the destination. The goal isn't to get to a million dollars, you need to figure out where you are going first and what does that look like and we can figure out the price of it later. We got to figure out where we want to go. What are we building towards – and it's not a million dollars! Typically, if you are really building generational wealth, you have to surpass a million!

So, let's get our Blueprint!

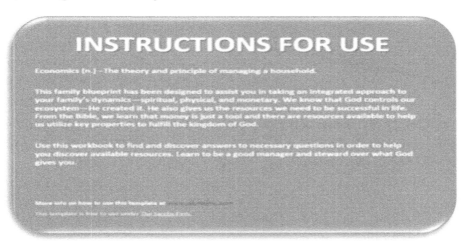

So, let me tell you really quick, when my wife and I first got together, three months into us dating, we actually did something that I have never done before, but it inherently became natural to us, because we were really serious about what we wanted to accomplish together. And even though we are not always on the same page, because you know in marriages and relationships, you got to work. The one thing that keeps our mind clear, is the fact that we know exactly where we are going together. So, it's easy for you to mitigate risk and to control relationships and to make sure that your mind is right, and everyone is on the same page if you all mutually know where you are going. So, what did, we created our own Jacobs Blueprint and it's the blueprint of what my family is standing on and what we are going to stand on for generations to come. We literally just wrote in a little journal, and by the end of this session, we will have them available for everyone to be able to get as we create them. But we literally just went into a journal, and we are going to do the same exact thing here, but we just literally went into a journal and created our blueprint, the very same thing we are going to do today together.

The very first thing we wrote down inside of this book was ECONOMICS.

We looked up the definition of **economics** as a noun and it says *the theory and principle of managing a household,* that's one of the definitions. Because a lot of us when it comes to economics, you think about macro-economics, economics of the government, economics of the world with other governments ... and you do not realize that the very first economic system that has to be managed and mastered, is the economic system in your household.

So, economics is the theory and principle of managing a household, because a household has many parts to it, and the family blueprint has been designed to assist you in taking an integrated approach to your families dynamics – spiritual, physical, and monetary. We know that God controls our ecosystem – He created it! And we also know that we don't own the resources that we have. The only thing that we can do is just manage the resources that are already given to us!

We have got to understand that money is nothing but a tool that is needed to be used to progress the Kingdom forward. And those are things we MUST understand! So, the very first thing we have to get done first is understanding how to manage your household.

Jake, let me ask you:

- ✓ **"What do I start with?"**
- ✓ **"What if I'm not married?"**
- ✓ **"What if I'm single?"**
- ✓ **"What if I am married and my husband or wife is not watching this with me?"**

Well if you are married and your husband or wife is not watching with you, that's problem #1! **GET IT TOGETHER!** But if you are single, the best time to create the blueprint that you want for your family, especially what you want to build, the best time to do this is when you are single. So, when you meet someone, either they can be on the same page or add value to that blueprint, or you know that someone is playing games with you. My wife and I, our third month dating, we got right into that blueprint, because we understood in order for us to make it, we got to get there.

Now you will need to begin writing down in your journal. **We are the <u>(state your last name)</u> FAMILY!**

Write down who you are! One of the best quotes out of one of my favorite books says, "That a good name is better than silver and gold." The reason why these banks and these institutions ask you to have good credit is because credit is a direct reflection of the weight of your word.

You are saying you will pay something back when you are supposed to and not trying to game the system! So, you starting this blueprint by saying **"WE ARE THE (_____) FAMILY**, that right there is letting you know that you are saying your name is going to mean something.

So, if you are a lady and you are single and you get a husband, then you all can start talking and change the last name but at this moment you put your last name on your blueprint. Now I know it's going to sound crazy but my wife and I we were that crazy, but let me tell you, we got some strong goals, and we're pretty sharp.

The next thing you need to do is **choose your family color**. "Jake, what does that have to do with building a bank?" **EVERYTHING!** Because building a bank is not the end goal. Banking should be a lifestyle. Like health – I'm not trying to **get** healthy, I'm trying to **be** healthy. So banking is a lifestyle, but before we do that, you got to stand for something. This family that you are building is a corporation. It is two entities, two businesses combining and merging to become one! So, you got to know what your family color is. Now what I want you to do, I want you to write down why you chose that color.

Now, write down your FAMILY COLOR:

• Is it green?   • Is it red?   • Is it yellow?

Then write down WHY you chose that color. Our family color is ARMY GREEN and the reason why we chose that color is, GREEN means new life, a rebirth, and ARMY GREEN because we know we are always at war! We are trying to increase our dominion, increase our kingdom, increase our territory, and we know that there will be opposition that's trying to stop our Jacobs family from moving forward. So, you got to know what your family color is, and do not just say it is your favorite color because this is what I went to school with, it has to mean something! Because everything that you build in this blueprint is absolutely critical in your journey to building a reputable family name.

The next thing you need to do is choose your family animal. If you think about how American is built, they went through everything – American colors are red, white, and blue, and the American Bird is the Eagle. Our family animal is a Lion! There are two animals that are described in my favorite book, it's the Eagle and Lion, that God identifies them as being. We chose the lion, because the lion is not the strongest, not the fastest, not the biggest, but the lion has the biggest heart and he has the most fear!

Why? Because of its reputation of not being scared of anything. It will literally go after anything! Not that it has the best kill rate, but the simple fact that every animal in the Savannah knows that the lion doesn't have a specific prey! It will go after any animal that seems to be vulnerable and enlarge its territory. So, the more specific reason we chose a lion wasn't because, oh a lion is a king, it's because a lion has respect!

When I walk into a room, I want the Jacobs Family name to actually stand for something and man something to somebody. That's the reputation, not just for a BILLION DOLLARS but we have a BILLION DOLLARS worth of influence!

So, write down why you chose your animal.

So, you got the name, you have the color, you have the animal – you are now **CREATING AN IDENTITY FOR YOURSELF!**

You can't be a person of influence that lacks identity. You see so many people become wealthy and they kill themselves or they are unhappy because they do not have an identity!

The next thing you want to do is create you family mission. A Mission Statement is a formal summary of the aims and values of a company, organization, family or individual. Your family mission is what you want to accomplish as a family.

What are you trying to obtain as a family. We will not go into it today, but I want you to write it down as this portion will be for your homework, but we will discuss in detail during our next session before we move forward to the next class.

Think about it – a summary of your aims and values of your family.

• **What are your AIMS?**

• **What are you trying to ACCOMPLISH?**

It needs to be in a summary, one paragraph that's able to determine and tie in your values as well as your aims, what are trying to do or accomplish?

For my wife and I, our family mission is that we be able to transform our generation to be able to help them become not only financially independent and free but to understand that freedom is through the God that we serve.

Let them know, let them see what a healthy relationship looks like; good, bad, and indifferent. Allow them to see people who have God inside of them, that are God like, that can have the best of both worlds, "Heaven on Earth!"

The next thing you have to write down is your

FAMILY'S VISION:

Your vision is your family's road map indicating what the family wants to become by setting a defined direction for the family's growth.

> ➤ What are you trying to accomplish?
> ➤ What are you trying to obtain?

So many black and brown cousins that we have, start businesses without a vision! Your business is not separate from your family – your business is a branch to the trunk of your family. The relationships that you have are a branch to the trunk of your family there is no separation.

Your banking and monetary system is not a separation, your spirituality or whatever God that you serve is not separate from the trunk. It's just branches on the trunk that create its own fruit. So, what is the VISION for your FAMILY?

MEN: It's very important – in the Bible one of my favorite books says that we are the head and not the tail. It does not mean that you are the boss of your family, it means you're the head. So, you have to be straight forward, upright and narrow. Upright means I am a man of integrity, and you have to have vision. And that vision that you have for your family has to supersede your existence. **"Well Jake, what if I am not married and I do not have kids?"**

Then it is perfect to do it now because it will keep you from **thotting** around and having babies with people you have no business having babies with! Yes, I am mad, and I am in your business!

WOMEN: YOU TOO! You will stop laying down with weak men. Weak men have no goals, no aspirations, unclear on what he wants to accomplish. That is a weak man to me, someone that is confused everyday about their future. **That's weak to me.**

- ✓ Your vision is where you want to go

- ✓ What are you trying to accomplish?

- ✓ Now notice I did not say the vehicle you are going to take to get there. There are many different fleets of vehicles that you can take to get to Florida!

- ✓ You can take the MEGA Bus, Greyhound, ride with your kinfolk, you can **try** to Uber, rent a car, take a van, ride a bike, ride a motorcycle, fly in a jet, commercial plane, or even an army fleet – but there are MANY different ways to get to the destination and we will figure that out later. **But you want to know is where you are going.**

I never said you had to figure out the car or transportation to get there but at least you have to be clear on where you are going. When your vision is clear, it is so much easier for you to be able to pick a significant other.

When I knew my vision and what I wanted to accomplish it was easier for me to go a year and a half (I know it's hard to do) without chasing no tail, brothers! And because I was so caught up on my vision, time just literally went by me. Women, it is so much easier when you are caught up on your vision. You can be alone! Along and lonely – are two different things. **Uh – OH!**

Being lonely is a dangerous place to be because you will settle for anybody. Being alone is a great place to be because that says, I am alone, but I am not lonely! I am alone and I am comfortable with me. Why? Because my vision is so clear it's hard for me to settle with these little busters, these little boys out here. If you are still sagging, you are a little boy!

The next thing you want to write down is your FAMIY VALUES:

Value Statement(s) – a declaration that announces a family's top priorities and core beliefs, both to guide their actions and also to connect with others.

I do not trust people who do not have values, especially If you cannot tell me what you stand for. What are your values? When somebody steps to you, how are you going to stand for your family? Are you somebody that will chase any dollar, chase anybody, chase any girl, chase any guy or lay with anybody because you do not have any values for yourself?

"Dang Jake, I didn't know this had nothing to do with money?"

It has everything to do with money!

Because if somebody who lacks value, you will go spend your hard-earned time, because that's what money is, a transfer and trade of time. You will go spend your hard-earned time, 40 hours of your life for some tennis shoes that you barely going to wear. You have got to understand your values, and the top priorities of what your family stands on!

Are you going to be druggies all your life? Alcoholics all your life? What do you all stand on? If someone sees your kid's kids, or they see you and they say, "Oh man, there are those McBride's?" I always admired those movies when people talk down about other last names.

> **"Man, those Rothschilds, they are dominating the word."**
> **"I want somebody to say that about the Jacobs!"** … **"Man, you're a Jacobs?"**
> **"Here go a $100,000 because I know your name is good."**

That is when you know you have good family values. What are your family values? It's a declaration that announces a family's top priorities and core beliefs. They are both needed to guide the actions and also connect with others on who you are internally. Or are you somebody that says, "Man, I'm where the money is**." That's a dangerous place to be!"**

"I will go be a trash man before I do some stuff when it comes to making money! I will go obtain a plumber's license and clean toilets with dignity before I go do some stuff I have no business doing."

- *Jake Tayler Jacobs*

All these things are important, this is how we run our company. When we first started the company, these are values that we stood on. Even when I had to start the company over three times, because of other stuff. The reason I had to start the company over was because there were certain things I just would not do. So, if that meant me losing everything and having to start from scratch to stand ten toes down on my values and what I believe in, that's what I was willing to do. And we have done it three times over! **WE ARE BACK STRONGER THAN EVER!**

The next thing is FAMILY MOTTO:

Motto (s) – **a short sentence or phrase chosen to encapsulate the beliefs or ideas guiding the family. Its's your motto! What do you stand on?**

Here at the company our motto is: The Truth is Good Enough. I do not have to lie, add no extra sales pitch, because the truth is good enough! That also means high accountability with my company. You cannot be around if you cannot take the truth.

- ❖ **You're lazy – the truth is good enough!**

- ❖ **You're getting big – the truth is good enough!**

- ❖ **If you do not start walking, you are going to die! – The truth is good enough!**

- ❖ **You are not helping clients; means you are not making money and I am not paying you nothing else – the truth is good enough.**

- ❖ **You are going to be working a job again – the truth is good enough!**

Because we live in soft world; you got to have a motto that your family stands on, like yo this is us and this is what we are about! I didn't' say your company motto, see your company motto and your family motto are two different mottos! My family motto is Jacobs over Everything! That means I am going to choose the progression of my Jacobs' name before I choose in getting a new car. **(You all are not ready for that!)**

15

This is important – your family motto needs to be something that is not made up in two seconds. I will give you until the next class (mid-day Thursday) to get this together! You will need to email me a report with this information. Your family motto is a short sentence, something that can literally just take the ideas that you have in one sentence of what you stand on. For example, like a motto like Nike: Just do It! But it has to mean something. If you are married do not try to come up with this on your own. Go to your spouse, because I just may call your husband or wife and ask do they know the motto. Do not try to come up with it by yourself.

The next thing you need are

FAMILY PILLARS:

Pillars – a person or thing regarded as reliably providing essential support for something, intentionally creating and fostering a positive family culture.

Your pillars are like, integrity, character, hard work, and resilience. You typically only need four pillars, four points of balance. Something that it stands for, and when you choose certain words, I will ask you why you are using these pillars.

They must be pillars that stand the test of time. Just because you change crafts, or change jobs or opportunities, or vehicles, your pillars should not change.

If your pillars can change based on where you work or how you work or how you get your money or how you have your career that is like having a cracked foundation with a beautiful house.

Every time you change the house you have to fix the foundation because the foundation is terrible. What we are building is the foundation of who you are. That would probably be the reason why I do not have a lot of friends, because a lot of people do not have any pillars.

> *"I do not know what to hold you accountable on,*
> *and my biggest pillar is INTEGRITY."*
>
> *Jake Tayler Jacobs*

Just be who you say you are going to be, and if I except you for your flaws, that's me accepting you. But don't be trying to be fake and be who you are not just because you think:

"Hey, listen, this is how you are going to be Jake's friend", and all honesty, if you just be who you are, I'm more likely to be your friend with nothing than I am with you having something.

"Half of you all are confused with money!" – Jake Tayler Jacobs

"The GOAL in marriage is not to think alike, but to think together."

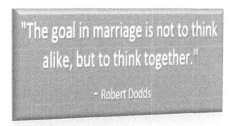

"Jake I'm not married so why are we talking about this?"

Well my wife and I, we do this for married couples, and I'm sorry the quote is there, and it is transferable with business partnerships and relationships.

The goal is not to think alike, but to think together, which means in order for you to think together you have to be on the same mission to go somewhere.

Let's think about an airplane at a terminal:

- you have someone doing the bags
- someone flying the plane
- somebody is the stewardess on the plane
- someone is in charge of fuel and oil for the plane
- someone is checking the engine, and the equipment on the plane
- someone in charge of fecal removal

But the point I'm making is that everybody does not have to think alike in order to get to the same destination.

My wife and I do not think alike, but we do think together, and her strengths and my strengths mesh. When it comes to building business partnerships, you don't want someone who thinks exactly like you, you want to be able to think together so you guys can be on the same page.

Which means you won't always come to an agreement on things, but at least it means we are moving together and moving forward. And we know that what ever we talk about, it has to at least meet where we are going as far as our destination.

If we have two different destinations, we are probably the wrong partners for each other.

I told my wife if you just want to make good money for us, and sit down and watch sitcoms, tv and movies all day, and travel and take pictures and make videos to show our friends we are all good, you are marrying the wrong cat!

Because I am for the people! I am going to do what I am doing until I die. I do not want to retire and go live on a beach while making passive income, there are only so many beaches you can go be on! There are only so many televisions that you can buy and watch.

I want to have a life of impact, a life of meaning and if you are not with that then, you need to get back! She said, hey baby, I'm with that jack!

Here is what we call THE BIG THREE –

The big three are your non negotiables, things you are unwilling to compromise on.

Everybody needs non negotiables, things you just will not cross, whether it's you lying to me – if you are going to lie, that's it! IF you lie one time, you will lie again, that's just you, and you are a liar! Whether it's cheating on me and cheating may not just be in a relationship, it could be having a business partner, doing business together and you find out they have some back deals somewhere.

These are things that **YOU ARE JUST NOT GOING TO COMPROMISE ON!**

So, if it's cheating, lying, abuse, emotional, mental, physical, spiritual abuse – not allowing you to express yourself spiritually, trying to put you in a box that they want you to be in – that's abuse!

In business, things that my company is not willing to compromise on is doing illegal business. Period!

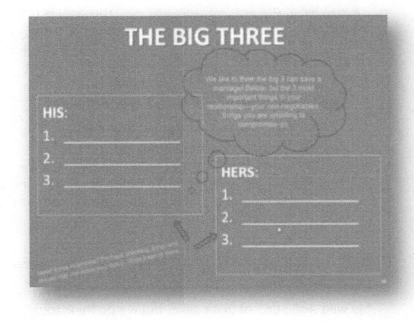

We are black and white – if you get approved, you get approved! If not, I am not signing for you, changing this, acting like you do not have any medicine, nor acting as if you do not smoke cigarettes. If you smoke cigarettes, then I have to put it on the application that you smoke cigarettes.

You will need to fix the fact that you smoke because it is making your insurance increase! That has nothing to do with me sir or ma'am, that is all you. If you are 100 pounds overweight, I am not about to chop your weight down sir or ma'am, you need to go walk.

It's ok – The Truth is Good Enough!

I love you enough to say this is not the time for you. We are not cutting any corners around here; we are not about to hire **somebody** just to hire **somebody**.

These are all things that are important and are non-negotiables, you need to make sure you write down all your non negotiables.

What we are seeing as we are building your foundation, write it down and make it plain so that those who see it can run with it. The reason that we want to do that is because you want your kids to look at all these non-negotiables and they know exactly where to go from there.

Now it is time to write down your three-month, six-month and nine-month goals:

These are quicker goals and I want you to start breaking down your goals quarterly.

Think of a year like a game, preferably basketball or football, just like they have quarters, you need to have quarters. And what I want you to do versus punishing yourself, I want you to create a rewards system for things you want to get accomplished in this three, six, and nine month which is 1st quarter, 2nd quarter, 3rd quarter, 4th quarter, and when you accomplish the goal, I want you to do this.

> Example: You hit a goal, whether it is something you want to accomplish. Such as I want to change my mindset or change my saving habits. When you have a goal or say I want to break this habit and I want to save this amount of money. Versus just doing it or going out to eat all the time you stop instant gratification – you begin to spend your money on memorable moments.

Some of us have dream cars that we want to buy but you never sat in the dream car. So, by the time you get the money and you go sit in the car, you are depressed because you have spent all that time working for a car that you no longer like because you never sat in it.

Don't focus on busying the clothes, focus on the experience. So, when you are setting these goals, whatever it is that you think you want to do, whether it is living in a mansion, at the end of that quarter, take a break, spend a day, or two, or a weekend living in a mansion.

Go to an Air B&B or mansion for the weekend. Go rent a Royals Royce or and I8, go rent a truck! You will spend a stack, two or three, if it is a jet, fly to California, whether the goal or reward, when you think about going out most families spend huge amounts when they eat out.

If you are going to spend $300 to $400 a month just for eating out on leisure food you can save that money each month and use that money to rent out a car and get a feel of how it really is to reward yourself. Get the experience and see how it feels versus, I am going to work hard to go to the beach. Work hard for that quarter, save you some money, do what you got to do and then go to the beach – live as you are going. You are rewarding yourself and it will make you want to do more, and you will stop eating your wealth away and you began to understand, that you like this feeling and what happens is your sub conscious mind doesn't know what is true or false and it begins to create the reality that its used to. So, if your sub conscious mind know every quarter, or two or three days, I drive my truck, it does not know that it is not your vehicle.

And what are you doing – INCREASING YOUR STANDARD OF LIVING!

.We Are about to Create your 1-Year, 5-Year and 10-year GOALS:

What are you trying to accomplish?

What checkpoints are you trying to knock off on your way to creating generational wealth or creating a family worth having a name with?

What are you trying to accomplish? Whether it's – I want $40,000 in my insurance bank – and the reason I am saying a number isn't because I am trying to reach these numbers, these are just milestones that you are trying to
hit because you are trying to accomplish something.
For example:

- ❖ I am financing my cars all through my insurance bank from now on in 10 years.
- ❖ In 10 years, I want to be self-financed, full outright.
- ❖ In 10 years, I want to refinance all my debt under me.

These are things that you have to think about so that you know you are always working for it. There is a quote in my favorite book that says, **Proverbs 29:18 "Without vision the people shall perish."**

Typically, the people who are dull, negative, upset, that beat themselves up, they have no vision. You have no vision! And your vision should be God like. The Bible says, (In my favorite book), there is a chapter and it says in **Psalms 82:6 "Ye are God's and we are made in the image of him."** And another verse in my favorite book, which is kind of like the re-write of my favorite book, it is a chapter called John, it's a man by the name of Jesus that also says, **John 10:34** "Is it not written in your Law, "I have said you are "gods"? **Jesus said that!**

Now I know for most Christians they don't get that word because only the real Christians read that type of Bible, that type of book, but what I'm saying is you do not have to believe that to know we are made in his image and we are God like. So, everything that we are supposed to have is supposed to be above board and above standard. So, there is no way you can have a vision that is not God like. In order for your vision to be a vision, it has to be vast, something that is bigger, something you cannot accomplish by yourself. It has to take God to accomplish it. If it not that big and you see yourself being able to accomplish it by yourself, then it is just a project and not a vision. Generational wealth just starts with you, it does not finish with you. It is your job to get it going but not to take the responsibility to accomplish it all. And that is the struggle that most people have when trying to create generational wealth. You have just got to get it going, it is NOT your job to keep it going too! Your job is to get it going, teach the people how to manage it next! THAT is your only job, you are going to be dead, you will not be here! Do your part to start it and let it carry on – **generational wealth**!

Just play your part, if you know that you are the person to start the generational wealth for your family, do your part, do not try to be the second and third generation. Do the best that you can do and maximize yourself and enjoy it along the process.

VISION

When you got a vision - that vision should be so big!

Be careful with giving your God like vision to small minded people! Now remember, your family's vision has to be a couple of generations deep. I'm not saying you have to accomplish everything in your generation, but it needs to be that deep! Which means, that you CAN'T give your FAMILY's vison to small minded people! People who can't see the full vision – they CHOP your vision up to what they can see! And they will have the audacity to tell you that the goals you have for your family are not realistic and can't be accomplished, only because they can only see the eye of the VISION! Your **family vision** should be sacred to you! You do not have to announce to the world your big ole vast vision! You say it in the sanctity of a safe place and then you go get it done.

The next thing we will discuss is Code Words:

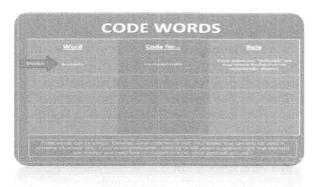

Does every Kingdom or Country have their own language? Yes or NO? If you are a king or queen in your own right, shouldn't your family, your kingdom, have your own language?

Things that only you understand and only you have the power to translate?

> So, my wife and I, when we first got together in the third month, we literally created our own language. I am only going to give you one word that we use.

Our language is growing daily; and I am going to tell you why – because when I am talking to my wife, I want her to be able to understand what I'm saying without the receptors of the enemy!

C'MON! YOU'VE GOT TO PROTECT YOUR VISION FROM THE ENEMY! YOU HAVE GOT TO HAVE YOUR OWN PLAY CALLING!

One of the movies my wife and I refer to is called Beetlejuice, and how you got Beetlejuice out the little small tank, is you say, **"Beetlejuice, Beetlejuice, Beetlejuice!"** and he comes out the tank – so what happens is, if we are out somewhere and my wife is ever uncomfortable or I'm in a place that is uncomfortable, and I don't want to be there and I feel like I am trapped in a tank somewhere, I will text her or I mouth to her **"Beetlejuice, Beetlejuice, Beetlejuice!"**

People around us they may laugh, but that tells my wife, it's serious and I don't want to be here anymore. So, we got a plan that says we got to remove my wife or myself out of the situation within 30 minutes or it's going to be a problem.

You want code words for your family so you all can talk out in public and no one will know what is going on, and the only people that know what is going on are the people that you let into your language. ***And I'm sorry but there is no Rosetta Stone for our language***.

Another language we that use is called **banchee - Banchee** is when we getting into it.

I'm talking about it's HOT!!   - It feels like I am literally on the **BATTLEFIELD!**
She got her gun. I got my gun – it's like Mr. and Mrs. Smith! She say something,
"I'm (aimed at target) **PEW PEW!** "I say something, she's (aimed at target) **"PEW PEW!"**

She say something, **BOOM**! We got landmines and stuff and I'm dropping low and hiding from her and I'm coming out like, **"yeah what about that, huh, you didn't think about that?"** **And we beefing!** Which means, we are not going nowhere. **She beefing, I'm beefing – we beefing together!** And it's one of the words that we use when we know that it's not going anywhere and one of us can recognize that the conversation and the argument that we are having is not beneficial towards our vision!

This is why having a vision is very beneficial for your company and for your family because when you are getting in to it with people you love and care about, if you have a code word like **banchee**, it can literally stop the conversation immediately and what she and I have to do immediately is drop our emotions and immediately think about is this conversation and is this argument going to hinder or move us toward our vision and our goal as a family? IF the answer is yes, you got 24 hours to come up with the reason why it will be, and it has to be written out. Because when you write out the communication – it is just like on the battlefield – a little telegram. It allows for me to read something without the **(The Neck)**. If I am upset with her I got 24 hours to communicate to her how I felt and why I think this is a big conversation toward our future. And it's not and we both can come to an agreement at that moment, we immediately drop the issue, ***now we still may be huffing and puffing on the inside,*** but we immediately drop the issue and we get over it a little. You know you got to calm down, you were just fighting, you got to calm down a little bit. You know – simmer down!

But the point is when we create our own rules to how we function inside of our Kingdom, we control the game! And in order for you to become a banker in the mind – to become the Kingdom or King and Queen over your monetary system, you have to create your own rules, as to what you abide by; not the rules of somebody else. This is the reason why most relationships and business partnerships don't work. Because you do not know how to communicate and talk to each other. This is important, when it comes to you building this financial fortress that you are trying to build, this legacy, this family banking system that you are trying to build. Communication is absolutely **KEY**! It is absolutely IMPORTANT! Because one person could be playing football, the other person could be playing basketball.

OFFENSE

Offense means to score, correct? Well, in basketball you score by shooting the ball into the hoop and in football you score by a touchdown. They are both offense and they both mean to score but it is a different mean or way. Defense in football, means to tackle and blast **YO BUTT**! Well some of you all grew up playing tackle communication, while on the other hand, this portion defense is – don't touch em! Don't touch, just stay in front. Basketball defense is motion – movement from side to side, guarding, blocking! You can't go nowhere, that's basketball defense, you touch me that's a foul! You yell at me that's a foul.. I'm going to the free throw line. Football defense is like (get that out of here!) And then you bump chests because you did a good job smacking the crap out of somebody!

What happens is, inside of you Kingdom, with business relationships, marriage relationships, one person is playing football and one is playing basketball, they both by nature have the same word, but the language is different!

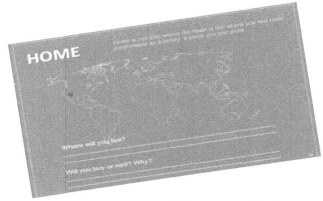

Yes, single people definitely needs a language, because when someone comes into your life, whatever your code or language is will be just what it is.

You need to decide where you want to live, do you want to buy or rent, you are building your Kingdom! Why? It's very important to understand that because that determines your financial scope.

- ✓ **How much do you want to have?**
- ✓ **How much capital?**
- ✓ **Where do you want to live?**

That is very important! If you currently live in Georgia, but you really want to live in D.C. you need to be trying to determine, how much does it cost to live there. And you probably need to go and start scouting the area. Look for Air B&B and Mansions around there. So that you can get a feel of where you are going. Jake, "Why is this important?" Because everything comes with a cost!

FAMILY LEGACY – WHAT DO YOU WANT TO BE KNOWN FOR?

My favorite book says, **"A good man leaveth an inheritance to his children's children; and the wealth of the sinner is laid up for the just." Proverbs 13:22**

Which means if you get right, and everything on earth will be given to you.

COACH'S CORNER

Recap of Kingdom Blueprint:

Just a quick review of the first class, we discussed the Kingdom Blueprint, and we know the parameters we stand on, we are starting to get an idea of who we are!

Psalms 82:6 says, "Ye are gods." – And we are made in the image of God. **John 10:34** let's us know that when Christ was about to get crucified, (**I know you all may not believe in the same thing that I believe in, but I am just telling you what I believe**)…

Christ was about to get crucified, because they were saying he was saying blasphemous stuff – (saying) he was the Son of God and that he was also God because he was the son of God.

And in **John 10:34** it says, "Is it not written in your word that I said ye are gods."

Which means – we are gods? If my daddy is a God, don't that make me a god, God is inside of me? And the reason why God is omnipotent and all seeing is because he sees through us?

That lets you know who you are and who you come from. That is the only point I was getting to.

So, if I know who I am, I know where I come from, and I know the strength that comes with being connected to God; with being a *being* that represents God – a Kingdom Ambassador on this planet, that's connected to a Higher Power, that means I have the ability to create things into existence. When I write down that blueprint, I am literally creating my life!

I am writing it down making it plain so that people who see it can run with it. The cars that we drive, the airplane that we fly in, the fact that we can talk to each other through internet that you can't see – is **A MIRACLE!**

So, we have the ability to create whatever life that we want, but it's up to you to take it serious.

NOTES

_____
_____
_____
_____
_____
_____

CHAPTER 2:

Know Your Enemy (Find your Stage of Financial Cancer)

So, we got the blueprint done but today we are going to be talking about the financial stages and habits, OK! We are going to be talking about the financial stages and habits and understanding the psychology of what happens when it comes to paying for stuff.

This is where we talk about how FINANCIAL CANCER IS KILLING YOU!

– I'm actually pulling the information from my book:
We are Sick: Surviving Financial Cancer!

In this piece what I am talking about is financial cancer is killing you, and in this portion, I'm literally proving, scientifically and statistically how financial cancer is the number one cause of your death. And when we talk about financial cancer, it's the lack of financial education, financial hopelessness, and debt – debt is the number one cause of stress, debt is the reason why you wake up, you are literally working to pay off debt. And the only way that I can be able to understand this kingdom that I am building, is I have to effectively be able to determine who my enemy is.

So, when I'm building my kingdom, in order for me to increase my territory, is it not true I have to be able to identify my enemy? Is that true? You don't have one country in the world that is a strong dominant country that doesn't know it's enemies – or even a weak country. So, we have to understand who our enemy is. So, as a family unit, in order for us to always stay on the same page, we have to have a common enemy that we are looking to fight every single day!

So, you can't have one day where we are talking about financial cancer and debt is killing me, and these financial institutions are not in my favor until I become a banker in my mindset so I can know how to use them properly. As a consumer debt is absolutely terrible. So, I can't learn this information, and I got my Kingdom down, but I am allowing people around me, allowing my family and my circle around me that's in this Kingdom Blueprint to literally go eat with the enemy.

So, once you consider something your enemy you have to fight like hell, to increase your territory, and take dominance over that enemy? Is that true? So, what we have to identify is who our enemy is, what is killing you and your family? Because I know me – if something is literally killing me and my family, that's my enemy!

My mother and my father are dealing with it right now! My father has not had a job in 12 years! Y'all are cousins so I got to let you in my business! My father has not had a full job in 12 years, when he Lost his job, I started selling candy in school. And what most people don't know when I was selling candy at school, I was actually selling it in four schools. While most of my friends were selling at just Cedar Hill, I was selling in four other suburbs. I was bringing home **$4,000** a month selling candy in school, as a necessity! I said bringing home, after paying expenses, and paying out all these kids that were eating my candy, but that's not the point.

Due to my father not having a job in 12 years, that **is** financial stress. He was laid off from his job that he was with for 18-19 years. Laid off from that job that he was a year and a half away from a full-time pension! He went from High School to this job that he thought would be there forever, that let him go and he lost himself.
Because of that, my father has a graft in his arm, teeth falling out of his mouth, and he's not even 50 yet, because of what stress is doing to his body!

Do you know what that stress has done? It put my mother in charge of the house financially. She was taking care of a household of 5, I was out of the house. On a teacher's salary, she has been doing that for 12 years, and literally, just this week, she has had four migraines that passed her out, woke up with a swollen eye because of this financial stress. She literally text me, **"Son you got to get me out of here – this is going to kill me!" "I can't keep the family up financially anymore!" "I can't do it – I am going to DIE!"** So, we got to figure out who our common enemy is! And understanding who our common enemy is, it's safe to say, if I know who my enemy is, it's a lot easier to fight. So, financial cancer is the number one cause of the death of your family and your Kingdom if you don't fix it!

I must define to you what FINANCIAL CANCER is – financial cancer is my discovery; therefore, you won't find it on any other concepts or anything online. I developed the concept financial cancer after I realized that there were four stages of financial cancer, just like there are four stages to physical cancer. You will find out more about that later as we begin to kind of talk, but I want you guys just like there are four stages to physical cancer, there are four stages to financial cancer and once I have any bit of diagnosis, or scan that says I have physical cancer, most of us will be scared! So that's the same scare or fear that you should have about financial cancer, if you don't get it together!

What I began to realize is – financial cancer, it does grow, and it interrupts or causes infection to other parts of our lives in ways that cancer grows! It metastasizes in other organs inside of our body, that's what cancer does, but so does financial cancer, it metastasizes in every other place in your life. It metastasizes in relationships, in your businesses, in your sleep, and in your health. That same type of physical cancer that literally can grow in every aspect of your body, is the same disease, that can grow in every aspect of your life, **if you do not control it!**

Based on the statistics from the National Vitals Statistics Report (Volume 67 - #6) from The Centers of Disease – the CDC has uncovered the top five causes of death in America.

Top 5 Reasons of Death Amongst Blacks:

- **Diseases of the Heart – 23.4%**
- **Malignant Neoplasms Cancer – 21.3%**
- **Cerebral Vascular Diseases Stroke – 5.6%**
- **Accidents unintentional injuries – 5.5%**
- **Diabetes – 4.3%**

 If you notice, KILLINGS are not within the top 5, but the media likes us to think that.

So, let me tell you what heart disease does – it transpires when plaque buildup thickens and stiffens the artery walls of your heart. It is kind of like the blood is hard to get through. This buildup can inhibit blood flow through your arteries to your organs and tissues. This type of clog, **atherosclerosis,** is the most common cause of cardiovascular disease. It is caused by correctable problems, like high blood pressure and high cholesterol.

When it comes to you clogging this type of artery, it can be fixed, but when it's not fixed it an become a problem. So yes, fixing your dietary track is one piece, but there is another piece that comes to it that most people don't talk about. When you want to ask, "Like what does this have to do with what's going on with my money?" What does this have to do with my enemy Jake?" I'm trying to follow, what does this have to do with banking?" It has everything to do with it, because there is no secret. The number one cause of complaints with adults, old and young – in the United States, is **STRESS!! Everyone complains about stress!** Is that not true?

That's why you see people meditating, posing like praying mantises, you see people sitting in chairs doing chants with wands using dialect language and smoke machines. They are either smoking ganja, smoking weed, drinking, and want to play the game because they call it a stress reliever, but it don't really relieve stress. All these things, the number one complaint for people in America, is the cause of stress! The physical effects of prolonged stress are numerous, including greater susceptibility of illness, lack of energy, problems with sleep, headaches, poor judgement, weight gain, depression, and anxiety. All of these other things that can literally cause you to stop from being able to be +healthy in your right mind. Many people blame their inability to maintain healthy relationships – on stress! You're tired! Like my mother, she's tired, and she's upset. She literally text me today, "Like yo, listen, you need to help me in my situation, because this is a lot for me!"

So, there is no guess that chronic stress can kill you, but what we got to understand is this, acute and chronic stress literally affects you in more ways than you think! When you encounter a stressful situation, stress hormones flood your bloodstream so that you can respond quickly and with strength. **Here's an example**. Watching your child nearly drown in water, it might induce a hormonal response that enables you to catch you youngster before any harm is done. So that energy that you feel with somebody is sick, or you see somebody that is about to die, or you see somebody that you got to save; that hormone that you have is adrenaline. And that's anxiety that you feel, and literally your body goes into action – when your body moves into action, you have more strength, your blood flow is moving through your body a lot faster, your adrenaline is pumping, your heart is racing, and you are literally rushing!

There is a story about a woman whose child was stuck under a car. This woman literally ran to the car, picked up the car, got her child free and put the car down! When the police asked what happened, people began to say the woman picked up the car! When the police asked the woman to come do it again, she has never been able to pick up another car again, and most people think that it was a phenomenon!

But the truth is, when your hormones are raging like that and your adrenaline increases, and your blood flow is up, your body is moving at a higher pace, and is literally injecting this feeling that allows you to be able to go do abnormal things. But the problem is – when this ACTH hormone – (Adrenocorticotropic hormone) enters the blood stream and it causes for me to have this almost anxious feeling. This feeling that you have, if it's not placed properly and then dispenses, and you get rid of it, then this stress literally stays in your body which causes us to have what they clinically deem as anxiety.

Anxiety and stress is not normal for you to have long-term. But when I have anxiety and stress about this one thing called financial debt, financial caner, financial illiteracy and when I'm stressed about this one thing, my anxiety, the same hormonal discharges that I get through my bloodstream, it's happening again and it is clogging up my arteries over time, it's going to kill you. When you see people dying, and people tripping, you got to realize is that you will be put in a situation that you can't get out! So, the enemy that you have is your lack of financial education. The enemy that you have is putting yourself in financial straits that you do not have any business putting yourself in. So, when I wake up every single day, I am literally working for money.

For example: This is the current ecosystem that we live in. It's funny in physical slavery, we worked in the cotton field, we were picking cotton, we working for cotton for the man! IF we didn't pick it up fast enough, we got chastised! We had to You had to turn in your cotton to the man, so the man could take our cotton and go make money from it.   We did this over and over again so the man could take   the cotton, sell it, and go make money off of it.

If you never realized it, money – (the dollar bill) – is made from cotton.

So, every day, we are picking this cotton, we are working for the cotton, then we go turn our cotton in, to these financial institutions, and tell massa – you go do something with it! So, the same slavery physically that we are in, we are still in - just financially. The same debt – indebtedness, where you are always in debt to somebody, that's the feeling of slavery. I'm always on you, always got to work for you – that's what an **indentured servant or slave was.**

An indentured slave worked for a certain amount of years, and after these years, we promise to set you free. And what they used to do as a trick to African Americans they used to do that to get us crunk, to get us excited, so that you work harder, because you know you got your end date, but at the end they say oh, "you still owe me for this, you just got to work it off!" They continue to increase the bid. That is the exact same thing that we are doing, every single time that we take out debt from these financial institutions, and not having the upper hand.

SO, I'M STILL PICKING COTTON!!!!! I'm still working for cotton – cotton is still the very thing I NEED to set ME FREE, and I DON'T CONTROL IT!

I know when I start talking about slavery and stuff, y'all be like – "There go Jake here he go again, "What does this have to do with banking?" It has everything to do with it. If I know who my enemy is, I draw the line and say, I will go with that before I put myself in that again. I don't care what the enemy offers me. If it's not my way, it's the highway. But we are still picking! Aww man, come get this car! OOOHHH come get this car! You still enslaved but you got a new car! Come ON! Let's look at money: it's ironic that we have all these white men on this cotton! You have George, Benjamin, Andrew, Lincoln, Hamilton,and Grant telling you what to do.

All these dollar bills say they want to go party, and you say **yes sir!** Let me put on my hat and working boots sir and I'm going to go help you party sir! So, you go out and party and you do not realize it, but the dollar bill has just became your boss! **"Well Jake, what do you mean the dollar bill just became my boss?"**

It's very simple, you finance your car, you finance your home, you finance the clothes you got on your back, your money goes to food, money going to all these other things you have no business doing – because you are broke! Oh, Benjamin – he is going to the movies! Everytime you get paid, he knows tha for a fact! Oh George- we getting singles, cigarettes! Andrew – the $20 bill, he may not go to Papadeaux, but he will definitely go to Chick-fil-A! Lincoln, the $5 bill, he will go to snacks! Grant- the $50 dollar bill, let's get shoes and some clothes. Let's look at Benjamin again, he is going to be on shoes, clothes, Pappadeaux, he is going to be on a lot! And Grant and Benjamin get together and they will be on mortgage, and your cars, that's what they want!

 **Singles – Cigarettes**    **Snacks**

 **Gas for Car**    **Chick-Fil-A**

 Shoes / Clothes / Mortgage/ Cars

 Movies / Shoes / Out to Eat / Mortgage / Cars

Those bills will say, "Hey Bubba, and you say, "yes sir boss!" "We want singles, movies, we want shoes, Pappadeaux, and mortgage." "And you say yes sir boss, I work for cotton so cotton can do what cotton want to do!" And they put you to work every single day, and they know every two weeks, or every month, or every day **it depends on it** and you're going to get paid and you are going to let them go party! Immediately when you get paid you are thinking about sending Grant to the car note. But you do not know that Grant's cousin is the person that owns the bank and so the money is getting flipped and you are just getting used!

Every time you get paid, your money is going to snacks! Every time you get paid you are like, "Sir, as long as you don't hit me sir!" "As long as you are letting me have the best clothes on my back sir!" "As long as I eat the good food sirs and look like I'm living good."

Your massa is saying as long as you are keeping that money cycling in my family's pockets, you are good with me. So, this money, this cotton, that we all greed over; (isn't that crazy) we worked in cotton fields, now we greed over cotton!
The money is your boss, you wake up every day – ooooh I hope I get paid today because I don't want to get repoed! I do not want massa taking my car. So, as soon as I get paid, I am just going to call massa and tell him – can you give me a week?

You are asking and trying to find a way to cover rent, mortgage, car note and many other things. Trying to find a way to pay your bills, or it will make your life hell and lower your credit. Once your score is low, the financial institutions will not lend you anymore money! Money is your boss! You wake up, money is running you! Money has you stressed out – cotton has you stressed out. Who owns the cotton? The same enemy that put you in slavery, owns the cotton. He gives you fancy stuff, as well as finances your stuff. You out here putting items on credit cards. "Well Jake what if I really want a home? I can't afford a home."
"Well if you can't afford it, you better go live in an apartment."

"There is nothing worth your FREEDOM!" – *Jake Tayler Jacobs*

If you really want a property and you cannot afford it, you better go split the property with someone that you love. Get a home and rent out three of the rooms, if you really want that property. "Well Jake I really want land." You do not want land because if you wanted land, you would've bought land in areas that you knew that would be worth something. Not in a little cul-de-sac.

"Jake what does this have to do with banking?" Everything! I'm trying to help you see where your enemy is! Interest and finances going against you is like a venomous snake that bites you on your heel and you didn't feel it. A week later you realize it because your whole leg has swollen up and you do not know where it came from. If you do not go to the doctor and get it fixed, another whole week later, now your whole body has swollen up! Now it's stroking out your heart – that is exactly what stress and finance does to you. Look at that – cotton is running us!

So, what we have to do, because we are living in their system, you got to get good at going from Bubba to **"that man" or "that woman", that has your own "whip"** – that's now making George, Lincoln, Jackson, Hamilton, Grant and Benjamin work for you! There is no way you can make that happen if you keep financing stuff without being in control of the way you finance. You got to control the deal. You have to go from crazy Bubba that is going around telling us you can have that car all you got to do is sign right here on the dotted line and work twenty more years for me. You an have that house and that land, but all you got to do is work five more years for me, and I am going to get my money off the top. But every five to seven years, you don't want your car anymore. They say, "Aww man, hey you need a new car don't you?" "Well we have been good masters to you!" Go ahead and Mastercard the next transaction. Now you financing again. We got to control the system!

If I am going to be in the system, I got to know how my enemies play, so that too, can know how to play the same game! It does mean that because you are the first one, you will not have the same the benefits that the next three generations will have.

So, what are you going to do? Are you going to go and sleep with the enemy and then try to build your Kingdom? That's treason! If you are the first generation, I am sorry, but you do not get the same benefits as the third generation. You can have a little fun along the way, but they will really see what your start is today! That's why the **KINGDOM BLUEPRINT** is very important. If you want me to lend to you, here are my contracts, here are my rules.

That's why I love using insurance, yes I am paying interest – but the deal is they are still paying me, so it's a partnership. You use me, I'm using you, but not to where I am just going to stay there and take it! Because I want to drive a BENZ to impress someone? Come on NOW! You know that BENZ is someone's family name? All they are – masters passing that cotton around and you do not own a piece of cotton, nor do you control the cotton.

We must understand the psychology around spending. There is no purpose of me teaching you budgeting if I can't teach you standards of your **KINGDOM** and I can help you realize that every dollar you allow to escape out your **KINGDOM** – they should be bringing you something back!

Here is my definition of an asset, your dollar bills, **a.k.a, your employees**, giving you their paycheck. You spend your employee's paycheck, don't spend yours. "Jake, who are my employees again?" Oh, I got you – George, Lincoln, Jackson, Hamilton, Grant, and Ben! You make them your slaves, and you use what they generate for you, and use their paycheck for your gain. That's what an asset is.

So, the house that you live in, that you are trying to purchase for your own good, you got to ask yourself, "Is this a house that is benefiting George, Ben, and Lincoln? Or is George, Ben, and Lincoln benefiting me for this property?"

How you know it is an asset, is if you can see their paychecks, which is cashflow coming in; that is how you eliminate debt! That is how you eliminate cancer.

WHAT THE HECK IS STAGING?

Before I can give you the four stages of financial cancer, I must first breakdown and explain what "staging" is so you can get a better understanding of the parallelism between the two concepts. Staging is a way of describing the nature of a cancer and how large it has grown.

When doctors first diagnose a cancer, they carry out a multitude of tests to determine the size of the cancer as well as the location, and whether it has spread to surrounding tissues. They also check to see whether it has spread to another part of the body.

Before proceeding, let's first diagnose how bad your cancer may be. The average person had these things before coming to me – the whole goal is that you don't have these things at least with other banking institutions, and you have it within your own bank. So, I'm not telling you not to finance, or not to believe in financing, and be in control of the *financing*. I'm not telling you not to borrow, I am telling you where to borrow from so that you are in control of the financing. If we owned a legitimate charter bank, you would still want to borrow from that charter bank, even though you own it, so you can pay it back to increase the bank's value. Same exact structure, the only deal I am telling you is, learning how to play the game the right way. I am still playing their game; the only difference is – it is on my **CHECKERBOARD**.

There are four key areas you must review before determining how bad your cancer is.

The characteristics are as follows:

1. **STANDARDS OF LIVING**: What is your income in regards to your standard of living percentage? Here's an example of how to calculate your SOL:
    i.   Total Home Gross Income (Married):
    $92,000 before taxes
    $ 85,995.12 after taxes/12 months = MI
       Monthly Income (MI): $6,454.78
       i.e. Cars: $958 (2 cars)
           Rent/Mortgage: $1200
           Homeowners Ins.: $135.45
           HOA Dues: $300
           Car Insurance: $216
           Utilities: $200
           Daycare: $1250
           Food: $275-$350
    Total (SOL): $4609.45

"People say well Jake, I want to own my property that I stay in, I am tired of just paying someone else's bill." You don't say that about energy. You pay for water, and you are using

33

electricity. You are not talking about you want to own that! So why all of a sudden you want to own that box you live in? For the land? Most of you all do not even have good land, you live in a cul-de-sac on a street that you do not even like that you have to pay HOA Fees for. You cannot build anything on the house or add anything without the permission of the HOA Association and the city you live in because you do not have control on what you can put on the property.

Now we must figure out how much of your income is going toward you SOL. So, take your monthly income and divide it into your SOL (standard of living) and that should give you the percentage of income going toward your SOL. Look at the example below:

This diagram shows that 71.4% of your income is going towards your standard of living, which let's you know you will be penny pinching everywhere else.

The reason why I am able to calculate this way, you have to know exactly to the tee, how much and where your money is going. This helps me figure out what stage of financial cancer you are in. I'm staging, this is what you do, like for a doctor – he will run tests to figure out where the cancer is, how big the cancer is, and where the problem is. That's what I'm doing right now.

An example such as this is obviously not good; it is saying that 71.4% of your income is going to standards of living before any other debt, bills, or gas is paid. The scary thing is that for most Americans, this is a reality.

2. **SAVING FOR FUTURE:** What percentage of your income are you giving to your future self? Take your monthly income and divide into the amount of money you invest or put aside for your future:

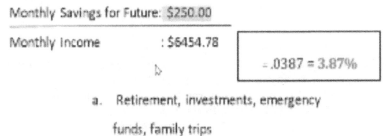

a. Retirement, investments, emergency funds, family trips

3. **FLEX MONEY:** What percentage of your income are you spending on "flex money"?

(Use the same formula that we used for SOL and future Savings): Flex Money: $$ / Monthly: $$

a. Entertainment, dining out, leisure activities, organizations, clubs, gym fees, side business costs.

Some people have never been taught how to look at their bank statement and that's a hard reality.

4. **SEED SOWING:** What percentage of your income are you spending on charitable donations? (Use the same formula that we used for SOL and future Savings):

$$\frac{\text{Giving: \$\$}}{\text{Monthly: \$\$}}$$

    a. Church, Boys and Girls Club etc.

Please put your percentages in the blank table below you will need theses percentage to help you determine what stage you are in:

I'm actually a firm believer in giving. I believe what you sow, you reap, and if you do not give or you are selfish and stingy, then your income will look real selfish and stingy! Please put your percentages in the blank table below you will need theses percentage to help you determine what stage you are in:

**This is just a random example:

	STANDARD OF LIVING	FUTURE SELF	FLEX INCOME	GIVING
EXAMPLE	71.4%	3.87%	10%	13%
YOUR #S				

Using these tests for staging is very important because it helps your treatment team know which treatments you need. If a cancer is only in one location, a local treatment such as surgery or radiotherapy could be enough to get rid of it completely; so, if you don't have cancer that has metastasized – like stage 1 physical cancer, where they typically can do an easy procedure, extract the tumor, pull it out the mass; a local treatment treats only one area of the body. If a cancer has spread, local treatment alone will not be enough. You will need treatment that circulates throughout the whole body; these are called systemic treatments. Chemotherapy, hormone therapy and biological therapies are deemed systemic, as they circulate in the bloodstream.

The same way a doctor tries to locate the cancer and snip it out, you too must locate your cancer and do the same. Why? If I have a spy or an agent that is in my KINGDOM that is literally killing my people and killing my kingdom, would you not try to find the spy or assassin and kill them? Would you do that? Would you kill them if you knew they were trying to kill you? The answer is absolutely, you would! So, to be blind to what is literally taking your wealth away is absolutely ludacris!

However, because cancer can spread to the body and require systemic treatments, you may need to rid yourself of the all little cancers that may be eating up your income: eating out, excessive leisure time, large entertainment budget, high car payments. Drastic times call for drastic measures if you really want to beat this beast. So, when people are like, "Jake, I can't eat out?" I can't do those things?" I say, "You can do whatever the hell you want to do, but, I'm telling you what's killing you!" "I'm not the budget man!" You are not going to see me on you tube or on videos saying, **"This is how you create a perfect budget, (sarcastic tone). I am not doing that! You know what's killing you and if you want to eat your wealth away – then have your BEST LIFE!"** I will not eat my wealth away, especially before I put my employees to work! Benjamin, Lincoln and the others, they will work hard – **I'M TALKING ABOUT HARD!**

I am going to work them harder than they have worked any of my ancestors, as long as I can, then I will use the paycheck they make which is their cash flow, then I will eat on their food and their work. I am going to eat on their work, I will eat on mine and that is how you explain delayed gratification.

Staging Systems

Staging systems use the TNM system to divide cancer into stages. Most types of cancer have four stages, numbered from 1 through 4. Below is a brief summary of what each stage means for most cancers:

Stage 1

In stage one, the cancer is relatively small and contained within the organ it started.

Stage 2

In stage two, the cancer has not started to spread into the surrounding tissues, but the tumor is starting to get larger than it began in stage one 1. The cancer has not spread in stage 2, but it is starting to get larger and become uncomfortable, while starting to move in other areas. It has not move yet but, it's starting to get too large.

Stage 3

By stage three, the physical cancer is larger and may have started to spread into surrounding tissues.

Stage 4

Once the cancer has reached stage four, it has typically spread from where it started to another bodily organ. This is also called secondary or metastatic cancer. Here in this stage most patients only have 5 years to live after being diagnosed with stage IV cancer; 80% will probably live for at least another five years, and the other 20% would probably not survive this period of time.

Just as physical cancer has four stages, so does **"Financial Cancer"**. The stages of financial cancer are based off a percentage system. Compare your income percentage in each of the given areas to know where you fall.

	STANDARD OF LIVING	FUTURE SELF	FLEX INCOME	GIVING
STAGE 1	45% - 50%	5%	33%- 35%	10%
STAGE 2	53% - 57.5%	2%	33%- 35%	5.5%
STAGE 3	58%- 60%	0%	34%- 40%	1%
STAGE 4	62%- 66%	0%	34%- 40%	0%

See Above Illustration: So, just like there are four stages of physical cancer (notice I have thought this thing all the way through), As you can see it for yourself, as the stages get more progressively down to stage 4 it starts to get bad. If 62% to 66% of your income is going to standard of living, you are in stage 4 cancer. You only have 0% for your future self. You are in stage 4 cancer! If you notice, these numbers do not add up as you are above 100% of you income, which is why you are in debt. Then you have 0% going toward giving.

So, let me explain –

STAGE 1

In stage one, the financial cancer is relatively small, making the extraction of this malignancy moderately easy to fix if you can refocus and pay close attention to your spending habits. So, if I am in stage 1 cancer, it's very simple, it allows and let's me know that there s a little small quick issue, that's it. Something that can easily be fixed. Stage 1 says I am spending a little bit too much, I am in the wrong area and I need to fix a couple of things and I am good. That is no different than having physical cancer.

STAGE 2

In stage two, stress levels are rising, and sleepiness nights are occurring increasingly. The financial cancer has not started to affect the flow of bills and activities being paid. However, the problem is larger than it was in stage one and you are probably looking at your budget knowing you are extremely close to having full blown cancer. The longer you wait to get ahead of this cancer, the worse it will become. In financial cancer, this is when somebody is approaching living paycheck to paycheck. So, they are not really paycheck to paycheck, but that one F'up one little slip, they are in paycheck to paycheck, and that is stage 2.

STAGE 3

By stage three, you are living paycheck to paycheck. You are most likely experiencing high stress levels in your home; you and your significant other are arguing increasingly. Sleepless nights are hardly the problem, it seems that rest is nowhere in your near future. You may be experiencing yourself getting more sick than usual and your mood is never constant. This is a red flag; your financial cancer is now larger and has started to spread. This is usually the tipping point, of alcoholism, drug addiction, botched marriages, and feelings of entrapment or worse thoughts of ending it all. At this stage of financial cancer, this is when you are extremely irritable, everything irritates you, you can't be constant at nothing. Stuff is not even coming off your tongue the right way. You're just snappy, and you thinking that it's the foods you eat – you fix the food and you're still an A*hole! You think that it's the people around you – you fix the people around you and you are still negative and dark.

STAGE 4

Once the cancer has reached stage four, this is what I call "the financial death bed." In this stage, most people only have 5 years to drastically change their habits or Occulta Mortem (death, creeps up on you) is sure to come. It's almost like having a virus in the city and you don't know what's killing you, it just sneaks upon you and kills you.

That's what stage 4 financial cancer does, kind of like physical cancer. You do not really know but you have stage 4 cancer, and 6 months later you're dead. Like my grandmother, she passed about 3 or 4 months ago, and that is exactly what happened. In stage 4 cancer this is usually where marriages end, physical health takes a big dive, faith in God begins to come in question, and everything in your life seems out of order. The truth is only about 20% of the people diagnosed with stage IV financial cancer make it out unscathed.

What I mean by unscathed, is marriage is intact, relationships mended, coming back from nothing and staying strong. Typically, people get divorces things fall down, they never fix their credit, and it takes forever to get themselves back on track. That is exactly what happened to me when I reached stage 4 cancer. Failed the first marriage, lost my place, lost my cars, and everything. Started from scratch and it literally took me five years to get back on track. **Facts –** these are no lies here!

Let me show you guys what **optimal health is** – when you are living on 30% of your income!

Illustration:

	STANDARD OF LIVING	FUTURE SELF	FLEX INCOME	GIVING
OPTIMAL HEALTH	30%	30%	30%	10%
AVERAGE	37%- 40%	15%	33%- 35%	5.5%

You really want to drop the flex income to 15% and put 45% of that income going to your future self, which is optimal health. Think about it if you are financing from your bank and you are still literally living the life that you want to live, but you are funding your future self because you're the financier. **You all have to understand that financial cancer is not your friend it is your enemy!**

When you begin to understand your psychology of spending and you begin to start negotiating things and how they are, and figure out your own stage of cancer that you are currently in. When you go through these stages and actually figure out what stage you are physically in, then we are able to figure out your psychology behind why you spend what you spend. It is very important to understand the psychology behind – a lot of it has to do with behavioral issues.

For example: If you were a child and you never got attention in school, and the moment that you walked in with new shoes, everybody was your friend, and now all of a sudden you think that it's a coincidence that you love shoes – it's not that you necessarily love shoes – you like the attention that the shoes bring you because you felt like as a child nobody considered your value! And so, you spend your money on shoes thinking that the shoes are the reason that people know you for, and you begin to find that those spending habits become almost like a drug or alcoholic addiction because you are looking for the attention of other people to seek you. So, then it goes from shoes and nobody is paying attention to shoes anymore because you are grown! So, then it goes from cars, then from cars to another thing, to another thing, all because you are seeking attention; that same endorphin that released inside of you when you were a child as the same thing that you are seeking.

> **Remember,** all of this is psychological, and you must understand all the behaviors that cause us to do some of the things that we do. It is very important to understand that when it comes to these financial cancers and things we deal with.

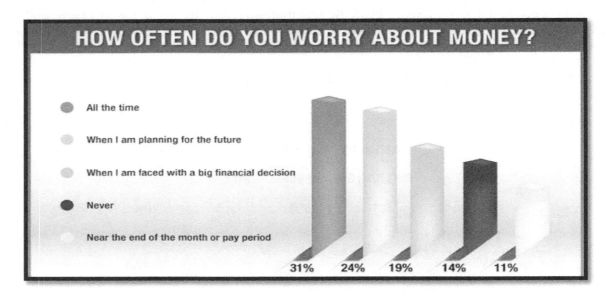

When you figure out your staging – Jake can help you understand and deal with your psychological reasonings and why you purchased the stuff you purchased.

If you think about it, that new car that you go and finance, you do not even like that car. You just get it because someone else got it! I remember in 2014, I financed two brand new 2015 BMW's, that I was renting from the bank, and the whole deal was, I do not even like BMW's!
I literally got a BMW because the people I was around, had BMW's – and I was like, if you can get a BMW, well, my favorite car has always been a BMW! I found myself at the BMW lot purchasing stuff because I had the wanting to fit in, and wanting to show people, I was successful. That was the number one cause and one of the top reasons why I lost my cars and had repos on my credit from BMW Finance – try to get that off your credit restoration, it is impossible!

There is this story of this man who got washed up at sea; literally a bad storm pushed him out at sea, and it cause for him to shipwreck on the island. All these people and islanders, they went to this man and said "Oh my goodness! The savior has come, we have had it in all of our history books! We are going to treat you like a king! They picked him up out the shipwreck. He woke up, going in and out, he heard them saying it, but he thought it was a dream. And when he woke up he was sitting on the throne. All these people began to bring him food, treats, and wives!

Talking about AMAZING – I want you to imagine that you wake up from a shipwreck and you are being treated like a king, like ROYALTY! And they are talking about – Oh my goodness, it was sent in our scrolls that you are the King, you are the Savior, you are going to help us achieve amazing things!

And so, he is liking it, "Like yeah! I'm the King! I'm the Savior!" Then what happened – time passed! As he was sitting down on his throne one day one of the servants walked by, he said, "Man I really do like you, too bad there will be a point in time where I won't be able to see you anymore." And he King looked at the kid and said, "Where am I going?" What do you mean, there will be a time when you will not be able to see me anymore?" The servant said, "Every five years there is a new shipwreck that always happens like clockwork, and when that person shipwrecks, what happens is, we make them King and then we send them off to the island to die by themselves. It's our ritual."

So, the King said, "Now, what's on this island?" The servant said, "Nothing King, nothing is on this island. It is literally bones and dried up kings that we sent." He said – dried up Kings? "Like how many people have you all sent over there?" The servant replied, "We've been doing it for years, over a thousand years, that we have been doing it."
The King said, "How much time do I have?" The servant responded, "Sir, you have two more years." So, the King asked, "While I am king you all have to do everything I tell you to do, right?" The servant said, "Yes sir we do. There is nothing we can say no to." The king said, "OK, you all do not kill me, you just send me over the hill, to the island?" The servant said, "yes sir, that is where we send you."

So, the King developed a plan. He said if my fate is to be sent on an island where there is nothing there, what I am going to do is prepare the island before I get there." He began to tell them to start sending ships to the island to start dropping off stuff that he was going to need to survive. He had them to start planting seeds of trees, they started building bridges, they started building a castle, he had them to start leaving people on the island. By decree he said there were some of the people that had to stay on the island. When two years passed, just like clockwork, they sent him off to the island and left him there.

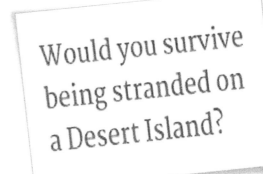

But the only difference from this king and others, is he knew his fate, understood his fate, and prepared for that exit.

I shared that story to say, one day you will get sick, one day you are going to get old, one day you are going to have kids, one day you will be a grandparent – these are things that you know to be for certain. And if I don't plan like the king, for my future, it is certain that my future will be dead. It is certain you will die! It is certain that your kids are going to need you! It is certain that your parents are going to need you! It is for certain that your parents are going to need you, and

I do not prepare today, for what I know is my indefinite demise – I know what's coming, I may as well say goodbye!

You are working a job, you work for somebody, and you know you firing is coming. You got your money in all these mutual funds and all this other stuff without studying it. You know a crash is coming! The market has been doing well for so many years, you know a correction is coming. You are driving a car, and you know you will get a flat tire one day.

You are having kids and you know that they will get sick. You are running a business, and you know that there will be dry spells. So, if I know that these things are for certain, why wouldn't I prepare like the king, for those things that I know are going to be for certain? So, that when I do get on this island, I am not lacking resources, and I just one-upped the game!

> **"My job isn't just to teach you this. My job is to be in your life for the rest of your lives, that's why I call you cousins. My job is to be the start, to teach you exactly how to take back control of everything that they have taken from us, and to be the catalyst; to not only be the bridge to this side of your island but to be here when you have kids, and grandkids, and to be here so that my kids can get introduced to your kids and we can keep this process going."**
>
> *Jake Tayler Jacobs*

But you have to want it for yourself! YOU have to want to build that island while you have the strength, while you have the ability, while you have the capability, and while you have the power to do it!!

Because, one day you will not have that power and you will wish when you were younger, and you had a lot more energy in your bones that you took care of what you knew was coming. You know you can't depend on certain family, and if they come through, they come through.

So, what would have hurt him?

He prepared the island. What if they said, "Jake, you can stay here." He just got two islands. **What if nothing ever happens?** "Great, I have prepared for the worse and I am enjoying the benefits of both preparations!" **Get yourself together!"**

Figure out your financial staging!

COACH'S CORNER

Recap of Financial Cancer: Staging

I'm very blessed for you guys to be on this training today. You guys did your Kingdom Blueprint and we did all that other stuff, and you were supposed to find what stage of financial cancer that you are actually in.

How can we take you from where you are – to where you want to go; if we do not know what stage of financial cancer you have.

Financial Cancer is the very thing that is killing the majority of Americans. I believe with all my heart that consumer debt is the number one cause of death in black America. We literally enslaved ourselves to thinking that the only way that you can be able to make it in this society is continuously borrowing.

That's exactly what the master who created the Mastercard created in our mind that the only way that you can get ahead is by using their resources and their money.

Now what does that mean in building your own banking system and what we teach?

These things, yes it takes time but the person who initiates freedom for your family is not always the one who gets to participate in the fullness thereof. I think It is very important to understand, people who started the Civil Rights Movement aren't the ones who get to participate in what the Civil Rights Movement actually created, and we are the benefactors of the Civil Rights Movement.

Either you are for legacy, and for your family or you're NOT!

There is no in-between, and that is what we got to understand and have a full understanding of what we are here to do.

43

NOTES

KINGDOM MANAGEMENT SERIES

The Spirit of Ownership

Why the Spirit of Ownership Will Kill You:

We need to be careful about ownership as It is dangerous. It is a dangerous spirit of individualism and it creates limitations, frustration and a spirit of depression and it creates lack. It will cause you to steal, and it creates poverty because people feel like what they can't get – they actually kill and fight to get it. The spirit of ownership is so dangerous that I actually creates sickness and disease and death because people are depressed over what they can't have.

We fight and kill ourselves working two jobs – can't sleep. You go from a day job, to a security job, you don't see your children, you don't see your wife, you don't see nothing, don't have time for nothing, don't see God, don't even have time for church, prayer or ministry. And at the end of it you got yourself a sick body. That's what the spirit of ownership does – it creates death. Ladies and Gentlemen, young men and great women, we have no idea how long we are going to live, but I hope you get this message before we leave this planet, there is no alternative except heaven.

And this is a reality to me, Jesus came to Earth to remove the spirit of ownership, but our culture is built, remember – on ownership. So we have a fight going on in our minds constantly! That's why it is very difficult to live in the Kingdom of God – matter of fact Jesus said it is hard for a rich man to enter into the Kingdom of God! He said it was impossible because the mentality is completely reversed because rich means "I" own. Kingdom means God owns! And to switch from me to him is a tough job. Let me put it another way – curse of eternity. Ecclesiastes says, whoever loves money, never has enough. Whoever loves wealth is never satisfied with his income. As goods increase, so do those who consume them. There is an economic lesson as the Bible is saying the more money you make – the more things you have to spend it on. You do not ever have any spare money left over; do you notice that? You're making more now and still don't have any money.

The Bible says it's futile. At what benefit are these things to the owner, except to feast his eyes on them? Just look at your car – you can't afford to pay the note. look around at your house – it's not yours, it belongs to the bank. It's frustrating! **Ecclesiastes 5:12** Whether he gets little or much, the abundance of a rich man means no sleep. **Verse 13**, I have seen a grievous evil under the sun. Wealth hoarded to the heart of his owner and wealth lost through some misfortune so that if he has a son, there is nothing left for his son. How many wealthy people do you know that are now broke? **Famous actors – famous boxers - famous wrestlers – famous musicians..**

All broke – nothing to leave to their children. Wealth hoarded to the harm of the owner. You can never hoard what is not yours. You can only use what is not yours. Lay this foundation in your mind – **verse 15** – naked a man came in his mother's womb, so as he came, so he departs. He takes nothing from his labor that he can carry in his hands and his too is a grievous evil. As a man comes so he departs and what does he gain as he toils for the wind. His days he eats in darkness with great frustration, affliction and anger. Most people are living that way. They work the whole week and at the end of the day they are frustrated because the check went directly to the bank.

Wake up! God is saying your system is not working. If you don't own – you have access. So the principle of Kingdom is lordship and this is why Kingdoms are opposite of democracies. In democracy – the prime minister owns nothing. The president of a country owns nothing, but in a Kingdom its opposite, and that is why God preached the Kingdom to us. In the Kingdom, Adam was given rulership but never given ownership. Because the source of our poverty is this idea of what I own. Ownership is what brings fear that someone is going to seal my stuff, that you want my stuff, and competition that you're trying to get my things.

You're trying to covet other people things that you don't have – all of that is from the spirit of ownership. That is happening right now in our country. One of the laws that God gave us is you should only covet if you think someone got something that you should have. IF you own or have access to everything, you don't have to covet anything. So covetousness is a sign that you think you own something, or you think someone else owns something. That's why God hates covetousness because it is a sign that the spirit of ownership has taken over a person. God told David, fret not yourself because of evil doers, for even if they seem to prosper, tomorrow they are like grass. Don't be jealous of people who think they are getting ahead. You own nothing. Adam was given access to everything that he needed.

We need to get back to **needs**. We are so motivated by wants that we forgot what we need. We need water, we need food, we need shelter. Do you need five flat screen televisions? I remember Abraham's son, just like your son may ask you a question – "Daddy how are we going to do this?" "Daddy how are we going to pay this?" And Abraham's son asking the same question – where's the sacrifice? And his answer was a good answer. "The Lord will provide."

If you have never prayed for anything – that's a good answer. In other words, Abraham abandoned the system and shifted to dependency on the **LORD!** Who is the **OWNER!** As Abraham was walking with his son on the other side of the mountain, there was a ram coming up on the other side. When you start moving in obedience, God starts moving all kind of things for you.

If you got faith, grab that right there and say – "Lord I'm moving!"

CHAPTER 3: MANAGEMENT OVER OWNERSHIP

Some people like to call that the Law of Attraction – you start moving some way, and when you move a specific way, and all of a sudden things just start happening your way and you start writing out your goals, when you start doing the work, when you start doing those things. Other people call it the Law of Attraction, and some people say it's God, other people may say it's Allah – but what I don't want you to get focused on is, that if you follow a certain doctrine or spirituality, get

the meat and leave the rest of the stuff. I don't want you to get caught up in all that and I am not trying to get into doctrine because we will be here all day. But what I am trying to get into is what was truth. All of us know, whether you believe in universe, whether you believe in trees, whether you believe in God, whether you believe in Allah, whether you believe in Elisha Muhammad, whether you believe in Minister Farrakhan, whether you believe in Jesus, or whatever you feel like you believe in – what we all come to an understanding is none of us created the world. None of us created the trees that we see, none of us created the fish, none of us created the sharks, none of us created the animals, none of us created the grass, and none of us created the fruit.

That wasn't man's creation. There was something that was larger and bigger than us and God created this world. And when I know that, that means there is no way that I can be the owner.

When I run a business, how can you say that you own the business when somebody can start your same company's name, in another country or another state? How can you say you own the business when you don't even own the people who work for you? How can you say that you own your house when the house belongs to the bank? How can you say you own the land when you have to pay the land tax to the state, the government or to the city, because if you don't they will seize the entire property? How can you say that you own money? **This is my money, or this is my bank account**. You see this **MY, MY, MY**… think about when a child is saying **mine, mine, mine**, they literally think that toy is theirs. And when you bought the toy and you tell the child to share, the child truly thinks that it is losing the only thing that is has when it doesn't know that right behind your back you got another toy for that child to have. This is an ideology that was forced down our throats to think that there is lack thereof.

"Man, he owns one insurance agency" There is no way I can own another one?" There is no shortage thereof and it's very important that we go from a mine, mine, mine, ideology to "there is no way I can take all of this with me." How many of you can agree that there is nothing on this earth that you can take with you when you die? How many of you guys can agree to that? Everybody can come to an agreement. Every single person can come to an agreement that there is nothing on this earth that you will be able to take with you in whatever next life that you believe in. Every person has a different doctrine and a different belief, and there is nothing you can take with you from earth, to the net level, to the next stage of life – there's nothing! **So, when I understand that, what exactly do you own?**

What do you own? So, we got to go from ownership to management! See, if I am managing something that I know is not mine, I'm going to do my best job to make sure I'm protecting what was given to me and growing it. See, if I don't own my wife and my wife don't own me, and I now that God or Allah or whoever gave it to me and I know that this person was given to me, then I am going to do my job at managing the gift that was given to me. I will do my best job to leave this gift better than what I found.

When it comes to the business, versus you thinking that this is my business – you are a MANAGER! When you die, that business is either going to die with you or someone else is going to take the realm of it. When it comes to your finances, when it comes to your bank, all these thing are finite, hey will not go with you. The money isn't yours, it has someone else's face on it. So, when I release attachment to things I don't even own, I gain authority! I understand I do not care about ownership, but I care about control over the situation, I want to be the best manager. The moment I released, that feeling of ownership was the moment my business grew, the moment my marriage to my wife went to another level, the moment my relationship with my ex-wife and my daughter went to the next level. The moment I realized; you do not even own time! You don't own your own lungs, you don't own breath, so, we are all chasing ownership and we are getting into debt – consumer debt, to own clothes? To own cars? And we are having sleepless nights, chasing this ownership thing, versus putting ourselves in better situations to control what we have; not to own it.

The reason why I love banking through insurance, and the reason why I love when money is getting drafted out of my account and going somewhere else, there is this piece of ownership that I lose. Because I am allowing currency to do what it is supposed to do, flow away from me and to me. So, I am allowing that draft out of my account, into my policy, into this banking system. Why? Because I understand for this period of time, I don't own my family and the best thing I can do is manage my last name the best that I can. My last name was given to me from my forefather; my father passed my last name down to me, and I want that last name to mean something to the next generation. Because I know I do not own my last name, but I can manage the value that I bring to my last name during the moment and time that I am alive. All of us are so committed to passing a business down to your children, passing land and real estate down to your children, and 90% of your children do not want half of the stuff you are giving. You're excited! Your calling was to be a doctor, your calling was to start FOREX, your calling was to be a DJ, your calling was to sell a nutritional product line, your calling was to make toys, your calling was to build that insurance or financial business, your calling was to build a landscaping business. But that's not your children's calling! Your job is just to build an estate, build cashflow. Grow the family's bank and net worth and leave that for your kids to figure out next what to do with it.

And that's why you see a lot of people that get rich, are lonely, not married, kids don't like them. Cheating on their spouses, allowing money and material things to control them. We live to own material things that have no value, no more value than you give it. The point is not the material things that lose value, it is to manage what God has given you. He has given me a wife, a child, a business that can generate cash flow that I can help move my family's net worth and grow it, and I want to manage that properly.

So, we got to leave ownership and start to pick up management. And when I realize I own nothing and I am only managing what was given to me and I want to move what I have forward, to grow this, what God gave me, so that I grow it so much the next generation can manage that properly. And that's how you grow generational wealth! That's how you build legacy and stability.

When you're building and growing a business, stop thinking it's yours. See that's why you are robbing yourself from your business. That is why you are stealing money from your business – the reason you do not have a savings account for your business. That's why you can't reinvest for your business because you are thinking it's mine. Dr. Myles Munroe said when you are literally eating or buying your wealth away, you built wealth and spent it on everything. You have nothing to pass to your kids.

48

I believe that in order to become the person who is completely in control of your entire life is to realize is that all you can control is what you manage. The grass is not green nowhere else it is green where you water it. It's not the industry that you are in, I's not the career that you are in, it's not the business that you are in, it is the fact that you got this false sense of pride of owning something that none of us own. Changing that philosophy in your mind, is a paradigm shift! Dang, even if you created a product, like the first laptop – how many versions of laptops are out there? Even if you created toilet paper – how many versions of toilet paper are there? Even if you created specific technology – how many versions of phones are there? So, no matter how much you trademark, no matter how much you copyright, no matter how much you LLC or ger licensed and do all this legal stuff to protect your quote on quote brand; it can be re-made, it can be re-done!

Nothing is new under the sun! One small change and it is a total different product, and someone took your idea and ran with it. It is not about ownership, it is about management, which is why we are talking about this as a **KINGOM MANAGEMENT SERIES**.

When you are on the computer and it's frozen and you just got to get the task manager up, because if I get the task manager up, I can delete anything! I can get off any app – so I want to **CTRL + ALT + DEL**! You want to **CTRL + ALT + DEL** and get some of that stuff off of there because what happens is, all of us, just like phones – technology is the craziest thing because it mimics real life. All of us came pre-programmed with apps, pre-programmed with a thought process. All of us came pre-programmed with ideologies, all of us came pre-programmed with how we think of ourselves.

All of us came pre-programmed with somebody called you shy since you were a kid and all of a sudden, you think you shy. You are not shy, nobody taught you or forced you to communicate. They allowed you to sit in your room. You know why I am not shy, and I can talk, my daddy made me talk everywhere, and when I tell you it was everywhere, it was everywhere. My momma made me talk everywhere, "Speak up boy!"

Just like phones come pre-programmed with apps, just like computers come pre-programmed with apps, just like tv's come pre-programmed with apps now. You come pre-programmed with your vision, your thought of who you are. And you got to **CTRL + ALT + DEL** all conventional thinking and ideology. You got to know your God for yourself. YOU got to learn your history for yourself, have an understanding of money and how it works for yourself. You got to **CTRL + ALT + DEL** all negative thoughts and everything.

But the first thing you got to **CTRL + ALT + DEL** is negative people! Negative people drain your time and your energy. If you don't believe in transferable energy, let me tell you – it EXISTS! Let me prove it – you wake up, say you are married or got a significant other, or somebody you care about. You wake up in the grandest mood, like nothing is going to mess up my day! And your significant other salty as hell! They are just off, and you say, "Hey babe, what's wrong with you?" "Nothing!... Like, Ok, you are still saying nothing will mess up your day and now you starting to get irritable. Like "what's wrong with you, "Nothing." Transferable!

You go to work, you go to your business, your employees or your team; somebody is irritated, and you get around and they are just irritated. Eventually you will become irritated. Or you're upset and you will meet someone, and they are just happy, they are thankful for the world, they are thankful for life, and all of a sudden you become grateful. Energy is transferable.

> ✓ **What if the negative one is a relative?** Just because you were born into a family, does not mean you are stuck with the negative people that came with it. You got the power to choose more than you realize. You got to cut them off. There are plenty examples in my favorite book, (*may not be your favorite book*) called the Bible, and there are plenty of times where people that God used were cut off and separated from his family. **Why?** Because growth happens in isolation! Because if you don't cut off those bad weeds, those bad weeds will cut you off.

Have you ever seen a plant try to grow amongst a bushel full of weeds? It's impossible, those weeds are going to choke you out! **Jake, "what does this have to do with money?"** Simple and it's easy, it has everything to do with money. I have people who has a negative thought when it comes to how to manage money; eventually I either have to adopt their doctrine, or they adopt mine. If I am not strong enough to stand strong and firm against people who don't understand how to become my own bank, and they got this warped ideology on how money functions and I'm looking at their life and the people and I am like it does not make sense. There are bunch of financial advisor that do not even do what they teach you to do! Check the stats – they are broke.

You have to cut off because If you start indulging in negative people and participating in what they have going on before you know it you will find yourself complaining and your whole entire day is ruined.

And what just happened? You just allowed that person to take over your space, your time, and your thought process. You allowed somebody to determine how you were going to handle your day. Typically, when people call me with a problem and I know they are about to ruin my day – (*call Connie y'all*) she can attest, I give them sixty seconds, I let them get it out in sixty, even if they didn't get to it and I say, **"Alright now, what's the solution?"** They say, "well I just want to.. ummh.. **Call me when you got a solution**." Well Jake, I don't have any money because I left this… **What's your solution?"** well I don't know it's because they left me and now I got the kids .. **No that is not the solution!**

The solution is you need to close your legs because you are having too many babies without understanding the repercussions that come with having babies. You need to close those legs sir and ma'am. The problem isn't the baby mommas, the problem is that you are too hard to guard.

You can't guard or manage yourself. So, now you got more money coming out your pockets because you do not know how to control yourself. The problem is not the job is not paying you enough, it's you living in a higher means than your job can pay. It's not the job, it's you!

You got to manage these things because you cannot get back time – time is too valuable!

We cannot allow ourselves to lose time in our day, so you got to cut off negative people. I know it's hard to cut off family, but you got to give the a warning, say, listen, this is what I'm doing and if you are not willing to watch the entire master class, and go through the entire master school and listen to the same guy, that is teaching me in full, and not your thought process of it. Because if you knew about it, you would have taught me! So, me telling you about me becoming my own bank don't tell me you already knew about it. IF you already doing it and you knew about it and didn't tell me, then that tells me who you are; and if you knew about it and you didn't do it, that lets me know who you are!

Managing Negative People

You've got to manage negative people. And negative people aren't just the things that they say, it is also their actions. They can talk good talk, but their actions are negative, meaning you got to manage people who find comfort in staying broke. You got to manage people who enjoy making bad financial decisions, you've got to manage people that are so short sided, that they can't see tomorrow past today! You've got to manage negative people!

Jake, **"I thought we were learning about money. I thought we were learning about currency, and the re-education thereof, and banking and investing "I am not going to teach you that until I can change your mind."**

Change your mind – change your life. My favorite book the Bible, says you can be in the world, but not of the world. Don't let the world control you – you got to be in it but do not let the world control you. So, typically if all the world is buying cars financing cars, odds are that is nothing you should be doing. And you probably should be doing the opposite.

Do not conform to this world but be transformed by the renewing of your mind. Which means do not tell me to do it this way, but you are doing it that way! I am looking at your lifestyle and it doesn't excite me.

You make ten, twenty or thirty thousand a year but you are living a twenty, thirty, and forty thousand lifestyle that should not excite you! What should excite you is somebody making twenty, thirty thousand a year and living on under eight thousand. What do you think they are doing with the rest of the money? That should be exciting! We should have "**save**" parties!

When women are dating, and people talking about all the cars. But do you save, doe? I mean, you are telling me about all the cars and how much you make let me see that savings account, doe? And don't go just by credit score because you know they can do the tradelines. And they can do that illegal credit sweep and get your trade lines on there for two or three months, which will boost their score to 780 but that is not the makeup of who they are.

But you do not want to hear about that because I am all up in your Kool-Aid.

We got to learn how to **CTRL + ALT + DEL** and manage our thoughts. How you deal with life and problems in business is important. Because in life, in business, in your career whether you realize it or not you are always going to be putting out fires. Let me tell you something as long as you are living life does not get easier. They say more money, more problems. Not because you are spending more and not because people want more of your money, but because the more money you make, typically, the more responsibility you have. People want minimum wage to go up and I get it.. minimum wage should go up! But the only thing you are doing is one thing. See, the reason why the CEO whether you like it or not, makes millions of dollars, is because he is managing thousands of people.

Managing Thoughts

So, the more responsibility you have means the more value you bring to society, means you make more money. So, if you are at your job, you say, "Man, I only make $40,000 a year, and I know I am worth more than this." Are you? So, I know an over achiever will reach the top of the compensation level no matter where they are. Whether they work for themselves or work for someone else. You are going to reach the top of the chain. So, we got to learn how to manage our thoughts.

Ask yourself these questions:

- **What system do you have to drown out negative thoughts?**
- **Do you shower or bathe every day?**
- **Do you brush your teeth every day?**

So, all of us are putting yes when it comes to hygiene – because we understand that stinking isn't cool.

So, let me ask you a question.

- **What do you do to clear, clean, shower, or brush that stinking thinking away?**
- **What do you do to bathe those negative, nasty, stinky thoughts?**

You got to have something clean, something powerful, something impactful, that is going inside of your brain, cleaning and washing away all those negative thoughts. You've got to bathe in positive thoughts.

So, how do you bathe in positive thoughts?

1. **Listen to audios that can progressively move you forward**
    - When you start off, you are going to fall asleep – they are boring. But eventually, just like vegetables, you start to have a taste for it, they get easier to eat, and then you start craving it. Because anything that is healthy for you – you do not want to do.

52

The point I am making is, such as bathing, it is not fun. You don't get excited or get a rush to bathe, you don't get a rush to brush your teeth, but you know that it's important to keep up a certain hygiene, because it is healthy for you. The point I am making is, you want to bathe yourself every day, so you listen to audios. I knew I did not come from a household or group of people that thought the way that I thought consistently. So, I knew that what I came pre-programmed with were thoughts that were taught and told to me before I could even gain consciousness.

So, those are things in my subconscious mind that I got to start getting down to and draining out. You have got to start listening to audios. Now I am not going to tell you who to listen to, you got to find who scratches your itch. Just like soap, you have to find which soap works for you because every scent is not good for everybody. Everybody got to have a different kind of soap that meshes with your skin good.

2. **Got to be careful and selective to the music you listen to, because you do not want to become a product of that environment that you are letting in your life.**
   - You want to control the music that you are listening to. It's very important the type of information that you are indoctrinating inside of your mind.

3. **Find ways to combat your negative thoughts.**
   - Some of you have said I do martial arts, and dancing – that is where you will add that. Find ways to combat your negative thoughts, find ways to release it. That's not what I would consider a mental shower, because you are finding ways to release it.

4. **Learn how to compartmentalize and weed out negative thoughts.**
   - Everything that pops us, every fire that is in your life, does not have to be addressed at the same time. That causes you to overload. You need to deal with the priorities and what matters at that moment. It is a skill set that takes time to develop. The best way to do it is to write down on a piece of paper, everything that's worrying you, and to deal with those problems as based on priority.

That is the best way we deal with financial problems in my house. If a bunch of stuff pops up at once, I am going to say**, "Listen, we are not dealing with all that right now." "What's most important right now? Everyone else can wait." "What would change our current lifestyle at the moment and that's what we will deal with right then?"**

Learning how to compartmentalize is very important. I got little blue me in my head, it sounds crazy, but I do. And any time I get fire and worry, my little blue men have like a little (musical) assembly in my head. They are passing papers to each other; I know it sounds crazy but this the way I designed it in my head. They have these little timers on their heads, and the timers are set up in my mind based on priority. So, I deal with things and problems as they come up based on priority.

53

Never deal with more than one problem at the same time. So, when the bill collector calls, I answer the phone. ANSWER! I don't have the money today sir, that's all I can tell you! You are not about to stress me, don't call me scam likely, just call me! I will pick up if you call me regularly – you cannot have my same area code, which is Dallas TX and it says Ohio TX is on the phone calling. What is Ohio TX? Call me – I don't have it.. it's cool we can talk. "Sir, at the moment y'all are not priority! My credit is already shot and there is no worse you can do. I cannot pay you today.

You're trying to mess up my area in my head and I got you on the 4th level with the blue men. But make sure you tell them that I corresponded with you, make sure you put that in the notes. Be sure tell management that I spoke with you. Don't go and say he went unresponsive; I'm talking to you. But at the moment that credit card has got to go. If you need to turn it off, turn it off if that's what you need because I'm not paying it today. Just letting you know that. Thank you sir and thank you ma'am, now don't be mean and put me in collections and close my account, because depending on how you treat me I may not even pay it; I may wait seven years and let it roll on off my credit. So be careful how you use me!

When you start thinking of stuff like that it's easier to manage your thoughts. Which now makes you not an emotional person and that type of person is a great manager to have, because we are going back to management. If you are the CEO or top Executive of the company and you got Regional Vice Presidents, managing regions of your company, you don't want nobody in high levels of management that is always bugging out when some stuff go wrong! But it's perfect when it comes to managing, if you are somebody that always loses, you can't sleep at night because things get out of hand! There is no way that the universe, God, Jesus, Allah, Muhammad, Buddha, the sun god, no matter who you represent; there is no way that they're going to bless you with more to have if you can't even manage the little bit you got!

> **It's like a father and a mother – you will never give your children more than you know that they can handle. You will never put a brand-new Ferrari in a 15 – or 16-year old's possession. You will go get them a little clunker car and you are going to make them wash it and take care of it because you that there are levels to responsibility. The higher the responsibility, the more you typically have. So, we got to get good at managing our thoughts so that we can control our environment. Controlling your environment is absolutely important, and it is very important when it comes to banking. Because when you start to become your own financer and your own bank, you can't control your emotions, you will borrow money from yourself and never pay yourself back and you will rob your family because you say this is my bank!**

5. **Get rid of pre-programmed apps in your life!**
   - You do not have to have those apps just because your mommy and daddy said that you should have them.

So that we know we do not own anything, we just got to get good at managing!
And I realized when I shifted from ownership to management – I realized:

- ✓ **How poor of a Manger I was**
- ✓ **How poor I was at managing relationships**
- ✓ **How poor I was at really managing a business,**
- ✓ **How poor I was at managing a team as a leader,**
- ✓ **How poor I was at managing my resources,**
- ✓ **How poor I was at managing my money**
- ✓ **How poor of a Manger I was.**

So, I started with managing my thoughts, washing them new every day, cleaning them as much as I cleaned my body and my mouth. So, when managing your thoughts, and managing negative people – the last thing is managing your life.

Managing Your Life

We got to understand is, if you do not manage your life, you cannot set proper expectations. Do not get distracted with life situations that take time away from your commitments. Learn how to be organized. Put things and processes in place. Remember, how you manage your life is how you manage your businesses, and how you manage your businesses is how you manage your bank.

- ✓ Life itself is a system – no matter what your belief is we all understand that there is an ecosystem. There is no doctrine or ideology that takes away that there is an ecosystem that we all live on. Any small piece of the ecosystem that is changed, taken away, or shifted, changes how everything functions.

Scenario:

So much so, I got bitten by an ant one time. Let me tell you, so, I was outside, and you know I'm in a fraternity – I'm a Que. And I'm out there hopping and hopping along, you know what the Que's do – and I realized that I was by an ant pile. I mean I was grown, but you know you are out there in the yard, and doing all that or whatever, you are not really paying attention like that. So, I was by an ant pile, and AN ANT BIT ME! Let me tell y'all, there is some stuff that I am just like, a mosquito bit me and I will be like, "ahh it's a mosquito, I'm going to sweat it out a little bit." But when an ant bites me, I get mad! Like WHY?" Like why does your little bitty bite hurt so freaking much?!" And I began to research why the ant was created, because I was going to find a way to exterminate all ants beyond existence. I just wanted to find some solution where I could kill every ant on site. And as I began to dig into the importance of an ant, I realized how valuable the ant is.

- The ant is the first line of defense to be able to eat away at things that decay for us. They help clean up our system, and stuff that we know that is not supposed to be on the ground, stuff that we leave, candy, gummies, gum, and all that. Ants dispose of all that for us.

- The second thing that ants do is dig holes. Inside of the ground, and they are typically by trees or in the grass. Ants dig holes in the ground that allows rain to be able to seep through the soil to be able to nourish the roots of plants and trees.

So, I began to see like, dang, if this small ant that I thought had no value to life, plays a big part in this giant ecosystem.

That means that the creator, literally put a system of something in place for everything. Which is how everything can function. Which leads me to the reason why it seems like your life is so unpredictable, it's because we do not have systems in place to manage our life. If the sun did not come up tomorrow, we would think that there was a problem. Because there is something about consistency, that we begin to depend on.

So, when I am inconsistent in my life, inconsistent in my business, inconsistent in the way I manage money, and inconsistent in my health; but the inconsistency is because we feel like we own time, and we own our life, that means we can control whatever! So, we are not responsible for being consistent. But if that sun decided not to come up, all of y'all would be like, "Oh Lord, the second coming!" "The Lord is back to take us all the way!" If there was ever a time when the universe began to be inconsistent, there's a problem. So, when you're inconsistent you should consider that to be a problem too. You got to learn how to manage your life like a system, everything should work the same exact way, everything has a place, and everything works best that way. You don't have to worry about putting up dishes all the time if you had a system to where you cook, you clean, you put away the dishes. You don't have to be frustrated – men your wife doesn't have to be frustrated if y'all had a system to where she cooks, you clean – boom you're done! Men, women, you don't have to be mad if you had a system of what you all did with the towels. Women love winning, when things got folded? Now you will be irritated because y'all are two people living together but the system of how everything works should be the same, and everything should have a place in your life. Managing your life is a system and everything in life has a system.

Jake, "what do you mean by that? What's the difference?" We got the system of the ecosystem but every ant, every plant, all the lakes, all the insects, all the animals have their own systems and ecosystem. So, an ant has its own function of life, different from the bees. Is that correct? The birds have their own function of life different from the eagle. So, everything in life has a function, and if I have so much arrogance to think I do not have to report to nobody and I can be where I want to be, how I want to be, but if you are not a great manager of time - you will lose time as fast as you blink your eye. How many of us, literally 10, 20 years pass, and everything was a blur. How many of us? 10, 20 years passed, and you cannot remember anything. We got the most intelligent brain in the world, but we can't remember a thing – **WHY?** Because you do not have systems in place, so you can't enjoy life in the capacity that is supposed to be enjoyed because you are so busy putting out fires because of the inconsistencies in your life.

So, **(the money that we have),** first if I'm a good manager of my resources, the money that I have is not for me to go buy Rolexes and Benz!

How cliché' and shallow do we have to be – that "I work, I trade time."

"Well I don't trade time for money Jake, when I sleep, money is made." Ok. Did you not have to develop a skill to be able to sleep and make money? Yes! So, the time that you traded to learn that skill and to be able to make money in your sleep, which you still have to manage is time you lost. So, money that you make is supposed to make your life's system easier. So, before you go buy a Rolex and a Benz – men or women how about you buy a maid or service to be able to clean your house to make your life systems better so that you can be able to enjoy life more. Versus going to get a $200,000 car, how about you get you a $40 or $50K SUV, sit in the back and hire somebody to drive so you will not lose that 30 minutes to an hour a day driving!

These are better places to put our resources. So, it is not you being boujee it's about you living like a King or Queen! It's you living in your ordained rightfulness to Kingdom ship to lordship – why would I drive? I'm going to pay somebody to drive? Why would I cut my grass? I'm going to pay somebody to do that. Oh, he boogie! NO! I enjoy and I appreciate life that much, that I am willing to pay to have a better standard of living to have a better type of lifestyle.

"I would much rather have you guys look at me and say, "Man, Jake drive that little used car – he look broke, does he really make money?" I would rather you look at me like that when I got a full bank account, I got full insurance banks, and I got systems and processes that take care of every aspect of my life."

"I rather you look at me like that and question my worth, based on what I do and don't have versus me continuing trying to buy stuff to impress people and keep living to a standard, trading my time and my life for things that have no value, like steel and cotton, polyester, and metal. Resources that we are supposed to service, we are spending the majority of our time serving them."

– Jake Tayler Jacobs

We have got to get good at managing our life and putting systems in place that make our life better. That's why banking is important and becoming your own bank. Because the more interest that you can literally lock up and control inside of this banking system, the more money you have to create a better system for your ecosystem of your life, your kingdom system.

And then you can spend more time (as they say in business) working on the business than in the business. So many of us are busy working in life, that we can't work on life in a macro scale, as there should be a system in life for everything. Wash, clean, this go here, this goes there – maid take care of this; if you got this whole ecosystem working for you, what are you really stressed about? You got more time to deal with real problems than deal with the small problems or beefing with your spouse over who put dishes in the sink! Who cares, Maria can come take care of that! Or Sholondria, they got a maid service.

You manage your life by finding the most efficient way to avoid small problems. When it comes to life, you got to start looking at life like an engineer. How can I build a system in my life where I can avoid small problems? Easiest way take negative people out that drain money. People that are always asking you for money, they probably need to be taken out of your ecosystem. Or you need to let them know, sorry I do not lend money anymore, I do not give money. Just because you make the most money in your circle, does not mean you always have to buy lunch. This is managing small problems.

Easy way to manage small problems – babies cost money, manage your libido. Manage your private parts adults because babies come with a cost. It's very simple, you do not have to go and save yourself for marriage just because of religion. It's simple – babies cost, and sex is for creating babies! That's simple math. Am I ready to spend $1,000 a month just on daycare? Not including everything else. Manage your small problems.

"If there are no systems, you are guaranteed to be unproductive... – NOT EFFICIENT "
                                                                                            - Jake Tayler Jacobs

I do not like people around me that are unpredictable, I cannot trust you if you are unpredictable. Just like when I walk in my house, I need that electricity to come on, I need to predict, because I paid the bill and it better be on. I paid for cable and wi-fi, it better be working. I paid for my phone bill it better be working. I don't need inconsistency in service, so I darn do not need inconsistency in people around me. "I don't go to work; I don't go to the office." "I am at the beach today, because I just don't feel like it." "I call life how I feel." You cannot be around me; I don't trust you. Because when I need you, you may not be there because you do not know if you are going to be there. I don't like those people. I don't trust people that want to sit on the beach all day and don't do nothing. I don't like those people.

You're not doing anything productive. Your life literally was made just for you. People that say I just want to make money on the beach and don't talk to anybody – I cannot stand those people. Those have to be the most selfish, ownership minded, covetous people I have ever met in my entire life. It's disgusting!! And if that is you – I am talking to you! Because you disgust me, as your cousin, I love you, but you discuss me! There is nothing you can do on the beach all day – nothing productive, but pretty much tell God- I own time.

All systems must flow and corelate in order to function. Everything has to work and flow together. Create systems for your life, for the consistent things that you deal with.
Create an ecosystem of your life.

58

CHAPTER 4: WHY WOULD I SETTLE FOR LESS?

LEGACY MANAGEMENT

I think it is very important that we understand where we want to go and that's why we talked about systems in the very last course. We talked about systems, because when you have those systems in place it's easier to manage your legacy, because everything has a place, and everybody has a part. And if I have a part and have a place, it's easier to be able to grow a legacy from one place to the next.

So, we talked about in the Kingdom Blueprint, the importance of having foresight, to be able to see something in the future, to have vision – **provision**, which is to be able to see something further than where you currently are. See tomorrow before it even comes and to prepare for that, so even if tomorrow is not a bad day you're prepared and you're good. **Habakkuk 2:2** says write it down and make it plain so that people who see it can run with it – so that men who see it can run with it. Basically, like the Blueprint, you're creating the Blueprint for your life so you can just run with the Blueprint! **Why?** Most of us, we're creatures of habits, we typically, usually follow the habits before we follow what we are supposed to do. We're easy at being told what to do, than we are at coming off the top of our dome. So, if we tell ourselves what to do, and follow our own rules, our own obligations, it's a lot easier for us to get to where we want to go.

When it comes to "Why settle for less", what I want you guys to see that I'm not telling you guys not to have the best of everything. I'm not telling you guys not to have good watches. I'm not telling you guys not to have nice cars. I'm not telling you guys not to lie in great places. But what I am telling you is one thing – **Don't have those things at the expense of your family's future!** See to get those things you want passive income to get you those things. Not your working income, not you slaving away at getting your freedom. That money that you have is to buy your freedom. That debt that you have; you want to buy your freedom! So, you want to get as free away from all things that can keep you captured in the traditional society or traditional financial trap. You want to stay away from the things that are traditional and put yourself in a position so that those things can purchase your lifestyle.

I want you guys to know that the God that I serve, the God that you serve; the manufacturer of who we are, who create us, the beings that we are – God wants us to have more than you can imagine! He wants us to live in abundance! He wants us to have quality! But the very first thing that we should be using our money for is quality of life, not quality of things. Oh, I'm talking to somebody! Which means a lot of us, we use these monies to buy material things so that we can look free but still be slaved. Yeah your cage looks better than your grandparents, yeah you got steaks, but your family got peanut butter and jelly – but you are still in the zoo, your cage is just bigger, and you are still trapped.

You still can't go anywhere – you still have to work to pay for things because of the debt that you have occurred over your life. See I don't want to look free; I want to be free! I don't want to look like I made it past the gun line boss – I want to pass the line.

The first thing I want to re-gear in your heads is not to use your money to purchase things that don't matter – you use your money to make your lifestyle better. To increase your livelihood, you employ, you give people opportunities. Versus you cleaning your house, you give somebody a job to clean your house. It's not you being uppity – it's you using your money to put back into the economy by employing somebody else, but then it gives you time to work on what God gave you to work on. You start employing people to make your job better, and to make your business function better,

In this piece of "Why Settle for Less" this is what I'm saying – don't settle for less! But the first thing, we got it misunderstood, it's not in the clothes that you have, it's not in the shoes that you wear, it's not in the ice that you rock, it's not in the rings that you wear, not in the cars that you drive, it's not in the home that you stay in. Do you know that we all are renters?

The goal isn't more money. The goal is the freedom the money will give you

Purchasing a home for an investment is a terrible move. You should be purchasing properties and homes for your compound for your family, to never sell. Not to purchase to sell, that's stupid. So, we got to change the paradigm of what we consider quality versus less. I want to eliminate as many things that stress me as possible. I want to get rid of those things that stress me, and if I could hire someone to eliminate that stress, that takes stress off me which increases the value of my life.

Don't settle for less, settling for material things are less than who you are. You start working for steel, steel that makes your car! You start trading in your time just so you can purchase steel or plexiglass. You trading in your valuable time just so you can purchase bricks – and mortar, i.e. your home. You are selling your time just so you can buy Gucci, Ferragamo, and all of these things that mean nothing. Ten years, that is going to be out of style, and you traded your time for things that are going out of style? Come on now! I'm trying to teach you something. I'm trying to help you, trying to shift your mindset! I'm trying to change your mindset so you can be able to see the value of not settling for less.

Lifestyle! How you live, how you are able to handle and deal with stress is what you should be spending money on. Not stuff that can deteriorate. You should be spending money on relationships, investing in people that are around you, because those things never die. Because that person that you decided to pout into, to help you better your life, you don't know that you bettered their life by hiring them, by employing them and giving them a chance. Pour money into them and they tell their kids how you impacted them – you may die but the lasting memory of what you done for them never dies. That's a lot better than purchasing things that people forget you had. Come on now! Don't settle for less. Why do you think God made people and didn't keep making trees? He created people because he understood the importance of where the value was and pouring into people. Don't settle for less. Your family, your legacy depends on it.

You teach your legacy the importance of:

- ❖ People Capital
- ❖ Relationship Capital
- ❖ Developing strong Relationships

It does not matter how much money you make when you implement! We don't settle for less. You don't sell out a person just to have a thing! You don't stab the back of someone that was rocking with you when you had nothing, just so you can have one up in the game to get a better car. Relationships matter more and when you begin to implement, ingrain that into your kids heads. You know what it does? It teaches them how to preserve the legacy more than you realize. If you teach your kids only money, only banking systems, only how to grow resources, they are going to be so consumed in growing the resources, that they miss serving the people! Come on! Don't settle for less! As I am teaching you these banking strategies, I am re-educating you on money and I don't want you to miss that. Which takes me to LEGAVY MANAGEMENT.

See it is very important that you begin to implement systems and processes in place to be able to manage your legacy. See I took you from ownership to management, now we are talking about legacy management. We need Wills, Trusts, and Insurance in place to be able to preserve what we are doing today for tomorrow. See, all of this means nothing if you do not have wills, trusts and insurance. You can start that business. You had intentions to start, but you never fully got it off the ground. You passed away and everything that you started with DIED! And everything that you sacrificed was for nothing because there was nothing for your kids to step up on – legacy management!

Legacy management means I am not going to sacrifice my kids tomorrow just so I can have it today! **Hello!!! Wake up!**

I am not going to sacrifice my kids' tomorrow just so I can have my **TODAY!** I am not going to put food on Bank of America's kids, or JP Morgan's great, great grandkids. I am not going to put food on their tables before I put food on my future grand kids table. See, y'all got two things in common, y'all future grandkids don't exist. But the difference is, you are putting food on their table before you put food on yours. You are willing to put yourself into debt, go into slavery today, so that you can have your luxury today; and you are robbing your kids, your legacy for tomorrow. **We're talking about legacy management!**

Let's use my shoes as an example – These are from Walmart! Do you know that when I walk around in fancy places, they do not know that this is an Avia Shoe – a Walmart Brand. If I am going to spend money on shoes, I would rather spend the least money going into tennis shoes, now the quality shoes I spend a little more, but these shoes, $10, $12, $13, $14 dollars. So, I can have the other $100 dollars I would have spent on tennis shoes and I can put that on my family's plate. That's what's important. It's important for us to understand that. See while y'all spending $20 grand, $30 - $40 grand, on stuff that died, I believe in putting my money in things that will continue to live.

When it comes to banks, we teach you how to do it and we show you. Versus putting money on stupid stuff, we could have bought a car and stunted on you, but we are in legacy management and I do not want my legacy to die in my hands.

I don't want to be responsible for that. So, legacy management means putting processes, and systems in place to make sure my legacy lives past me. "Well Jake, I don't want kids." Well your last name is a legacy, so you better partner with your sister or brother that got kids, and you make sure the legacy moves forward.

So, legacy management is: Wills, Trusts, Insurance, Blueprints of your family's legacy, and the game plan on how to apply everything that you are learning. Everything that you are leaning, you should be writing it down so that your kids can be able to see how to do certain things and they do not have to go to YouTube because they can see from their mom and dad. You should have policies and procedures for you family. Just like Grandmama, she passed down her food manual, her recipe book – you should be passing down policies and procedures on how to open up bank accounts, and how to properly set stuff up, how to set up a business. You should be writing those experiences down so that your great, great grandkids have something to fall on. It's called legacy management. You can't manage nothing that doesn't have a system and a process. What are you managing? You don't know how to determine if the legacy is moving forward or if the next generation is actually growing the family's name. You can't have **KPI's (key performance indicators)** in place to be able to determine if the next generation is actually succeeding or failing; other than the eye test, if you do not have policies, procedures in place to grow it.

Legacy Management every single day!

This is how I monitor my legacy – I make sure that everyday I am moving my family's name forward. Everyday I am doing something to progressively move our family's name forward:

- ✓ **I write my goals down**

- ✓ **I put my quote of the day or the month of the year that I am focusing on**

- ✓ **I write my targets and what I want to accomplish for the day**

- ✓ **I write my successes – what I actually accomplished for the day**

- ✓ **I write down my goals again**

And you know what's going to be important? All of these planners that I have for my kids, you know what I am going to do? I am going to put them down, these all are going to be in my will, and my kids are going to be able to follow their father, from when he didn't have anything to when he had the world. And they are going to see the growth of their father from one place to the other. Legacy Management, you got to keep receipts of growth of your business.

62

See, my last name I consider it a business, I'm moving the legacy, the name forward – I'm moving my family's name forward. It's important, I'm moving my legacy forward. I'm managing my legacy by putting processes and systems in place.

I will not be the same generation that shoots from the hip and expects life to be predictable when you are not predictable. I won't do it. So, in this segment, I want you to be intentional because we are about to go into the re-education of money, we about to get into the meat of things. But, what I want you to do – I want you to get serious about your future and I want you to make the decision that from this point on you are going to be tracking your family's legacy, and that you are going to be moving forward, because now we are about to get into the money of things.

I won't be talking about legacy and family generation as much, but you cannot leave these segments without being fully focused an intentional with moving your legacy forward. **Wills, Trusts, Life Insurance, Blueprints, and Policies.** Those are the five things that you need in order to guarantee that your legacy moves forward.

Scenario:

> **Jake, "What are Blueprints?"** Blueprints are how you built it from scratch, what to do, what is step one, what is step two, so that your voice, your words can be passed down from generation to generation. Just like you look at grandmama recipe book on exactly what she did. Your kids should be able to look at exactly how you handled certain situations – they should be able to see that. They should be able to go to chapter 20 when Grandma built that real estate business from scratch – her failures and successes, what she did right, what she did wrong, what to check for, who to go see, all these things should be there, that should be the blueprint, your family's blueprint. And then the application, how to apply the blueprint now.

Remember: Wills, Trusts, Life Insurance, Blueprints, and Policies.

Applications of policies to dictate how they should be, how they should be behaving, how they should function, how to maneuver in society to make sure that they have the upper hand and not the underhand.

Kingdom Legacy over Everything!

COACH'S CORNER
Recap of Legacy Management

I want you guys to know that the God that I serve, the God that you serve; the manufacturer of who we are, who create us, the beings that we are – God wants us to have more than you can imagine! He wants us to live in abundance! He wants us to have quality!

But the very first thing that we should be using our money for is quality of life, not quality of things. Use your money to purchase things that don't matter – you use your money to make your lifestyle better. To increase your livelihood, you employ, you give people opportunities. What does it mean to leave a legacy? Do you have things in place that will leave an impact for your kids or your family?

In order to define your legacy, you must know what that means and how to get started. When we started off our lessons with the Kingdom Blueprint, those pages helped you see the foundation of how you wanted to leave your legacy. Your legacy does not determine what you do while you are here – that's just the beginning. Your legacy determines what you leave behind and how much you wanted the generation after you to continue carrying on your name and your vision.

Legacy starts with you, and you are the designer to help create generational wealth for your family. Leave something at the expense of your family's future. We should make sure that all the milestones set in place will continue to carry on and that your kids, kids can say that they are second and third generations of something great! What legacy will you leave behind? Will people have good things or bad things to say about you?

Your name should be one that leaves a permanent stain on a person's memory when they think of you and that is the **impact** you want to leave behind.

Guys this is your Coach Jake Tayler Jacobs and I will see you in the next segment.

NOTES

FINDING THE MONEY: WHAT'S IN YOUR WALLET

CHAPTER 5:

The Evolution of Money: Value, Wealth, and Income

In this segment, we will be talking about how to make money your slave and not your boss. So, we are going to talk about that first, and before we get into the meat of things, I even got PowerPoints so you can kind of see visuals of what we're talking about and also I will provide a link of the book that I used for the illustrations to be able to help me pinpoint that. I'm a firm believer of giving you guys the sources to where I have learned this information or that helps me better teach it so that you can be able to gain that knowledge for yourself. I think that the true way to uplift people, is not only to educate them; but to give them the same sources that educated you. I think I want to give you to the plug – I want you to be a part of the plug source too. So, I am going to give you the information of where I got some of the clippings for this PowerPoint today. Always remember, that I am always going to give you the game as much as I can give you if I can. So, before we get started there is one thing that I want to go into, I want you to understand that money is supposed to be your slave.

Write this down – MONEY IS MY SLAVE! It's your servant – money is supposed to be serving you, not you serving money.

The majority of us; we've talked about this in our other segments, how we've all been around this system, but we have been backwards. It's like we're all enslaved, just in another way.

So, you've got to get ingrained in your thick head, that MONEY IS YOUR SLAVE! You've got to let money go to work for you and stop working for your money. Money is not your boss! And how do I know that some of us think that money is our boss, it's very simple, I can tell how uncomfortable some of us get when it comes to us communicating about our finances. It's kind of like that boss that walks into the room and you're scared to talk to the boss because you don't want them to fire you.

You don't want them to hear that you have been talking s*** about them. Because you do not know how they are going to feel about you. That's the exact same way we feel about money, but somebody that's your employee, somebody that's your servant – you don't get nervous to talk about them, because that's just the deal, and that's just what it is. You've got to get real with understanding, that money – **YES**, it can make your life better – **YES**, it can enhance the quality of living, but money IS NOT your boss!

❖   MONEY IS YOUR SLAVE!

❖   MONEY IS YOUR SERVANT!

❖   MONEY IS YOUR EMPLOYEE!

And when you get good at understanding that it is a tool that's supposed to be used over, and over, and over again, your budgeting will get better! So, you got to let go of master –

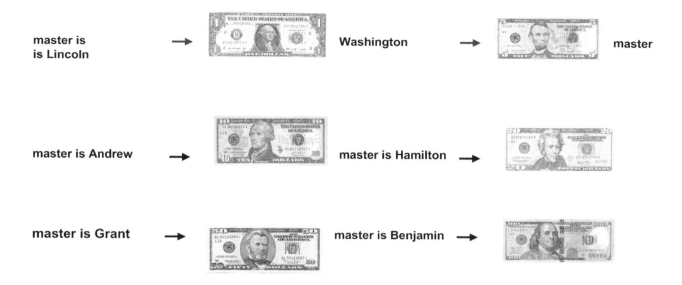

You got to stop serving master and start making them serve you! The Bible says that you are the head and not the tail. It tells us to lead from the front, it tells us that we are the lender and not the borrower. It says in Deuteronomy 28:12, I believe – it says that we are supposed to be lending to nations, not borrowing from them! Come ON! So, that means one thing, you got to get in your head that this money got to be serving me, and I got to get good at detaching my emotions from money.

Detach your emotions from money! That is the only way that you are going to be able to break free. Because when you think that money is the only thing, when you think you are serving money or you're working for money. Think about it – while you're working a job: "Man I'm trying to get this money!" "Man, I got to get this money so I can get that car." Think about that!

The majority of the decisions that we make is **"because of this money."**

- ✓ Why do you get married to a man that's stable, but not the person that you really love? "Man, cause they got money/"

- ✓ Why do you take that career?

- ✓ Why do you find yourself in bad business opportunities? "Cause I'm trying to chase this money!"

Why? Because you think that when you get to money, money is going to save you. Money cannot save you if you don't learn how to make money your servant, and how to make money your employee. It's very important that we understand that. We got to get good at understanding that, the moment that we do, your life will begin to start changing.

You will detach yourself away from money and you will begin to make money work for you. We got to see and understand – if money is going to be my employee, that means – every single dollar bill, or all money has to have a role. You are not going to hire employees or a staff and not have something for them to do.

That's a waste of money!

To hire people, not give them a specific job, a specific requirement, something that you know that's going to be comparable to the pay that you are giving them. So, if you do not give money something to do, it's going to find something to do. So, you know like some of y'all employees that work those jobs and you be stealing from your boss cause you really don't work all eight hours? You know you got stuff to do but you not going to do it cause you're going to try to prolong it? And then you find other stuff to do? And you're spending money from your boss money that you didn't work for, but you know you are going to get that check, so you are spending that money somewhere else. That's exactly what our money does. That's exactly what our employees do. And I've wasted so much time putting too much clout into money. I've been giving money too

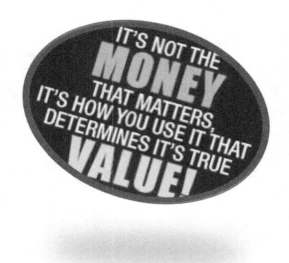

many cool points and too much status all my life. You've got to make that money work for you, make it go do something, you've got to give it something to do. And know that in return of giving that money something to do, it's going to do something back for you as it is going to bring you back something in return. So, the reason that you hire people, is to make the load lighter. Now watch this, if money is my servant, and I am not supposed to be working for money, versus going to get a car note – how about you use money to make your life better?

Scenario:

> **Jake, "What do you mean by that?"** Well if I'm a husband, or I'm a wife, and my husband or wife cleans, and I know the best way to ease the load on my wife or my husband would probably be to get some help. You know you don't have the time to get help; **versus** spending **$300 a month on a car note** – why wouldn't you spend $300 a month on someone to come clean your house?"

It lifts the load; money is supposed to make your life easier, not harder; It is supposed to serve you. The more you have time, not working on smaller things; now what am I doing? I'm not putting my money in material things; I am putting my money – investing it back into my community. WHY? Because my wife and I have a cleaning specialist who comes and cleans our house, and she's a black woman. So, versus us spending money or time on a car note, or some stuff that's frivolous, we decided to invest and pour money and time into a cleaning specialist who is a black woman that's able to help her family by doing a job or providing a service

So, versus spending my money on material things, I just made my life a lot better and a lot easier, we just want her to come a lot more frequently.

But just imagine how much more time you have to think, and to grow, and to develop and to expand your business organization thoughts and creativity if you had people helping around your house. Some people call it boujee, I say it's common sense. Some of us are spending $800 a month on a car note, and you're stressed! I would much rather drive a beat-up cash car and have people serving me at my house. Imagine if you are married, and you have someone to cook the food, clean the house, to cut the yard, helping with minor stuff, even with driving. The typical average person loses up to two hours a day just driving. Just imagine if you had someone just to drive you. I'm not talking about using these things as a way of growing in class like you are better than somebody, I'm telling you a better way to use your money. And the majority of us, we have plenty of money to make our lifestyle so much better, but we decide to put our money in things that depreciate than things that appreciate. Why? Me putting my money into a cleaning specialist, who come and cleans my house – it appreciates my lifestyle. It gives me more clarity and more time to work on my marriage and work on our lives. Think about it – we have a lot of crazy arguments just on cleaning. Your wife or husband mad because there are dishes in the sink. What if there were never dishes in the sink and there is nothing to argue about? We got to get good at understanding how to use money as our servant. So, every dollar has to have a responsibility.

When you began to think of your dollars as employees this money is going to cleaning, this money is going to this, and all things that are going to make your lifestyle better; I guarantee that nobody will think about trying to put money into a house or car. Because if I am going to spend that money, I am going to spend it trying to upgrade my life, not causing more stress. So, the money that you are spending on drinking and weed, taking this chick out, taking that guy out; did you know you can use that same money to enhance and grow your life?

The more time you have to concentrate on your creativity, the highest form of Godliness is creativity! God created the world with words, then he put it on paper. Christ came down, for some of you guys, you may believe in something else, but Christ came down, he was a carpenter, that would be a new day architect. He took things from trees and made them into tables and chairs.

He built houses from wood – carpentry! Architect thinking! Creativity! The highest form of Godliness is creativity. The more time I spend on things that aren't creative, the more I'm losing the power of my Godliness! It's just simple, simple math.

So, while we are growing up in poverty, thinking people are boujee, and asking:

- ✓ **Why don't they drive?**
- ✓ **Why don't they take care of their kids?**
- ✓ **Why don't they do this?**

It's simple, while you're spending your money on material things they're spending their money by circling money within their same community but making everybody's life better! Simple math to me! So, money has got to be your employee! So, versus thinking about budgeting, start think about employees so all your dollars are literally going out and partying. It's going to party! It's partying everywhere, all of our dollars. I'm not the best at it yet, I'm not perfect at it, but all of us, partying.

We want out money to go to shiny objects versus enhancements of life. If you fat and out of shape that money you are spending on a car payment could paid to somebody to train your butt to let you lose weight so that you could live longer. IF you eat bad and you need a health specialist, the money that you are paying and going out to eat and drink is the same money you could be spending on somebody that can help keep you on this earth longer. Got to be your employee, when we rearrange how we see money – everything in life changes.

Example:

How families spend money

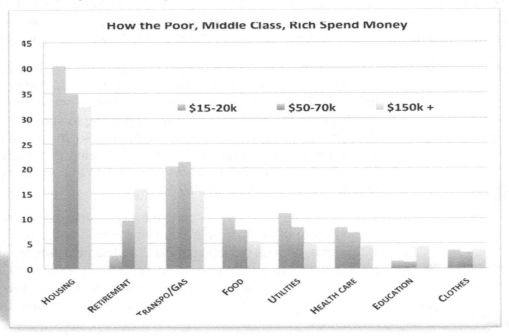

- Poor people spend more of their money on essentials than richer people. But how much is left over?

- After essentials – housing, transportation (incl. gas), food, utilities, and clothes – the poor have 15% of their disposable income left over, and the $150K+ crowd has about 40%.

You start to realize, "dang, I traded time, or I traded creativity so that I could create currency – only to take that currency and dead that currency on stuff that's not going to be of value in seven years.

- **There's going to be a new car!**
- **There's going to be a new house!**
- **There's going to be new shoes!**
- **There's going to be new pants!**

**You are always going to want the newest thing!
But one thing you can't get back is TIME!**

Money is supposed to buy time back first – before it buys you anything. That's why you hire employees in a business to help buy your time back. Yes, you lose scale and profitability, but the lower your profitability, the more employees you have, the more time that you have to be able to grow the business; but that's going to be in the business segment

AUTO DRAFT IS KILLING YOUR CASH FLOW!

Jake, what do you mean by that cousin? It's simple, and what I mean by that is a lot of us have our life on auto draft!

- **your car note – auto draft**
- **your mortgage – auto draft**
- **your phone bill – auto draft**
- **your credit card bill – auto draft**
- **you going out to eating fast food is pretty much auto draft because we don't even think when we swipe.**

I say we; we don't think when we swipe – **"I'm hungry – SWIPE"** forget how much it costs, just swipe. So, our entire financial ecosystem is on auto draft and it's killing the control we are supposed to have on money. Why? When the boss tell us what to do, we just do it without question. If a boss tells you to work on a task, you just do it without question. That is an auto draft moment. The boss tells you to do something, you go and do it, you don't even think. A lot of our transactions are auto draft, there is no filter in between. My wife and I do not have nothing on auto draft. My phone bill goes off every month. Every month, I'm going to work or to go work out or doing something and try to get on the Wi-Fi, and it just won't connect, and I have to think about it, "I got to go pay the bill."

I'm ok with a little interruption for thirty seconds to have control over **MY EMPLOYEES**, so I can pay you. My phone bill is off every month! They say, "Hey, Mr. Jacobs, would you like to pay it all right now?" Absolutely not, put me on a payment plan." I have it, you won't to pay it?" NO!" My wife says, "Babe just pay it." NO! They can't tell me what to do, this is my money." You got to get in control of your money – stop auto drafting your life! Wake UP! In the Bible, it says Christ was raising people from the dead. You know that doesn't always have to be physical, I'm trying to raise you from the dead, you have been walking zombies.

What if you have all your bills written down and the draft date, it comes out, and keep a tight schedule on your bills?

> *I know that most people don't do that though. My wife is a beast like that, and we still don't do it. But let me tell you about auto draft – they be double drafting to see if you are going to check. They double draft on accident all the time. And the only thing they say is, "Oh, I don't know how that happened, let me correct this for you. We will send it to you right now, but it will take 48 hours." It did not take 48 hours for you to draft it! Send me my money back right now, it is my money and I need it now!*

You can still have your date; you just be the one in control of your employees. Even when it comes to you setting up your insurance policies, or your insurance bank – even when they say it has to be auto drafted, you still have control of that entire system.

Don't get so blind. If you are good at keeping up with the, just make sure you check. Don't just think that people have high integrity and will not pull out of your account. – just to see if you are awake and looking. So, if you know your stuff drafts on a specific date, and if it says the 14th, you check your bank account on the 14th to make sure your employees are doing what they are supposed to do.

You got to make sure your employees are going to work on time. I have never met a boss that just allows their employees to come and leave as they please without ever checking on them. I have never met one. Have y'all met one? Let me know. I am unemployable, but I may need to go work for that person if they are not going to check, ever. I will go clock in and come work here and then go clock out. Your money is your employee and it is your job and your fiduciary responsibility to make sure you know what your employees are doing, or your employees will rob you blind, like the majority of you all are doing at your jobs. That's why I don't have employees because people don't work. You work four out of the eight hours and got the audacity to be mad if the boss tells you to stay later. You didn't work the eight! – so no hourly stuff over here.

Now, I want to re-educate you on money, and I want to teach you some stuff when it comes to saving money, how to get wealthy, and how to eliminate assets versus liabilities. The very next course we're running right into what strategies that we can do to be able to get rid of some of the debt and some of the bad decisions that we made financially, and what we can kind of do to upgrade our lifestyle. What I mean by upgrade our lifestyle is, to increase cash flow, and drop liabilities, that's an upgrade in lifestyle. Buying new shiny objects and driving around in a Ferrari, Maserati, Benz, or Lexus, is not an upgrade in lifestyle. The increasing of cash flow is an upgrade in lifestyle. I don't care what you drive, the cash flow is your lifestyle. Are we all on the same page? So, just like when you are hiring, none of us would ever hire anybody without knowing the history of your client. **Is that true?**

All of us would do some type of reference check, we want to know your background, where you came from, what did you do, what do you specialize in, what is the function, so I can make sure I hire you and put you in the best place so I can get the best value for my dollar? **Is that true?**

If that is true and we would go that far to be able to hire somebody – why don't we go that far to study the history of money? Because if money is my employee, I need to cross reference, I need to check. I need to know where you come from, how you got here, where we're going, what it looks like, so I can know exactly how to best use you during this point and time. So, we got to find the money, find the history of the money, and where the money comes from so that we can know exactly how best to use it so we can increase our wealth, and we can increase our success in life, financial success, relational success, spiritual and emotional success. All those things are achievable as long as we can know exactly how-to best use all of the tools of our life.

Now, we are going to talk about Money Basics, and we are going to grow. When we finish this, we are also going to go into the budgeting software.

Let's talk about the evolution of money. I think it's very important that we talk about this because in this evolution of money, we got to figure out where money came from, how it got to where it got to, because we're devaluing the space of where money is with us. We're devaluing the space and where money has supreme authority in our life. When I know where money came from and I know the history of money, I know what money is supposed to do, I don't put as much value on money, meaning, I'm not going to allow it to take over my life. Am I making sense?

The first thing I have to understand is:

There is no shortage of money. There is $80.9 Trillion dollars of estimated money in existence today. Which means all you got to do is find somebody with the cash flow. So, before money even existed, **there was a system called the bartering system**. It's where people originally traded surplus commodities with each other in this process known as bartering. Which means if you had fish, and I had water, we would trade or barter.
The value of each good traded could be debated. However, money evolved as a practical solution to the complexities of bartering hundreds of different things. When it came to bartering, if you had fish and you needed my water, and I didn't want your fish, there was a problem.

You really needed my fish and you wanted to barter with me; the problem was how can I barter with somebody that does not value what I want? That's why bartering only works when there is an equal transaction where both people will want each other's services just as equally or need each other's services just as equally as the other.

So, it went from bartering to evidence of trade records in **7000 B.C.E**. where pictures of items were used to record trade exchanges becoming more and more complex as values were established and documented. So, pictures of items, when things were traded, they would have this trading system and sketch the picture of the item and put your name by it. But as you began to trade more and more it began to be a lot more complex and people couldn't really keep up because there was a lot of pictures and items. So, they kept trying to find a better way.

Then it went from evidence of trade records to **precious metals**, that was later formulized as **coins**. So, then they used to trade coins, but the problem with trading coins was people began to trade their own coins. There was nothing set in stone, like this was the coins that we use and there was no unity in that. So, everybody made their own coin, so it really didn't matter. If you gave me a coin or fish and didn't want fish – and I don't even eat fish, but you want my water; that's not an equal trade. I don't want your fish.

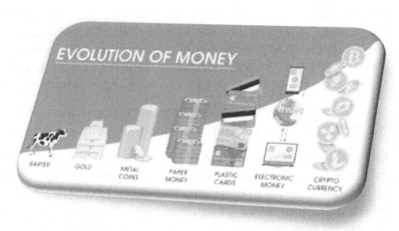

So, now I got to find somebody that wants your fish – I'm going to trade your coin fish to somebody else, it's like trading Pokémon cards or something or like sports cards. I got to find somebody that wants your fish coin and trade them for something that I want. It gets too complex. That's why in the 1100's and 2000's the states began to use bank notes. Your dollar bill is nothing but a bank note, it's a paper **I.O.U.** and that was traded as currency. It's when the country or countries got together to be the note that represents this value. So, it doesn't matter what you purchased with it, this bank note will allow you to ;purchase something else. But in the early **1100's** that bank note was backed by silver or gold. (Write that down!) That bank note was backed by silver or gold.

The U.S Government removed that money being backed by silver and gold which allowed for them to print more money because of the Federal Reserve which allowed them to print more money at an increased rate which also took down the value of the dollar because it was no longer backed by silver and gold. Every bank note, every I.O.U. had to be backed by silver and gold. I'm getting to a point that what we think about money *isn't* what it is. So, when I understand that, I can better use it to my advantage.

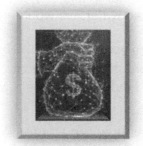

So, it went from bank notes, paper I.O.U's, to digital money.

Digital money is our debit cards, our credit cards, money that doesn't exist, it gets transferred virtually. You guys can literally today pre-order a Blueprint book, that digital money will be transferred to our digital bank account, that digital money will then pay for the printout of the book. So, digital money can be exchanged without ever exchanging bank notes – this is the evolution of money.

Jake, why is this important when it comes to banking?
Why is this important when it comes to me controlling my finances? It's very simple – when you understand that money doesn't have that much value, you are going to be like, "Oh, ok I get it now.. I get it.. This make sense.

So, I am literally sacrificing my time, my life for digital money that doesn't exist, and purchasing things that don't bring value to my life. How ludacris is that? So, if someone wanted to trade cows for wheat, they could literally trade cows for wheat. But the problem is – that both parties must want what the other party is offering. So, if I did not want cows, like I said, "I don't want your cow." So, if you want my wheat and the only thing you got is a cow, we can't trade or barter business, which stifles the growth of an economy. It's hard to establish a set value on items. So, if you feel like your cow is worth a thousand wheat bushels, and I feel like your cows is worth fifty wheat bushels, there was nothing in place to be able to determine the true value of that exchange. That's why it was very important that in this complex trading that there was some sort of I.O.U. system or bank note allowed for it to be the same value. So, when I traded I didn't have to be landlocked for getting some type of clothes, or only getting wood, or only getting apples, or only getting fences. I had this I.O.U. paper going around. A lot of us are literally saying, "I'm about to get this money for I.O.U. notes. **YOU ARE COLLECTING I.O.U. NOTES!** Stop collecting I.O.U. notes.

Values, Wealth, and Income

What we have to understand when it comes to wealth – wealth is a measure of the value of the assets owned by an individual. And an individual's net worth is the value of any assets owned minus debt owed or personal liabilities. So, when you got a bunch of debt, that decreases the value of your wealth and your net worth. So, just because you mortgaged a home, doesn't mean that now you got a $500,000 net worth. No, your net worth is your assets minus your debt. So, that's why it's very important for you guys to understand, I despise debt. I feel like every time we get into debt, with somebody other than ourselves, it's like we agreeing to go back to being an indentured servant or slave or something. So, that net income, that net is your income that's produced by your efforts or your income produced by your assets.

So, your income produced by your work ethics – you working, or your income produced by your assets – minus your liabilities and minus your debt, that will establish what position you have in growing your wealth. So, we got to determine what our net is. And the problem that we have is, the majority of us – we don't run our households like a business. That's why it's very important to write [Week 1 Kingdom Blueprint](#) down right! Because you got to get good at running your household like a business. The problem is the majority of our households have never been net positive since we been alive! Ever! You have never been net positive! At the end of the year, you are in the red. You got a bunch of overdrafts, living under check to check, and you wonder why your life is stressful. It's very simple – your household is an economic system.

One of the definitions in economy is a household – managing your household. People ask me, they say Jake, how can we change the world? First control your house first, and then teach other people how to control their house, like you control your house, and voila' – the world is fixed! Whoop your kids, punish your kids, get your kids together before you try to go march about everybody else kids! You got to run your house like a business.

Let me ask you guys a question:

Would you ever for your business – take 40% of your business's cash flow monthly to rent or to lease, or to finance business transportation?

The majority of us would say no. We would try to find any way to spend as little bit of money on cars. So, why is it when it comes to our income, you got the audacity to only be making $90,000 a year, and you want a third of your income to go to a $30,000 to $40,000 car? Would you take a third of your business income, if you are thinking logically – and spend it on feeding your employees? Just bringing food every day? Most of us would say no. So, why does the average person spend the third of their income on food? When you think about it, you will say, "You know what Jake? You got a point there. That makes sense." Let me ask you one more question. "For the location of your business, where your business is located – would you take a third of your business' revenue to rent out space for your business? Or would you find the cheapest most economically pleasing place for your money so you can increase your profits and where your business is? Would you spend a third of your income just on space? No – the majority of us would say H E L L NO!

The majority of us would be like, Naw man, we are going to find us like a little office, we are going to work out of this office as long as we can, then we are going to maximize it. You want to use all the space. I told my staff we are not moving until everybody is uncomfortable, when everybody has three people in their office, then we will move. So, if it makes sense to not do it for your business, why do we do that for our house? Why don't we do that for where we stay? I make the same dumb mistake? Why do you need a three-bedroom 2 bath house? Why? And the only thing you are using is the kitchen, the bathroom and your room, and sometimes the living room. And most of us in business – we want to find someone to co-share with us. "Hey man, I'm about to get this office, and I know you need an office, let's just office together. You run your business from over there and I will run my business from over here. And if people come we can have an assistant – that be like "ok, who are you here for?" Most of us will co-share, so why are you too boujee to co-share where you stay?

Oh, you don't want to share the kitchen? So, you sharing the kitchen means more to you – so you rather be extra broke to not share a kitchen? Well, if y'all room together didn't you know you can get a maid every day? Two roommates – you know y'all can purchase a maid, right? So, your kitchen is always clean, and you don't have to worry about anybody being stinky! Jackie, which is our cleaning lady will come and clean and be happy. So, when you think about your household like a business – I'm just trying to wrap my mind around the dumb decisions that we make. I'm talking to myself too. When you think about it, all because you want to be aesthetically appealing, cause you want people to come and they are not crowded, and you don't even invite nobody to your house. In order for us to get a hang of wealth we got to understand that you can't pass that responsibility off to a financial advisor or somebody else to help manage the very thing that is going to bring you financial independence. So, the first thing we got to do, we got to assess the situation, we got to assess where we are, which is why we do our staging.

In order for us to get a hang of wealth we got to understand that you can't pass that responsibility off to a financial advisor or somebody else to help manage the very thing that is going to bring you financial independence. So, the first thing we got to do, we got to assess the situation, we got to assess where we are, which is why we do our staging.

Write this down:

The first thing to wealth is assessing the situation – we got to calculate the value of our assets minus our debts, loans, and mortgages. We got to calculate that, and it's very simple – you are struggling.

The second thing we got to do is set financial goals. That's why we did the Kingdom Blueprint – so if you skipped the Kingdom Blueprint because you didn't want to do it, you half A S S did it, you missed the whole entire point. There is no business that can grow if the business does not have a vision. So, if you want provision from God, you need to be provision for your family and for your business.

You got to be provision! And to be provision means you create a financial goal and you got to start by establishing at exactly what age do you want to be released from responsibilities of working or doing the legwork for your family.

> **Jake, what do you mean by released from responsibility?**
> The reason why you go to work everyday is no different than the reason why somebody starts a business – to provide income. But, at some point in time, you cannot just work in the business all your life and expect for you to be healthy. You got to graduate from working in the business, to working on the business.

> **What do you mean by that Jake?** You got to be from the person in the field, to the person running the field, from the person running the person running the field, to becoming the chairman of your oversight. That's why you got to put money aside. You got to put your employees to work, so that you have enough cash flow coming back in; pay stacks coming back in from your employees, i.e. your dollar bills, working for you, so that you can be able to take more time to spend on working on your family and working on your spiritual walk!

So: Assess the situation - Set the financial goal!

The next thing is you got to increase your savings from your income. My wife does this really well. She creates little goals for us to hit when it comes to our savings. We want to do this – this month or we want to do this – this year; or focus on that. I don't want our checking account to ever go below this. We got this little game, and she has this really cool way – of where I literally have to eat my words of what I teach, every single day. My family we jus don't come from that. So, she has these cool little games, these little milestones, and we are both competitive – we got these games of where we eliminate debt " I paid off that debt – you paid off that debt! And before you realize it we got this game going and eating up debt. So, you got come up creative ways to increase your savings from your income.

> **How do you know a business is doing well?**
> You check the end of the year and see how much profit they have. It's simple! So, you got to find ways to increase your savings from your income. You got to save from income and evaluate that savings regularly to ensure that they are performing efficiently, so at least you want to make sure that your money is being saved in the right place.

Have your money saved in a banking strategy; saved in properties – your money is being hoarded in places so that the cash flow from those properties or those businesses or from inside your insurance bank is bringing you back enough dividend or whatever for you to be able to live on.

The next thing you got to do, once you understand you need to be increasing savings – you got to manage your debt. You got to get rid of debt as soon as possible – and never take your narrow behind back! (That's what my mama used to say). You want to look for cheaper, lower interest rates, for bringing down the cost of life. It's funny when we run a business we want to find the cheapest labor.

But when it comes to running a household, we settle after one person gives us a pitch. After one person shows you a car, you say ok I don't want to look nowhere else, we going to just go with this person. But for your business, you are like – "NO, uhh uhh, he expensive! I know we can find somebody cheaper!" You got to run your house, like you would your business. So, you increase those savings, you get that debt under control. You can't really manage debt until you can start to increasing those savings. Because I can look at my debt, but if I'm living check to check, barely making it, how can I manage debt and my savings account is not where it is supposed to be? So, I got to focus on selling stuff, getting rid of stuff, and getting on Facebook Marketplace. We real good in my house at selling stuff – Facebook Marketplace queen, is AJ. She will try to sell something in a heartbeat. So, you got to increase that savings, find more efficient ways to get that dollar to stretch for you, before you can think about and start to figure out how to manage that debt. You got to deal with one thing at a time, ok!

The last thing is that you want to use those investment payouts, those property payouts, that business payout to start helping you use that business income and reinvesting that money that you were saving. You want to take that to start washing down your debt. So, you want to build up that savings and move that money somewhere so it can start to generate cash flow and then use that cash flow to start washing away your debt. So, that's how you want that thing to happen, you just want a fluid motion of that. That's how we get that water cycle that you guys saw. After you have done all of that, now you've reached what I call financial independence. If successful at doing that, this individual can maintain a good standard of living without the need to go exchange time or money.

Analyzing & Calculating Net Worth

So, what I am trying to do – I'm trying to get y'all to stop thinking so highly of these weirdos, talking about how much they make and how much they revenue. Stop getting so excited about that, anybody can make up numbers.

I have even made up numbers before and have made up numbers so much I started believing the numbers. Somebody said, 'Man, you know my business did **$100M** this year." Great! Awesome!" But if they are in the negative $100,000 and you got $100,000 in your insurance bank, who's richer? Them because they made $100M or you because you actually have more liquid assets than they do? You are richer! Don't allow people's revenue to get you to start thinking that you are lesser than. Because the more money they make, the more money they spend – the more money you save, you've got more money than them.

If y'all were to go to the bank, your net worth would be more than theirs, not just because the make revenue, or because they making money – stop being so impressed by these weirdo Instagram and Facebook people. They're weird y'all.. and I think it's real weird to always brag on your revenue. Weird! So, a person's wealth or net worth can be calculated by adding up all the assets that they own and subtract that from the total amount of debt that they owe. Notice what we are talking about, debt. **NOTICE** what we keep talking about – DEBT!

Trying to get it into your head, that if anybody tells you that the road to happiness is through debt, they're a liar! I don't care how much money they make. Because the book that I read and I know God to be true, it tell me that if I'm in debt, I am enslaved to the person that lent me the money. So, I don't care what society says, the Bible tells me, (that's my favorite book, it doesn't have to be yours) that to be in the world, but not of the world. It means that I can function in the world, but I don't have to adopt the psychology and the theology from the world. Don't allow people to make, just because they look like you, just because they got nicer cars than you, don't allow them to dictate what your common sense should be.

So, this is the formula you always want to use:
ASSETS – DEBT = NET WORTH

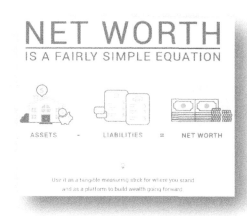

Well, Jake what is assets? I don't have like properties, and businesses. Ok, liquid assets –

- **How much cash do you have on hand?**
- **How much cash do you have in your current accounts?**
- **How much cash value or cash reserve do you have in your insurance policy?**
- **How much money do you have access to for short term investments?**
- **How much money do you have in your CD's?**

That's liquid assets, that's valuable – because your net worth it tells financial institutions and a lot of people about an individual's financial status. Your net worth is a more relevant indicator of your financial health than the income that you make. You get wealthy because of your net worth not because of the income that you make.

The next type of asset is an investment asset that can be convertible to cash. Notice all assets have to be able to be translated into cash. That lets them know that's an asset. So, your investment asset:

- o Term deposits held at the bank
- o Securities
- o Stocks
- o Shares
- o Bonds
- o Investments in real estate
- o Businesses
- o Endowment policies

The last type of assets are your **personal assets**, it can be sold for cash but may take time.

- ✓ **Your home – if you want to sell for downsizing**
- ✓ **Additional properties – i.e. vacation home**
- ✓ **Art, Jewelry and other valuables**
- ✓ **Furniture**
- ✓ **Collectible pieces**
- ✓ **Vehicles – although they lose value quickly, if it's paid off, that is an asset**

What are your debts? Your debts are your short-term liabilities

Short-term Liabilities – that means it's payable within the next twelve months.

- ✓ **your credit card interests and capital repayments**
  – these are your repayments on personal and student loans
- ✓ **your current monthly household bills**
- ✓ **your unpaid personal income tax – those are debts.**

Long-term liabilities – payable over more than twelve months

- ✓ **Your mortgage**
- ✓ **Your rental properties**
- ✓ **Child support**
- ✓ **Alimony**
- ✓ **Children's Education through College**
- ✓ **Payments to a Pension Fund**
- ✓ **A Higher Purchase Contract**

All of those are things that you got to understand – we will go over the rest in the next segment and start on strategies to eliminate those liabilities to increase cash flow. Start thinking about your business, all of us in some form or fashion believe in God, and there is no way that God will give anybody, as it tells us that God will not give us more than we can bear, that's also wealth. Because if I can't manage my business at $20,000 – why in the H E LL hockey sticks would God allow me to have a $1M dollar business, to have a million-dollar household. If I can't manage this, and I can't grow this, why do I have the audacity to complain and to cry, and to pray, and to beg, and to be frustrated, with what I don't have, and I don't even take care of what do have. It says don't despise small beginnings. DON'T DESPISE SMALL BEGINNINGS!

I have never met somebody who focuses on growing what they have, ever be somebody that never achieves success. I only see people that are focused on what everybody else has, are the people that stay stagnant. Stop worrying about what your cousins got! Just because they got a new Benz and BMW, just because your employee or your staff or somebody on your team got a new car – doesn't mean you got to get one.

Stop worrying about everybody else garden, you trying to analyze everybody else garden and you neglect your own. The grass is greener where you water it – not where they are. So you worry about cultivating your relationships, you worry about cultivating your household, you worry about cultivating your business, worry about cultivating your income. You worry about eliminating liabilities and increasing your assets. It's very simple – it pays to mind your business.

The more you mind and tend to your business, the more your business grows.

So, that will be the conclusion of this lesson, but the biggest thing I wanted you guys to get was that value, that wealth, that income – to understand it and start thinking in terms of the Kingdom Blueprint. I hope some of you go back to the Kingdom Blueprint and say, "DAMN – I need to go back and really, really, do it right. Let me think about this, man I have been going about this wrong! That's why I have been struggling." And hopefully the majority of us, together we can literally start to grow and go where we need to go. But it takes one step at a time. All of us working together, holding each other accountable to get there. But it starts with you at home, looking yourself in the mirror, saying Man I have been a bad manager.

Like we talked about last session – to go from ownership to manager; I've been a bad manager.

> **What can I do to grow what was given to me?**

> **How can I be good at taking this what I have, and leaving it better than what I found?**

I've never found a broke person who does that.

COACH'S CORNER
Recap of Finding the Money: What's in your wallet?

Last session, we talked about that value, that wealth, that income and understanding the history of money, but we got to continue the conversation – there was like a "to be continued" with a commercial in between. Because I really want to dig down on that net worth and understanding how it works. I want you to kind of see it.

I want you to feel it. So that when you start to think – you're starting to think like somebody that doesn't like liabilities. See it's hard for somebody that actually has the cash to when they are really thinking about net worth, and when they are really thinking about increasing their assets, it's hard for them to purchase stuff.

I was telling my wife just the other day, I said, "Babe, there are things that I used to dream about purchasing when I was broke, but now that I got the money, and I know how hard I worked for the money and how disciplined we were with the money.

I don't even want to spend the money. Because it's like dang, all that sacrifice is pretty much for nothing. And she busted out laughing, like you know what – we are in a good place.

So, I think it is very important for us to understand when you begin to value you more than you value money – HELLO! When you begin to value your sanity more than you value purchasing things, your life begins to increase and your value in life increases which means, guess what?

Your net worth also increases. So, we got to make sure we're understanding to do that.

Guys this your coach Jake Tayler Jacobs and I will see you on the next segment.

NOTES

CHAPTER 6:

Finding the Money Part 2: Income, Wealth, and Budgeting

Turning your Income Into Wealth

Today we are going to talk about converting income into wealth and understanding that your income is not wealth. It needs to generate and turn into wealth and that's what we got to understand. So, we are going to talk about converting that income into wealth, we are going to also talk about the difference between income and wealth and the different types of income – like passive income versus active income.

And what we all have to understand is that in order to get passive income there is some type of active income or active activity that's required in order to turn something passive. And that's the piece that most people have to understand, and we'll get to that in a moment. But the very first thing I want to talk about is:

"HEY!" Welcome back to PBB – PRIVATE BANKING BLUEPRINT MASTER CLASS! And we're going to take you from consumer to banker, I want you to say, "I AM NO LONGER A CONSUMER – I AM A BANKER!" When somebody asks you your name or ask who you are – say THE BANK! Say I'm the Bank, that's who I am, I'm the Bank!

Let's talk about income and let's talk about wealth. Two of the key concepts of personal finance is income and wealth. They both represent different stages of an individual's finances. Income is always moving and often unstable while wealth mainly is static and stable. So, income is that money that flows in and out and it always changes. But, your wealth is something that can't easily be moved.

So, if I were to give you an example of income vs wealth –

I want you to think about a little speedboat vs like a titanic cruise boat. It takes longer to turn a titanic cruise boat then it does to turn or flip over a speedboat. See what would flip over a speedboat would make the titanic cruise boat laugh. So, when I'm talking about wealth, we are talking about building that titanic cruise boat that can be able to handle the small ups and downs of life. That income like that speedboat – if your entire life is depicted upon your income, you're in a scary situation, because one large wave and it will wipe you out and you better hope that you don't die from it. Follow me now, follow me! So, what we have to understand is that income is money that flows into a household, money that is used to pay bills, it's money that is used to pay for food, it's money that is used for the essential needs, as well as the non-essential needs, such as like vacations.

So, what we have to understand is that when I am talking about income, that's the money that's flowing and that's the cashflow. Your cash flow is not wealth.

Write that down – MY CASH FLOW IS NOT WEALTH!

My cash flow is not wealth, so a lot of the people that go around talking about make this, I make that, I do this – I made $100K this month, I made $50K this month. I made $20K this month then you look at their expenses and be like – yeah you made $20K but you need to make $20K again or you are going to be just as broke as me. So, I want you guys to get that in your thick head, that the money that you make I am not impressed with. What I am impressed with is what is at the end of that. Remember we talked about your house being a business. And at the end of the year you want to be profitable. And it lets me know how your loans, your debts and expenses are and how you manage that household business will let me know at the end of the year how money you are saving and how much you have in cash reserve and your savings account, ok. So, we got that understood.

Now let's talk about how wealth works. Wealth is the value of a person's assets – it's your savings and your investments. Wealth is the value of your assets. So, while income is the money received regularly from work or for work, for the investments, your income is received so that it can work for your investments but your investments, the cash flow – from your investments are where your wealth lies, ok. So, what I'm saying is money that is coming in – your income, is only after it goes through the expenses and using the money before it can actually turn into wealth. So, we have to definitely understand that.

So, income that is closely managed and carefully invested can create wealth over time. So, we got to make sure that we are really protecting that income coming in, and we're really protecting that cash flow and we are not taking it for granted – because guess what? One day we are going to be too old or one day society is going to shift on us, and what we used to make money on – we're not making money in that fashion anymore, which doesn't make us as marketable in the marketplace. So, we have to make sure that we are prepared for the shift of time, the shift of life, and the shift of circumstances. There are people that had legitimate jobs in New Orleans but when Katrina hit, their income changed, they had to move to Dallas, to Houston, or to the surrounding areas, which what; changed their income, their cash flow, what they were bringing in. But people who were saving and had money and assets didn't really feel the hit as much as people that were depending on the income.

So, if we were to give a definition for what wealth is, wealth is the value of assets already owned by the household or individual – wealth is the **value of assets already owned by you or by your household.** It can be a savings or loan, or it can be a mass of savings as well as investments and inheritance. Wealth is rarely used for your day to day expenses.

So, what I am trying to get through your thick head is to stop judging yourself based on what people saying that they are generating in income. Because your wealth – you could have a lot more money as far as saving your assets or your cash reserve than they actually have saved in their cash reserve which means you are wealthier than they are. Now they generate more income than you, but they are not as wealthy as you. And you want to be wealthy because a person who is wealthy can maneuver through trying times. Remember, we're building a cruise ship – a titanic size cruise ship. The key is learning how to turn our income into wealth. So, unless people inherit a large sum of money or win the lottery or you know, get lucky in a business, typically, most people rely on their wealth through your savings, so it is what you can put in that cash reserve.

Based on your active work, your active activity – what you're doing to be able to create that money and create that activity. What we are saying is this – unless you got lucky, the majority of us average Americans or average folk, we got to depend on our savings in order to be able to start amassing wealth. If you are not building your savings you are actually damaging yourself even more because you are putting your household and your Kingdom at risk for trying times to come. Remember your savings is not supposed to take care of your day to day activity. So, it's very simple, the amount of money – going out every week, or every month, must be lower than the money coming in. Right? Is that simple? And that difference that you have should be stored away. It should not be, "Ok I have free money this month, let me go ahead and get me something – like shoes or something because I deserve it."

The easiest solution is have more money in the house than you have going out and store the rest. That's simple. Now the question is, "Jake, how can I turn my income into wealth?" What do I have to do to get my income through all the of the defenders to get to wealth? I want you to imagine yourself as a football player. And your job as the football player – say a running back, is to get the ball and get to the endzone. You have got to score a touchdown. And there is a lot of people that want to stop you from scoring that touchdown.

Do you know how amazing it feels to score a touchdown or to score a ball or to do something miraculous in whatever sport that you are in?

It's a great feeling because you know what you had to do to score. So, I want you to think of yourself as the running back, and the football as your wealth, as your money or as your income. And in order for you, every single month, every single day, every single week – it's when you get that money to your bank – that's that football getting handed to you. And it's your job to dodge, to duck, to truck, to keep running, to find your way to the endzone so you can take that football, your money – and you can put it in the endzone to be stored away for wealth.

The better you are at running your ball – the better you are at getting to the Hall of Fame, becoming somebody or a big person of wealth! The better you are at scoring touchdowns with your money – the more successful you will become, the more money you will make!

Jake, what's income? Income is your earnings after tax, which includes benefits, tax allowances and your returns on investments.

Your income can come from:

- **Interest**
- **Dividends**
- **Salaries**
- **Rental Income**

We got to get through the costs of life as well as debts.

86

Now I want you to think about debt like that big ole line backer that is like 6'5, 260 – grown, grown man, fully looking like a thumb. You know some people around my age, you remember a movie called Spy Kids, and there were these thumbs out running around. These football players look like thumbs. You just look at them and they look scary, they just look greasy, they look stanky and they look like they'll hurt you.

That's what debt does, and you got to run through them to score the touchdown!

And the bigger your debt the bigger that person is. Uh Oh! So, if you want a smaller person that you got to run through – you got to make sure that debt is real small and non-existent.

The first thing you got to get through is costs, that's your household expenses, which can actually be regulated by a budget. So, the plays, to get around your household expenses is a budget. Put a budget together and stick to the play. So, when you put the budget down, that's like the play call. You stick to the play; you are guaranteed to win the game. You get off the play, you are going to lose.

For the ladies that got kids, it's like you telling your kid what to do, get off the bus and come straight home. Because you know as long as they get off the bus and come straight home there will not be any problems. But when your child wants to get off the bus and go to Jimmy house, and go to Susie house, and go to lil Kirk Kirk house up the street – you know that there are a lot of different variables that happen, and you can't control that variable. And the odds of them getting hurt or the odds of them doing something crazy has just increased because they got off the play. You told them to come straight home.

So, you need to tell your money to come straight home. Don't go out and play, no you cannot go to your cousin's, no you can't go to Chick-Fil-A with your friends, and no you can't spend the night at your aunt's house because all they do is spend money!

So, some of us need to put our money on punishment. Your money just need to be in a room just reading all day.

Expenses are food, housing, transportation, and clothes. You get through your expenses to get to debts, and your debt should be paid off as quickly as possible – i.e. credit cards, mortgages, loans, and education and all of that.

And when you finally get through your costs and you finally get through your debt, now you have whatever is left over to save. People always say all the time, "well if I do all that, I don't have any play money." Your play money should have been inserted in your costs of living. That's your play money – and it should be on your costs of living!

So, savings is what's left after the debt and that's when you should invest it into assets, insurance, property, art, jewelry, equity in companies.

Converting Income Into Wealth

We're talking about converting income into wealth. So, what you are going to find out is that high earnings along do not guarantee wealth, you have to keep your outgoings lower than your income. Accruing savings and investing them wisely are the key components to long term financial security. There is no formula to determine how much wealth is enough.

Can't nobody say 10x's your income, times this – that's enough. Nobody can determine how much wealth is enough. I say think big, think larger than life. I believe in abundant God. I believe in overflow. I believe in more than enough. I believe the more wealth I have, the more people I can help, the more people I can serve, the more I can do God's will for my life – the more I can explain the Kingdom, the more I can increase the family's name, the more I can be a Kingdom Ambassador – I need it all! I need as much as I can get, and I need a jet too so I can just get on the plane and just get all the way over there. I used to be like you don't need a jet – but now I need it! I know I need a jet; I need the fuel and all.

So, we got to start manifesting this stuff into our life. But faith without works is dead – people without vision shall perish. People that don't have a vision will never get anywhere, they are always Debbie downers, they are always angry, and you don't like to be around them – they're always woe it's me. I hate being around sour pusses – I mean they just sour, they always got something to complain about. It just drains me. Lordy, lordy, lordy!

There's no formula to determine how much income is needed to build wealth. It depends on the individual. High earners – people who make more money tend to have a higher lifestyle, and expectation than others. So, if you don't make a lot of money, people don't expect for you to have a lot, but the more money you make, the higher expectation for you to have more things. Don't fall into the trap! Now, listen, I'm not telling you to not go get the Bentleys, I'm not telling you to not go get the Benz, I'm not telling you to not go get the big, big house. I'm not telling you to not go get the biggest building with all the stuff, but what I am telling you is – you do not need to do that at the demise of your wealth.

- **You getting those things should be as insignificant as you buying a burger. So, if you think, "Oh, it's just twenty dollars." You need to think well I need to save this twenty dollars until I can say, "Ooh, that's just one hundred thousand." See that's the game I'm on. So, that means we must sacrifice today so that we can live like no one else's tomorrow. We got to do today what people won't so that we can live tomorrow like people can't.**

So, it is very important – the more income you make, the more you have to be disciplined to store that cash away. And the problem with people who make a lot of money – that danger for that group of people, is that high income earners, it can lead to them feeling a sense of affluence, resulting in big spending and a big lifestyle but little set aside in savings. So, the more money they make they say, "man I'm affluent, I'm making half a million a year." I be like, "cool, great, I see you making half a million a year. It looks amazing." But just because you make a half a million – it doesn't make you affluent! To be affluent means to have a supernatural overflow of wealth. Remember what wealth is – wealth is after expenses and debt. I don't want to look affluent; I want to be affluent! **BE AFFLUENT!**

My wife and have a goal – our goal in life is to literally save 50% of our income. We want to save 50% of our cashflow. That's our goal. Now the truth is, being a high income earner – you are talking about 40% of your income gone, so that means we got 60% of our money left to play with, and we want to save half of that, so 30% of our income we want to completely save away, so 10% of that money we want to absolutely give – and the other 10% we want to just be "STUPID!" We want to get to the point – 10% we are giving. I want to give $10 million away, and I want to spend $10 million a year – so that means I'm storing $30 million. I want to spend money like with no regret. That's what I want to do so that means I got to sacrifice a little bit.

We are about to look at two case studies.

I'm going to show you somebody who is affluent, makes a lot of income – but doesn't save money for wealth. Then, I am also going to show you somebody who makes the same money but saves and stores money for wealth. Because a top salary won't ensure wealth, because saving habits are poor and you think that it will always be there, and it provides this false sense of pride. Just like people who walk around with muscles and think they can fight and don't know I will whoop the draws off of them! You go that false sense of vibrato, but we know you are soft as tissue. We know you soft as Charmin.

So, I am going to give you two examples of two senior managers, which are senior executives, they both work for the same company and they both earn identical income. However, they use their money differently. So, we got Case study A and Case Study B:

> **Case Study A:** See what they do00, they make that money and they want everybody to see they're making money They go buy the nice car – the Lexus, they're living good. They are getting debts, they have mortgages, rental houses, they got this, they got that; and all of it is financed. They got Gucci, Prada, they got the red bottoms – oh it looks gorgeous!

> **Case Study B:** She is storing as much cash as she can away.

> **Case Study A:** She got the attitude of debt! She says, "Oh I believe credit cards are revolving, so what I am going to do, I am just going to make the money – put it on the card! Make the money – put it on a card, no big deal." "I'm just going to finance the car, finance the house, I am just going to finance my entire life because I got the income to pay for it. So, it's no big deal, I need the credit anyway. I got to get debt right, because I need the credit."

> **Case Study B:** She says, "I don't know about what she is doing, but we are about to get us a little budget, ok, and we are about to manage our outgoing and our incoming – and we are going to just make sure we are good."

> **Case Study A:** She got a high income, so she don't feel like I need to save, which is what most business owners do, most entrepreneurs – "I make money." Especially network marketers, it's a bunch of network marketers I see make a lot of money, and then they are really broke, broke, broke, after that company drop – most companies that are network marketers don't last past ten years. Most businesses don't last past ten if it's really good. They say man, "My business is going to retire me, I am not going to ever quit, I am not ever doing that – everybody is going to always want what we got."

And then guess what? You don't save any money for retirement or you penny pinch retirement by five or ten percent. Your lifestyle was 80%, but you have been saving five to ten percent.

How do you think that is going to sustain you and your standard of living and your image that you have created when you retire, or you can't work anymore?

So, when retirement comes for **Case Study A**, this executive – she has no wealth to rely on, and she is spending the rest of her money in poverty. Matter of fact, she will probably be on a Wal-Mart greeter plan. Hello! We say, "Ma'am, you are back working?" She responds, "I just miss people, I just got to find something to do." No, ma'am, you're broke!" That's what you got to do because you are broke!

Now **Case Study B**, she says – "No, I am going to manage my money – I am about to go buy me some properties. I am going to go buy me some properties and from the cash flow from these properties that are debt free – because I own the debt and I didn't mortgage them. The cash flow from these properties or these investments endeavors, they're what? They're paying me in retirement. So, I am not worried about it because I know I got units and properties that are taking care of me – I got investments that are taking care of me. I have passive businesses that are taking care of me and paying me dividends, paying me owner share, while I am cooling and the other person who was all this and all that, she has to have her cars repossessed and I am buying her same cars brand new, CASH WITH IT!

"How much confidence one must have to not have to feel the responsibility to look like what you get paid?"

Now I am not telling you to look bad forever, I am telling you to look ok until you can look like, "whew!" So, when people say," How you get a Rolex, isn't that out your – that's expensive!" You can say well it is expensive to you, but me getting my Rolex is like you getting a three-thousand-dollar cash car, no big deal, right?

You have to have confidence to not look like what you get paid – now that is confidence, that is commitment! When you have seen poverty, and you have worked hard – you realize working hard isn't enough! We live like nobody today so we can have what nobody can tomorrow! So, after we understand that difference we got to understand the types of ways to generate income.

Generating Income

In order to capture and trap wealth, you got to have income coming in, and you can't be lazy. You [go]t to get creative in generating extra cash flow, [the] wealth can be built in various ways. But [...] all wealth is **dependent** upon income to get [...] ou need income to get to wealth. You can't [...]ome – you can't say, "Man, I'm going to be [rich], but I am not going to work a job!"

You got to find anyway you can to generate enough cash flow. If you are not that good of an entrepreneur – you need to put your ego aside, go work for somebody, generate cash, and use that cash to build your wealth. Use their money to build your wealth, so that you can make sure that you are building a dam on the other side.

You are making the money, you are generating the wealth, but you are only as good until they want to get rid of you – but it is only the people that prepare for your exile that are the ones that actually build wealth. See some of y'all are saying, "I get it – I get it Jake. I have heard you say this before," But I don't get too many that say, "Jake I have heard this before, but I get it. Or, "Jake I want more in the bank, I want to sacrifice more, I get it." That's what we got to understand. I don't care what people think of me today, because I am preparing for my tomorrow, it is very important that we understand that.

There are couple of ways to earn money:

Active Income – money that is received in exchange for work, and there are a variety of ways you can get that:

The whole notion is you have to be there in [order] to make it function. There are a lot o[f peop]le who only believe the only way you can genera[te] passive income is through real estate. [That] is a lie! Your business can generate passive income if you set it up correctly and you do what you got to do.

All passive income had to be started by active activity – which means you had to gather the income or gather the capital through active work in order to be able to pour it into something that can generate you passive income.

So, people that sit around and tell you that you do not have to do anything to generate passive income, they're crazy! People that sit around and generate money through Forex and day trading, can say, "yeah you can say I making money in my sleep," but you had to make the trade in order to make money in your sleep; so therefore, it is still **active income**. You had to make the trade! "I got internet stuff and it make money," yeah, but you still have to make the videos that you put out all the time through your social media that generates cash flow but – that is still active income! "Well I got properties." If you are the managers of those properties – that is still active income and that is one way to earn income.

The second way to earn income is passive income.

Passive income is money that is received and exchanged for little to no effort.

So, investments and businesses that require effort to start up but nothing after that to really manage. When I think about passive, I think about when I am building up ABS Brokers, I'm building up Assets Before Splurging or Financial Institution – my goal is not to have to be the active CEO forever. My goal is to groom somebody to be in the company for ten or fifteen years and then pay them to be the CEO of the company and me to move to Chairman where they can just bring me reports and I can just monitor the business and give advice on keeping the vision to where the company should go. That is passive income – where I can be missing for a year and the business is still cutting me a check.

My idea of passive income and what passive income is, as I build a real estate portfolio and I generate enough cash flow from my real estate portfolio to hire a management team that does the payments for me to the mortgage – or sends my money to the mortgage team that pays the mortgage and lets me just see the numbers and cuts me the checks. That's passive income, otherwise known as money making income.

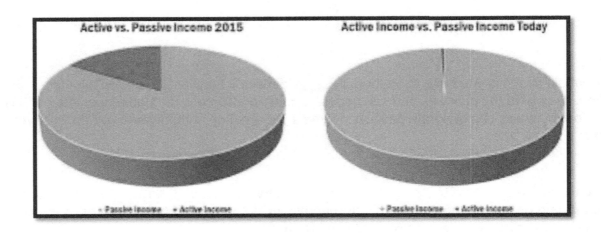

Passive income are savings accounts through our cash accounts through insurance – but what most people don't know is that the portfolio – and we will talk more about it as we get really into the insurance banks; the portfolio of the insurance company, they have to grow the money. That's how they guarantee the 4% plus dividends. It's not just insurance, so, their portfolio is based on lending to corporate, commercial, and residential multi-family homes. It's corporate bonds, government bonds, financing companies, and then it's like 2% into the market to buy options. So, the majority of the money is going out to lending and things with assets – that is what is going out; things that have hard assets. So, the money that I have in my cash reserve is making money without my effort. The 4% dividend from the portfolio of the market or the insurance company which means I am part owner of a residential lending company through insurance – THAT'S PASSIVE!

What's passive income? Rent from a spare room. Some of you probably need to turn one of your rooms into a place that you can rent out. My wife and I were going to inherit a four-bedroom house from my grandmother, but you know family gets involved and screws everything up. But were going to inherit this from my Grandmother before she passed in September 2019, and we already rented out two of the rooms at $800 a month. Me and my married wife with a daughter, already rented out. Why? It already had the same amenities as an apartment. They had their own bathroom, and with the $800 I was going to even offer a maid service to come clean every day, because I could afford it. So that's $1600! You rent your room out and then you use that extra cash flow to enhance the living environment, so now they got a maid, someone to make their beds, someone to wash clothes, and help keep the house clean. You got someone to help clean the kitchen, and the bathrooms and we already filtered the type of people we wanted to room there, which are people that are already responsible that just wants to limit costs. These are people that have good jobs, and people with good paying history. And we were going to rent that out making $1600 a month on a house that we were going to inherit. Why? Because we were not going to use all four rooms. What were we going to use all four rooms for? To say we got a four bedroom – for **WHAT?**

Passive Income! Here are some places you can make passive income:

Blogging – put blogs up, do it one time – those blogs pay forever.

Royalty payments – do something one time – get paid forever

So, when we are generating wealth, most of the billionaires that appear on the annual lists of the world's wealthiest individuals, they may have built their empires in different ways, but most, almost all relied on starting with a little cash to invest. Most people begin to build their wealth, unless you inherit, like we talked about, from their earnings, from their income, and saving a large portion after wealth, ensuring they have financial security. So, making small changes in your lifestyle can cut spending and increase savings so that each person can be able to live at the lowest margin that you can and have an overflow.

So, even when you are making a million or ten million a year, if any of you are blessed to do that, if I am living on **10%** and I am making a million a year, that mean **10%** of a million is what **$100,000?** So, you got a **$100,000** living lifestyle. You can afford certain things, and still have an overflow. Converting your income to wealth is absolutely crucial, you got to find ways to eliminate the outgoing, but you got to make more money. Most of our problem is that we don't make enough money and in entrepreneurship you have to sell. Whether you are a janitor, whether you are a cleaning lady, whether you are a caretaker of the elderly – you have to sell yourself in order to do it, or find somebody's service that you can sell that you believe in. **I.E. PBB Masterclass and Financial School, you can do that all day!**

So, the first thing is earn your income, the second thing is you store that savings, and you track your spending, you set your budget and you build your credit within yourself. You build that confidence from yourself. You invest the money wisely, you maintain and manage wealth, and that's the process and the cycle that you go through over and over again.

Investments for Income

Warren Buffett says this, "Risk comes from not knowing what you're doing."

A lot of say, "Man entrepreneurship is risky. Putting my money in insurance is risky." It's only a risk when you don't know what you are doing. But if I know what I am doing it's not a risk. So, when people say, "Man Jake, it's risky to start your insurance business all over again after you lost all your agents and you lost everything, and you started from scratch. You left your apartment, uh and you got kicked out your building and you had to move back into your apartment, are you sure you don't want to get a job?" "NO! Because there is no risk! I know exactly what I am doing – I've done it before, and I can do it again."

The risk is leaving your job because you feel like God told you it was keeping you away from your vison. God didn't tell you that. Because you just told people God is the one who got you the job. Just a year ago, you were thanking God for getting you the job, now you are telling everyone God told you to leave. So, God told you to leave without a plan?

That's what he told you? Come on now! So, when it comes to moving and investing your money, I got a rule – if I don't understand it, I am not giving my money. People say, "Man if you spend more time – you will get it. Ok, I work eight hours a day, there is sixteen more hours for me to get it. All I need to do is sleep and eat eight. Well, sleep eight, and eat thirty minutes here and there. I got six hours to learn what I need to do, if that is not enough time – I don't know what is."

So, when it comes to growing your wealth you cannot depend on this – "Man my gut say this one good." You got to say, "Naw, I'm going to filter this one out – if this is me missing it, I am not really missing anything because I never really got in it. Listen, if I missed it, then I missed it but I want to mitigate all risks. When banks give you money, they typically give you money by locking up some assets. You got people that say, "Man, you can go to the bank; they will give you money" They will give you a bunch of unsecured credit lines, or credit cards at 15 to 20% because they don't trust that you are going to pay it back. That's money they're willing to lose. But if you want big, big, money – you got to secure and anchor assets.

Why would the bank do that? Because they want to mitigate the risks. Now I am not a fan of borrowing from the bank, but I know they're not just discriminating on you because you are black. You are going to the bank on a business idea that hasn't been proven.

You going to the bank and saying, "Man they are discriminating on me!" "NO, you don't have any assets dummy!" So, you don't have nothing that the bank can say, "Ok if I take that asset it will mitigate my risks. Why? They don't want to gamble and hope that you are going to pay them back. They want to know! So, your credit score is not the only indicator to give you money and if somebody is telling you that, they are lying! Your credit score just says – ok, they are good at paying things back. If you don't have anything on your credit report, they say, "Hmmm. Your credit is high, but you have not proved anything! Which means you have nothing for me to have evidence to know that I know you are going to pay me back." That's why they tell you that you can get tradelines and stuff, y'all con the bank system and then y'all end up bankrupt and crying and stuff, because you did not build up the discipline to take your time. But y'all don't want to hear that because some of y'all do credit, and I am in y'all Kool-Aid – My BADD! Yeah y'all doing trade lines, skipping the system and wonder why all the tradeline people be broke! There is only 1% of people that do tradelines on their credit and actually made it out.

So, the lowest of risks are more of the guarantees:

- Savings accounts
- Insurance or cash reserves
- Bonds
- Term deposits

These are things that have lower risks and good potential for income.

The higher risks are:

- Property
- Real estate
- Rent from residential, commercial and industrial
- Profits from buying and flipping homes

  Its not a risk if you know how to:
  - look at a property
  - evaluate a home
  - evaluate and find good tenants
  - find the best management company

    it's not a risk when you know:
    - you have the right acquisitions team
    - that you have trained correctly

That's not a risk – that is me saying I know what I am doing and let me put money on the fact that I know it. I know it is going to grow and I know the risks that are at hand and I have mitigated that risk to protect and hedge me.

That's why Warren Buffet says, **Rule number one** – never lose your money.
Rule number two – don't forget rule number one

Because he is never going to a deal that he doesn't understand!

So, that's why when people ask me, "Jake, why don't you have real estate?" It's very simple – I am not in a rush! Why? If I can't finance it from my bank and I am not ready for it. So that gives me enough time to store my cash inside my cash reserve, so if I do want to get in real estate, that gives me ten to twelve years to be able to really look at the type of properties I want and learn how to read properties, how to read foundations, how to read roofs, how to read tenants, how to find and invest in education. So, when I do make my move – I am making the best move with the money that I have.

I have friends that come to me and say Jake it's a great idea. I listen to all their ideas, I look at all their deals, and if it is not simple and easy for me to understand, I'm like – "Yo, I want to know the whole process and if they cannot explain the whole process and they can't prove how they have done it, they can't prove how they have generated or can't show me, and I do not care if it was two hundred dollars – I am not doing it! Because I know how hard it was for me to accumulate my cash. Like today – I did a **$24,000** deal today, that will pay me like **$8,000** in commission. It took an hour for me to do an $8,000 deal. And some people may say, "Man I make **$8k** an hour." I say, "No, I didn't make $8K an hour – that took me seven years to learn how to make $8k in one hour." So, I am not about to give money away just because I know that I can make that in an hour. So, no – you just got in the industry, no you can't do what I do, because it took me all this time to learn how to do it.

I remember when I got in the industry and I just wanted to make **$100** dollars. Just wanted to do a **$1200** dollar deal that would pay me like **$800** – I just wanted to make **$500 to $800** dollars. I just wanted to learn how to do it. I got really good at the $500 and $800 and I said, "Man I just want to do like **$2,000 dollar deals.**" "Man, I want to do **$4,000 dollar deal**. "Man, I want to do **$6,000 dollar deals**. Then, dang, "I got a $6,000 dollar chargeback – dang I didn't do that deal right, because clearly they didn't want to keep the policy."

So, you begin to get better and you develop yourself. When I look at investment deals, I am asking it worth the time that it took for me to accumulate this cashflow to get into that deal? I don't think so! I don't care if it is passive income, that passive income came from some activity that I did actively. So, I traded time at some point in time to get me to that passive income. I don't know if I want to do that. You have to get to that point and stage so you can be able to do that. You got to get to that point to where you are like you do not want to shortcut stuff.

I don't judge myself against people that are forty, fifty, years old that's been in the game twenty or thirty years. I don't judge myself against someone that's thirty-seven or been in the game for fifteen years. I don't judge myself against somebody that's even been in the game five years, but they got funding – I don't judge myself based off what anybody else and what they got; I judge myself based on my road and what I'm doing. People that are financial gurus – it is not Jake's time yet, but guess what? You better believe this is the decade of ascension. The world is going to know Jake Tayler Jacobs' name! Because I put in my bid and I put in my time. I have been teaching this same concept for the past three or four years when we lost our company. I started teaching out of a room in my apartment! I turned one of the rooms into my office when I lost my company. These same principles, the same blueprint, same concept – three or four years ago!

The same exact strategy that I used to grow our company to over nine states now – and we are going to continue to grow! It is the same exact thing I did when I lost everything. I had to put in my time, and I am ok with that and you have to be ok with that too. You got to be ok with looking at everybody and say, "You know what, he got off to a really good start because he was good at making good friends and building relationships. I just started to learn how to do that. There are some people around my age, and I am like, dang, they not better? How are they not, they were popular? They knew friends, had a bunch of friends, they mingled – they talked, and I was a loner, I like to chill. So, their road to success was a lot faster because they had a bigger network. Mine – I had to develop some stuff. I had to learn how to communicate and talk to people because I would rather just be inside myself and just talk to my friends. I had to learn how to get out there and communicate. I go out there and be like "No I really don't want to talk to anybody."

I had to learn those things. You got to get out of yourself and say however he got to wealth, - good for you! There is no lack in God's world and there are only two beliefs. You believe the world's belief, or my favorite book says be in the world but not of it. Do not conform to the world's view – be transformed by the renewing of your mind. What it tells me that – you have made your million dollars and I am going to applaud you, whatever I can do to help you grow it – because there I no lack in the world that I live in. And I am either going to believe what God said or I am going to believe what the world said. I am going to believe what God said about abundance or I am going to believe what the world said and there is not enough to go around. I am going to believe what God said that I am a King, and I was made after his image and likeness. I am going to believe what he says? Or am I going to believe what the world says that just because you are black – you got different rules? NO, I don't have any different rules. I am going to believe in what God said. You got your wealth, that let's me know that mine is on the way.

You got to get good at celebrating people on their way to the top! You want people to celebrate you. Hit the likes, share their videos and stories, because those celebrations are what will yield your celebration in life. Start celebrating them, as God qualifies you in darkness so you can be elevated in the light – he builds your character in darkness – you will be ascended in the light because you have been built when no one was paying attention. Allow God deal with you in the darkness, allow God to keep you in that dark place, allow God to make you understand the importance of discipline, prudence, and value. See I can build myself and not have to go purchase anything because I know I am a person of value. And I rather make purchases on lifestyle becoming better and making my life function better rather than purchasing some stuff jut to make people think I am making money. Gratitude will take you a long way.

Now we understand income. Now we understand passive income, we understand wealth, we understand the difference of net worth, the difference of assets, difference of liabilities, and we know we have to get our expenses down. Some of you need to get out of your pride and you need to downsize like yesterday. Are you going to keep making the billionaire richer or are you going to build your next egg. What are you going to do? You may say, "Jake my credit is going to go down." Well, you will never hear me say go get debt, you can go do it on your own. I am not the only financial person you are going to listen to, and I am not going to get in debt for nobody. There are financial people that make money and say get debt, if you want to use that as one of your tools that's fine, but me – no!

Teach the World that Freedom lives within you!

CHAPTER 7:

Finding the Money Part 3:

Balancing your Kingdom Budget

What's going on cousins – Welcome back to PBB Master School, in this session we are going to be talking about the Kingdom Management System and the importance of budgeting.

When you think about a Kingdom you think about a domain of a King or a Queen. What you are going to imagine is it is hard to think about a King or Queen if you do not have anybody running it without barriers and walls that surrounded the city that they were protecting. Because it is hard to protect something if you don't have walls to protect it – and they had guards at the gates to be able to detect who comes in and who goes out. But when it comes to our monetary system, we have to think of it with that same understanding.

If I don't have some type of barrier, some type of system protection around my money and I control when it comes in and when it comes out – I can't protect what I already have. So, when it comes to our cashflow, when it comes to our income, when it comes to us growing, I can't grow something that I do not know how to check. I can't tell you how long it will take for you to become financially independent if we don't even know where you already are. It's very important that we understand the Kingdom Management System and we stick to this.

The first thing to understand with the Kingdom Management System is you have to set up a time where you literally manage your income where you set up a financial meeting with yourself with a mirror or with your significant other and you sit down once a month at the same time – you set that appointment up and you run through your numbers.

And the best way to run through your numbers is not from the top of your dome, but it's the last month's bank statements – see what you swiped your card for? So, when you go get those statements from your bank or your online banks and you print out those bank statements, you can actually look at what you spent your money on. At the beginning of the year or the beginning of the month – you set your tone on how much money you plan to spend and all the areas of how much cash flow that you think you are going to have.

At the end of the month, you monitor that by getting your bank statements and you check over everything. It's no different than running a business. You would never allow someone to manage your business or run your business and keep track of your books without you double checking them. So, it is very important; in order for you to grow this monetary system, and become financially independent to grow your wealth, you have to be the
one that is always looking at your money and looking at your numbers.

I am going to go over briefly what you do for your budgeting system and it's very simple for your management system. Where you see expected monthly income, this is money that you expect to make that month.

Kingdom Management System Worksheet								
Enter your monthly income and expenses to better understand your personal budget. If desired, insert new rows to include new income sources or expenses, but do not enter any information in the grey boxes or columns with icons, as these cells hold formulas.								
EXPECTED MONTHLY INCOME	Income 1		✓ $4,500.00	EXPECTED BALANCE (Expected income minus expenses)			✓ $4,500.00	
	Extra income, SPOUSE		$0.00					
	Total monthly income		✓ $4,500.00	ACTUAL BALANCE (Actual income minus expenses)			✓ $0.00	
ACTUAL MONTHLY INCOME	Income 1		✓ $0.00	CASH FLOW (Actual minus Projected)			✗ ($4,500.00)	
	Extra income		✓ $0.00					
	Total monthly income		✓ $0.00					

HOUSING	Bill Due Date	Expected Cost	Paid Cost	Difference	ENTERTAINMENT	Bill Due Date	Expected Cost	Paid Cost	Difference
Mortgage/Rent		$0.00	$0.00 ✓	$0.00	Netflix/Hulu		$0.00	$0.00 ✓	$0.00
Phone		$0.00	$0.00 ✓	$0.00	Music		$0.00	$0.00 ✓	$0.00

So, if you expect at your job to bring in $4500 a month and where it says extra income, it could be from your spouse – so say you expect your spouse to bring home $2500 you can fill it in there or it could be extra income from your side business, if you don't have a spouse. But if you do, place the amount you expect them to bring home for the month. So, after adding, I know that $4500 + $2500 = $7000. So, between my wife and I, it is safe to say our monthly expected income is $7,000, and everything is where it is supposed to be.

Kingdom Management System Worksheet								
Enter your monthly income and expenses to better understand your personal budget. If desired, insert new rows to include new income sources or expenses, but do not enter any information in the grey boxes or columns with icons, as these cells hold formulas.								
EXPECTED MONTHLY INCOME	Income 1		✓ $4,500.00	EXPECTED BALANCE (Expected income minus expenses)			✓ $7,000.00	
	Extra income, SPOUSE, SIDE BUSINESS		✓ $2,500.00					
	Total monthly income		✓ $7,000.00	ACTUAL BALANCE (Actual income minus expenses)			✓ $0.00	
ACTUAL MONTHLY INCOME	Income 1		✓ $0.00	CASH FLOW (Actual minus Projected)			✗ ($7,000.00)	
	Extra income		✓ $0.00					
	Total monthly income		✓ $0.00					

HOUSING	Bill Due Date	Expected Cost	Paid Cost	Difference	ENTERTAINMENT	Bill Due Date	Expected Cost	Paid Cost	Difference
Mortgage/Rent		$0.00	$0.00 ✓	$0.00	Netflix/Hulu		$0.00	$0.00 ✓	$0.00
Phone		$0.00	$0.00 ✓	$0.00	Music		$0.00	$0.00 ✓	$0.00

Now when it comes to housing at the beginning of the month, what do I do? I set my expenses and I know that the mortgage is going to be $1400. But lets say for an example that is what I expect to pay – but I actually paid – let's say $2000 because something broke or I was late. As you guys are going to see your cash flow right here was affected. So, notice if I paid $1400 even, I expected to pay $1400 and I paid $1400 – **my cashflow is at zero.**

EXPECTED MONTHLY INCOME	Income 1		$4,500.00
	Extra income, SPOUSE, SIDE BUSINESS		$2,500.00
	Total monthly income		$7,000.00
ACTUAL MONTHLY INCOME	Income 1		$4,500.00
	Extra income		$2,500.00
	Total monthly income		$7,000.00

EXPECTED BALANCE		$5,600.00
(Expected income minus expenses)		
ACTUAL BALANCE		$5,600.00
(Actual income minus expenses)		
CASH FLOW		$0.00
(Actual minus Projected)		

HOUSING	Bill Due Date	Expected Cost	Paid Cost	Difference
Mortgage/Rent		$1,400.00	$1,400.00	$0.00
Phone		$0.00	$0.00	$0.00
Electricity		$0.00	$0.00	$0.00
Gas		$0.00	$0.00	$0.00
Water/Sewer		$0.00	$0.00	$0.00
Cable/Internet		$0.00	$0.00	$0.00
Waste/Trash		$0.00	$0.00	$0.00

ENTERTAINMENT	Bill Due Date	Expected Cost	Paid Cost	Difference
Netflix/Hulu		$0.00	$0.00	$0.00
Music		$0.00	$0.00	$0.00
Movies		$0.00	$0.00	$0.00
Concerts		$0.00	$0.00	$0.00
Sporting Events		$0.00	$0.00	$0.00
Social Outings		$0.00	$0.00	$0.00
Theater		$0.00	$0.00	$0.00

But if I expected to pay $1400 and I only paid $1100 that month for some reason, then my cash flow is at $300. Your cash flow change based on what you actually paid. Let's say for example, I expected to pay a phone bill and I expect it to be $125 but I actually had to pay $145. That means I am negative $20 cash flow already. Ok, that is what I am expecting. My balance has literally just dropped down to where my balance is $54.74 left from my $7000.

I already know that my cash flow has been interrupted. So, let's just say $125. Let's say of my gas I expected to pay $150 but I actually paid $225 this month, let's say my cable bill was supposed to be $75 this month but somebody ordered movies and I ended up paying $105. So, after paying those bills my actual cashflow is $5,145.

EXPECTED MONTHLY INCOME	Income 1		$4,500.00
	Extra income, SPOUSE, SIDE BUSINESS		$2,500.00
	Total monthly income		$7,000.00
ACTUAL MONTHLY INCOME	Income 1		$4,500.00
	Extra income		$2,500.00
	Total monthly income		$7,000.00

EXPECTED BALANCE		$5,250.00
(Expected income minus expenses)		
ACTUAL BALANCE		$5,145.00
(Actual income minus expenses)		
CASH FLOW		($105.00)
(Actual minus Projected)		

HOUSING	Bill Due Date	Expected Cost	Paid Cost	Difference
Mortgage/Rent		$1,400.00	$1,400.00	$0.00
Phone		$125.00	$125.00	$0.00
Electricity		$150.00	$225.00	-$75.00
Gas		$0.00	$0.00	$0.00
Water/Sewer		$0.00	$0.00	$0.00
Cable/Internet		$75.00	$105.00	-$30.00
Waste/Trash		$0.00	$0.00	$0.00
Maintenance/Repairs			$0.00	$0.00

ENTERTAINMENT	Bill Due Date	Expected Cost	Paid Cost	Difference
Netflix/Hulu		$0.00	$0.00	$0.00
Music		$0.00	$0.00	$0.00
Movies		$0.00	$0.00	$0.00
Concerts		$0.00	$0.00	$0.00
Sporting Events		$0.00	$0.00	$0.00
Social Outings		$0.00	$0.00	$0.00
Theater		$0.00	$0.00	$0.00
Other		$0.00	$0.00	$0.00

So, let's move down the sheet and look at the section for both car payments. For both cars, we are expecting to pay $695 and we actually pay $695 – lets say we took an uber that month and we didn't expect to pay anything to uber, but we paid $105. As you can see we are now over $205 for the month of what we expected to pay.

We expected to pay $125 in gas but this month we spent $175 in gas and we realize we are $25 dollars over. You will start to see where the money is going with each expense and it is adding up. So now we are $260 over. Look at insurance, we only expected to pay $60 for renters insurance and we actually paid $65.

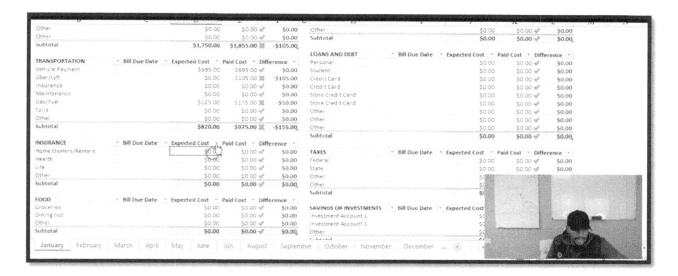

For health, we expected to pay $180 and we actually paid $180. You will notice we are right on the money with that, and this will help you try to stay in balance. At the beginning of the month we expected to pay $185 for groceries but we actually ended up paying $325. We expected to spend $100 dining out, but that month we actually dined out $450. We don't have any pets. For Hair grooming we expected to pay $80 but we actually paid more than normal for haircuts and hair grooming. As we scroll up you can see we are $795 off from what we expected to pay over what we actually pay. So, this lets us know that we are $795 off for the entire month, right.

So, let's look at this column which is **Netflix** and **HULU** - **$45** is what we expected to pay and that is what we actually paid. Movies, we expected to pay **$50** for **movies**, a couple of good movies came out and we took everybody out – we actually paid **$250** for **movies**. **Social outings** we only expected to pay **$75** but we went to a couple of parties and we ended up spending **$312** that month. So, as you can see we are **$1232 over** what we expected to pay for the month. So that means what? We have a leak in our system, and it got to be fixed. Lets talk about credit cards, we expected to pay **$125** and we actually ended up paying **$125** for this **credit card**. And for the next credit card you pay **$300** a month and you actually paid the **$300** for the month. For **student loans**, we expected to pay **$250** a month and we actually paid the **$250** a month.

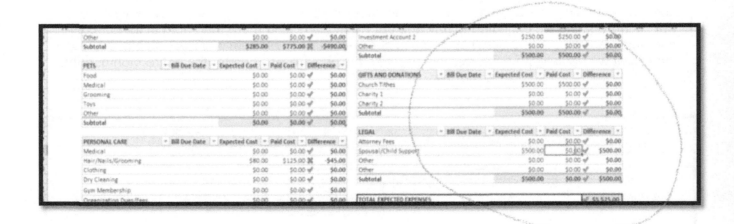

You don't have any personal loans. **State and Federal taxes let's say you have investment** accounts - **$250** goes to that account for you and for your spouse. Say you gave to charity such as **tithes**, you were expected to give **$500** and you actually gave **$500**. Your spouse has **child support $500** a month and you actually paid the **$500** for the month. So, we will start to pay differences in what you expected to pay based on what you actually paid.

102

We expected to have $1475 over that month but what we actually had was our real actual cash flow was $243 and we paid $1232 over what we expected to actually pay for the month. Which means that month we went over and beyond.

Kingdom Management System Worksheet					
Enter your monthly income and expenses to better understand your personal budget. If desired, insert new rows to include new income sources or expenses, but do not enter any information in the grey boxes or columns with icons, as these cells hold formulas.					
EXPECTED MONTHLY INCOME	Income 1	$4,500.00	EXPECTED BALANCE (Expected income minus expenses)		$1,475.00
	Extra income, SPOUSE, SIDE BUSINESS	$2,500.00			
	Total monthly income	$7,000.00	ACTUAL CASH FLOW (Actual income minus expenses)		$243.00
ACTUAL MONTHLY INCOME	Income 1	$4,500.00	DIFFERENCE (Actual minus Projected)		($1,232.00)
	Extra income	$2,500.00			
	Total monthly income	$7,000.00			

So, you will do this every single month and at the end of the year you will be able to see that your average monthly income will be more but it will total out your average monthly income as well as your average monthly expenses and you will be able to determine if you are positive or negative. But this says we are positive $243.

Kingdom Management Sy			
Annual Average Income vs			
INCOME		**EXPENSES**	
January	7,000.00	January	6,757.00
February	-	February	-
March	-	March	-
April	-	April	-
May	-	May	-
June	-	June	-
July	-	July	-
August	-	August	-
September	-	September	-
October	-	October	-
November	-	November	-
December	-	December	-
Annual Income	**7,000.00**	**Annual Expenses**	6,757.00
Average Monthly Income	583.33	**Average Monthly Expenses**	563.08
Net Gain (Loss)			

But let's just say January was a hectic month for us and we went out to some sporting events and spent $300 for the month – we will realize that our cash flow got immediately ate up! If you keep that habit up you will soon realize your negative gain $57 – you are negative for the year, which means your Kingdom is not profitable.

INCOME		EXPENSES	
January	7,000.00	January	7,057.00
February	-	February	-
March	-	March	-
April	-	April	-
May	-	May	-
June	-	June	-
July	-	July	-
August	-	August	-
September	-	September	-
October	-	October	-
November	-	November	-
December	-	December	-
Annual Income	7,000.00	Annual Expenses	7,057.00
Average Monthly Income	583.33	Average Monthly Expenses	588.08
Net Gain (Loss)			

You will need to do this assessment every single month – you put what you expect to pay at the beginning of the month and at the end of the month, you get your bank statement and put what you actually paid. And that is going to help you determine exactly what you need to do in order to keep a check and balance over what you already have.

It is very important that you are calculating all changes to see what comes in your Kingdom and what is going out your monetary Kingdom so that you can manage what God has already given you.

104

BECOMING THE BANKER

CHAPTER 8: It's a Financing Game: The mind of a Banker: Choose your Side

Welcome back to PBB Master School. I am extremely excited to share and talk with you all about taking your mindset from consumer to becoming the banker. And I want you guys to start transitioning your minds as we take you down the process of becoming the Banker.

We want to make sure that we understand that this life is nothing but a financing game and it is all about cash flow first. **Why do people invest?**

he truth is we invest for one or two reasons – cash flow and capital gains. When it comes to cash flow and capital gains – the problem that we have with most people when it comes to purchasing stock or purchasing investments; we only purchase stocks and investments. A lot of people like to preach capital gains which is your stock or value grows but you miss out on the most important thing which is cash flow gains. The wealthy understand that they need cash flow to pay for their living expenses and lifestyle and that is something we all must understand. The wealthy also recognize that investments for capital gains are nothing more than money that will buy more income producing assets in the future.

So, you have those capital gains like you buy a stock that goes and turns into $50 and you bought it for ten dollars – that's forty dollars of capital gains but it does nothing for you until you liquidate. So, a lot of people like to say, "I'm in stocks, I'm in this, I purchased that – but they are not getting cash flow, which means they have paper equity and that equity is not generating them cash flow so they can be able to grow from it. The first thing we got to understand is that step number one is: **Success in life is about Cash Flow.**

The wealthy understand that it's about cash flow – but the problem is, the middle class and the poor tend to invest for capital gain only. For example: Investments such as buying stocks for long term – ('the buy and hold" strategy), are all very typical. The general public has been conditioned by the financial institutions to think this way. Bankers and other wealthy people realize that it's about cash flow first.

- ✓ Why do they teach us to buy and hold stock?

- ✓ Why do they teach us to put our money somewhere and just let it sit there without generating cash flow? Why do they teach us that?

    We will talk about these questions later on.
Benjamin Graham – (was Warren Buffet's mentor) and is known for creating the best blueprint, which is his book called **"The Intelligent Investor"** Warren Buffet learned from Benjamin

Graham, is never to make investments for capital gains. You make investments for cash flow. That's why the majority of Warren Buffet's investments, well all of them are dividend paying investments.

When it comes to banking inside of insurance, we use dividend paying insurance companies. Notice how those work the same. I want you to understand that middle class and poor class, we invest for buying whole strategies: 401K's, IRA's, Sep Funds, and Roth IRA's. All these things were financially created to have our money sit there while they move our money. I hope this is making sense to you.

How do we generate Cash Flow? Cash flow is about arbitrage (creating a spread between the cost of borrowed and used money and what an investment pays). Arbitrage is nothing more than a leveraged strategy. So, when we think about arbitrage – it's the money in between. If I borrow money at 4% and I sell my investment that makes me money at 7% that means that my arbitrage – the cash flow is the 3% in between. Because the difference between seven and four is three. So that's where that cash flow spread is. In order to create this arbitrage opportunity, we need to have the following criteria, which is a simplified formula for passive income:

> **A: Income producing asset –**
> rental properties, insurance policy, business, bonds, apartment building
>
> Jake, "Insurance is an income producing asset? Absolutely, you didn't know?"
>
> **B: A lender that is willing to lend against the asset as collateral (obtain leverage)**
> As you all know when it comes to us borrowing money from our policy – the lender i..e. insurance company is willing to lend to us based on collateral.
>
> **C: Income that is larger than the loan payments and expenses related to the asset**
> That's the arbitrage in the middle.

The difference in the cost of the money – which is the interest you have to pay the lender, and what you make on the money, that's what we call the **cash flow spread**. So, if the money costs me 3% and I charge my customers 12% - the difference in cash flow is a 9% spread.

Let's look at three case studies and determine which one we would actually prefer :

Case study 1:

An investor buying an apartment building and he will use the apartment building as collateral for the loan. Now what we do know is that anything that' already producing cash flow or guarantees to produce cash flow, you can easily find a lender because they know that you can pay the loan. So, the investor puts some money down and borrows the rest from a banker. That was criteria number one – you need an income producing asset to use as collateral, and he uses the apartment building as collateral. The second thing you need is the lender that is willing to lend against the collateral. So, we know that he is able to get the bank to give him money for that apartment complex – so that settles criteria number two.

#1 **You need something that can produce passive income –**
#2 **you need someone that is going to lend you money on criteria #1**
   -which is the cash flow – that's what creates the arbitrage.

The arbitrage is how we get to all three criteria above: we have an asset that produces income, we have a lender that is going to allow us to borrow money – which leads us to arbitrage – the cash flow in between.

Case study 2:

A business owner is buying, let's say a car wash, the business is the income producing asset – which meets criteria #1 because they know the business is going to generate passive income. Why? Because people will come and get their car washed without the added help of people. So, the lenders would be willing to lend against the business – because they know the business will be able to pay back the debt. Criteria #3 is you hope that the income that you are making is larger than the loan payments. So, if I were to do arbitrage by numbers, what I would say is, if you got to pay the bank back $2000 a month on your loan, you better hope your business is making more than $2000. **For example** – your business is making $4000 a month and you owe the bank $2000 ea. Month. This is arbitrage – the difference in between $**2k.**

Case Study 3:

Let's suppose that you can buy a black box from a retail store and you could place this box on a shelf in your home. Let's also suppose that this black box generates $1000 a month for you. So, this box that you bought from a retail company, you can put it on a shelf in your home and it makes you a $1000 a month. Let's just say that you are able to buy that. And let's say the bank lends you money to purchase this box that generates you the $1000 a month, and let's suppose your loan payments are $700 a month – so if you got this black box that generates you $1000 a month, you owe the lender $700 a month, then the difference between $1000 and $700 is $300 a month. You met all criteria.

Now remember, this black box is headache free without any hassle, all you got to do is place it on a shelf in your home. You don't have to worry about any employees, you don't have to worry about any staff, you don't have to worry about any customers, you know that it is going to generate you $300 net profit every month. Would you want that box? A bunch of us would be like, not only do I want this box – but I want to see how many I can get! And most of us would prefer to own a black box that generates $300 cash flow every month, then we would an apartment complex or car wash. Why? Because it is less headache and less hassle. Most of us would want that right? You would just go purchase more black boxes to meet the capital you would make for rental homes.

The point of this is to illustrate that the main reason that we buy some of these assets – the car wash, the laundromats, the rental properties, self-storage, etc., is for the sake of generating passive income first. We don't buy them simply for the sake of saying I just want to own them. We don't buy it just to say I own a car wash – if that car wash is not generating you income, what is the purpose of saying you own it. So, when I hear people say how excited they are to own real estate or how excited they are to own businesses – I realize that they don't own enough real estate or they don't have enough businesses for what they are talking about. Typically, when a person says they own a business, the business is not generating you cash flow. You may say I own real estate, but that real estate is not generating you cash flow. Or you may be in network marketing but it is not generating you any cash flow. So, the purpose of owning businesses and owning real estate is for passive income first.

That's what we want to get to and the problem that we have with most businesses is that we never get to the point of where we are enjoying cash flow of our businesses. It's always hard active income.

All of this is important because I am shaping your mind about becoming the banker and the difference of it, so obviously we will choose the black box, right? Now, unfortunately this black box doesn't really exist. But the question is what is the closest thing to this black box? The answer I'm going to give may surprise you. Unfortunately, you can't find this black box anywhere. It's ok, you can cry later. But the question is, "**Jake, what is the closest thing to this black box where I can have little cash flow with more headache?**"

THE BLACK BOX IN REAL LIFE

Let's look at an example: Suppose you have a borrower that borrows $50,000 at 10% from a lender and this borrower signs a mortgage to the lender for this 10% charge at $50,000 The lender now has an income - producing asset (the piece of paper – the interest – for them). This asset is producing income just from a piece of paper. This easily meets criteria #1.

Now let's think about it. We are going to realize why the banks are the ones that are winning. Because when you look at it, you are going to be like, "dang, I'm getting got!"

What I am trying to impress upon you is that there is life after business owner. There is life after real estate developer or real estate investor. I'm trying to get you to see that the life is to be the banker! So, now what this lender can do – this lender can now borrow against it's asset, the mortgage paper, at a lower rate. **This is called hypothecation** – in our example this lender pledges the mortgage as collateral for a loan of $50K, let's say at 7%,and they make a 2% spread.

Let me show you the power of being a banker. I'm about to show you what a banker does. The person borrowing the money put their name on a piece of paper, they loaned them the money at 10%. The banker lent the money ($50,000 @ 10%) – now this banker, they can take this piece of paper, it is now a mortgage, they can take this piece of paper to another lender and can sell this piece of paper to another lender at 7%. The lender gives the first banker back the $50,000 and is now charging him 7%. This first lender charges the borrower 10% and he takes that same piece of paper to another lender that gives him $50,000 for the paper and charges him 7%. The difference between 10% and 7% is 3%. So not only did the first lender get his money back that he invested on the property, he shifted all of the risk to the next lender and he took all his money back. And he is still getting the difference arbitrage between what he charges and what he got to pay the second lender. The $50,000 was a loan and it was tax free!

I am trying to impress upon you why you got to learn how to BE THE BANKER and to stop settling for borrowing money from entities while you get your money re-used. I'm trying to get you to see what arbitrage looks like when you see a bunch of people moving your money. And it's no different than you saying, "Hey, bank can I borrow $50,000? And the bank saying, "Ok, cool. What assets do you have? I will give you $50,000 if you give me control of the asset until you pay me all my money back. If you don't pay my money, I take the asset. If you pay me my money, I release the asset. That's why you get your titles to your cars, and the deed when all the debt is paid. So, the only thing lender number one did – he just gave what he had as collateral, his asset. It may not have been a home, but it was the contract to the home.

So, he literally just did what? He gave his contract, his deed – it is no different than having title loan companies. When you need money real quick, you can go take your car title to a title loan company and they will give you a loan for your title. But you have to give them the title to your car. If you don't pay the loan back, they take the title and the car because now they own possession. If you pay the loan back, they get what? They give you the title back.

Jake, who or what is an example of lender number two?

All banks are lender number two, as they all are reselling your debt. But we will talk about that more a little later. That's why they want you to keep your money in a bank.

So, you have people that are investors. Investors have to buy physical structures, such as properties or businesses, to use as collateral to get leverage (borrowed money) so they can generate cash flow. So, the only way an investor can generate cash flow is if they go and buy a home. When they are going to buy a home, it is only when they are in agreeance with the home that they go to the bank and say, I got an apartment or I got a home, that told me I can be the buyer, I just need somebody to lend me the money. The bank says ok, "let me see the specs on the home, or let me see the specs on the apartment complex." The bank says, ok, "it's a generating asset, it has 90% occupancy, that's a safe place for us to put our money. We will lend you our money, you can lock up the assets and we will just get the deed."

But the deal with investors and business owners, yes, they do get the money from the bank. Yes, they do make the spread from what they borrowed, from what they charged to make the difference of the spread – so if the bank is charging me $3K a month, and I am making $8K a month, then yes I am making a $5K a month cash flow difference.

But they are forced to deal with the aggravations of these assets, such as tenant problems, overflowing toilets, employee hassles, inevitable lawsuits, and a myriad of other nightmare scenarios. Bankers simply print a piece of paper – call it a mortgage – and as long as someone is willing to sign the paper as a borrower, it serves as collateral for the borrowed money. While the business owner makes cash flow off the property, the bank makes cash flow off the paper. The investor needs to have a renter in the property to make cash flow difference. A banker with a filing cabinet of 40 mortgages that are each generating $300 a month is just as equivalent as the landlord with a lot of homes each generating $300 a month.

So out of the two which one is closer to the black box? The banker with the filing cabinet of mortgages or the landlord that got to manage all these homes?

The banker is closer. The banker literally created collateral out of paper to borrow against it and created an arbitrage cash flow opportunity immediately. This is power, but it gets better. Other investors, as you will find out later in the class, take a bigger risk than the lender, but they also got to play by the lenders rules.

"Jake, is that why you don't want to get in real estate?"

"No, I don't want to get in real estate. I want to get into lending. I want to lend to the real estate developers because the real estate developers got to play by my rules – Because **I'M THE LENDER!**"

And if you don't pay the bank like you are supposed to, guess what? The bank gets to seize all of your assets and your properties. So, when I tell people, you are the slave to the banker, people get mad at me. They say, "Jake, but I can make money. You got to borrow to get wealthy." I respond, "Dang, you sure are thinking like a producer. You're not thinking like a banker." You're thinking like a producer, somebody who needs my money to make your life work. "Jake but you need to borrow money," I say, "Dang, that's how you feel?" Keep thinking that way because I almost got enough in my reserve to start lending to you.

"You feel that you are not a slave and that you are the one controlling the deals?"
You are no controlling the deals – the person who controls the deals is the person who lends the money. So you're jus a high paid employee to me. You're managing another person's debt, you got to deal with all of the headache, while the banker only has to deal with you. You have to report to the bank! I'm trying to transform some of your thinking!

If you see the big picture, you're going to realize that you create your own arbitrage opportunity as the lender by creating collateral out of thin air. You are shifting the risk to the borrower and putting yourself in a safer position. If I lock up a property and I'm the lender, I'm moving myself to a safer position. Because not only does this borrower have to pay my interest first, that's why they got the amortized interest rates so you can pay the majority of your interest in your first 15 years of your 30-year mortgage. Because once the fifteen years are up, guess what? I'm out the game. Not only do I lock up your asset, now I have my money out of the deal. All my money I gave you in the firs 15 years, I got my money out. IF you dare decide that you can't pay the mortgage or you dare decide that you don' want to pay me the rest of my money; I'm going to foreclose the home, sell it, and then make my money and interest that I was going to make anyway.

Generating cash flow is what you are looking for and writing the rules by which the borrower has to play. You accomplish the same thing as the investor. Arbitrage the cash flow, but more easily and less hassle. I would rather someone come to me and say, "Hey Jake, I got a property." I say, "Man let me hear the deal, let me see what you got!" He says, "Man I got this development idea, I got this, I got that." I ask, where are the buildings?" Ok, you got to many this and too many buildings, and I'm doing the calculations" And I say, "How much money do you need?" He says, "I need $500K." "OK, let's do an appraisal on your buildings." I find out that the buildings are worth $500K. I tell you cool. Why? I lent you $500K and the buildings are worth $500K, so I know off top – I'm getting my money back. I put myself in a safe position and then I charge you ten percent interest – so I am really good!

Bankers, we realize and recognize that generating cash from spreads is nothing more than a financing game. Most real estate investors think it's about real estate but it's not about real estate at all. It's about financing. It's a financing game for them. The only reason that they purchase buildings is not to say, "Man I own buildings." I hate to hear people that say, "Man I'm buying back the block." Is that block making money for you? Or you just want to say I bought a building? The only reason they purchase a building is for sake of creating a spread. To buy a building and to sit on it and say, "Man, one day the equity in this building is going to be crazy." **THAT'S STUPID!!** It's not about the physical property, it's not about the tenants, it's about a building that can simply be used as collateral, to a bank, so that the investor can make that spread. The investor trying to figure out how big that spread can be when I purchase a home. So if I ever were to purchase a home, and what I would do is look at its spread. What can I make in cash flow from all the rooms versus just trying to sell one door? If there are four doors in our house, I want to sell every door. I want to increase my spread versus just selling one door.

Similarly a business owner buying a business, such as a laundry mat, most people would think it has something to do with the laundry mat. You don't start a business for a job, if that's the case, you may as well just get a job, its less headache. You start a business for cash flow so you can build it and get to a point where you don't have to physically be there but you can enjoy the fruits of having it. That's why most people only talk about real estate because real estate is the only thing they can get in their head that it's a possibility quickly for passive income.

Your business can generate passive income, you just don't want to get out the way of it. It's not about the laundromat, it's not about the hair product you make, it's not about the nutrition product you make – it's about the cash flow and generating that spread. That's what its about. Bankers recognize that because life is about financing, and they play it quite well. They create the need for the collateral, from a piece of paper. They create the spreads all day long and how they want. They know that they are in a business of financing safety and it makes a lot of money. They want to put themselves in the best position. That's why they don't lend to black people – not because they hate black people, they don't loan to black people because you don't have any collateral! You want to go in there talking about a business idea that has never made any money. The more your business makes without your efforts, the more chances you have to leverage.. and to get leveraged money.

I'm not someone who would tell you to go to the bank and get money – I'm not that person, but if you were to; that's a tip. When you are able to go to the bank to say my business makes $5K a month without me, that is a better proposition than someone going to the bank saying my business makes $15K with me. Because the bank knows with or without you, you have enough money to pay that loan. The bankers have the best position and they know it. They shifted the risk to the borrower and they're in the right position to make the money and they tied up the borrower's collateral just in case the borrower slips. They're in the business of finance and safety. In order for the bank to work they need borrowers and need to use other people's money to create the spread.

That's why the tell you to sit your money there, to sit it in the bank, and you need to keep investing an keeping your money for the long run; keep it in a 401K until you are 65, because they are using and abusing your money and giving you back the pennies left. They condition the population to borrow money using good collateral and shifted the risk to the borrowers. They've conditioned everyone to invest for capital gains. This allows the invested money to sit with the bankers and make even more money, because the money is "dead." It's not moving for the rest of us. So these hedge funds, and mutual funds, they're teaching you to keep your money in there – dollar cost averaging over thirty, forty, fifty years, and what do you think they're doing? They're becoming the banker, lending the money, purchasing companies that pay them cash flow while telling you to keep your money with them fifty years.

They condition the population to save their money in their banks, which then becomes a chunk of their money source they can use in creating spreads. They know they have the most powerful wealth-building strategies ever know to man. But they keep it a secret – otherwise we all would become bankers and no one is left to be a borrower! Welcome to banking family. Welcome to the other side. In summary, what we got to understand is that generating cash flow boils down to the following specific formula in The Wealthy Code:

A) having something that can get collateralized
B) having somebody that can allow you to use that collateral
C) being able to make a spread

111

"Jake, why would you use insurance?"

Because insurance allows me to use my money as collateral. I don't have to use my money. They charge me 4-5% interest to borrow money from them, and they are already paying me 8-12% so I am getting paid to borrow from them. And I am using their money for an investment to generate me cash flow so that I can be able to make the difference.

So at a basic level generating as flow requires two things, income producing asset and the leverage to buy the asset. For business owners and investors, the income producing asset typically turs out to be a physical structure with many aggravations. For bankers, the income producing asset becomes a piece of paper they print and the borrower signs. Business owners and investors think they are in the business of doing what the structure the bought do but the reality is, they are in the business of generating a spread using financing. Everything in life is financing. That's what the bankers recognize.

Now that we know the truth, we have to pick a team. We have to choose what team we are going to be on. The world is divided into three teams: consumers, producers, and bankers.

> Consumers – use products and services. They are the ones who buy the latest electronics, smartphones, and impressive cars.
>
> Producers – provide products and services. They're the ones who manufacture and/or sell the latest gizmos: phones, cars, televisions, food, and more. Everything a consumer uses comes from a producer. The producers are the ones who create jobs and hire consumers to work for them. They are masters of systems that generate profits. Many believe that this is the most interesting position to be in because it is always challenging and, with the right mindset can be seen as a game for adults.
>
> Bankers – finance both consumers and producers. The consumer uses that money to buy products and services from the producer, and the producer uses that borrowed money to produce those products and services for the consumer. The bankers don't have to laugh all the way to the bank. After all, they own the bank, so they laugh while sitting in the bank! They are master of shifting risk to the borrower and financing.

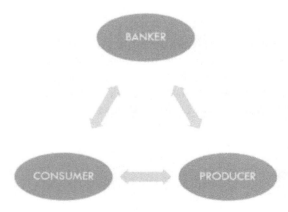

Every person has the option of choosing which side to play on. Most people think they are limited to being a consumer for the rest of their lives. But if you really want to make the right choice you must decide if you want to be the banker, consumer, or producer. If you are smart, you can choose to be the banker and the consumer. When you are the bank you can be your own consumer and your own producer. Because you own the entire ecosystem. You control the money and if you can afford it – lend to yourself and pay yourself back because you ARE THE BANK!

CONSUMER

Have to work hard all their lives to pay for the financing of goods and services. They make up the majority of the world, and without them, producers and bankers would suffer. So it is everyone's best interest to have consumers working hard in jobs and using borrowed money to buy goods and services. They aren't aware that they are always being conditioned to buy stuff or being persuaded into buying certain brands. They aren't aware of how producers and bankers team up to influence them into buying.

When you find someone that is sponsored by Capital One, be very weary of the advice that they give you. Because nine times out of ten they are probably of the top tier of borrowers from Capital One.

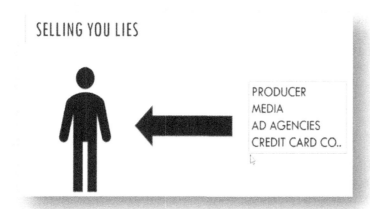

Producers partner with advertising agencies, credit card companies (bankers), and the media to condition the consumer to spend borrowed money on "stuff." Hundreds of millions of dollars are spent on conditioning the consumer to spend money. The biggest companies in the world partner with experts to ensure that consumers spend.

If you got a financial advisor that keeps telling you to borrow, borrow, borrow – nine times out of ten, the more they keep telling you that, the more the banks are what? Giving them more money. Why? Because they want that person to tell you – "I go through Capital One, or I go through Chase Bank, or I go through Bank of America. Why? It's in their favor that they keep telling you to borrow money. Because the more of a celebrity they are, the more clout they have, the more the banks are going to give them. The banks want to be on their side. Come on y'all, its common sense. Everybody is working together.

PRODUCER

Producers borrow money from bankers, use it to generate products and services, and pass on the cost – along with hefty profits – of the borrowed money to the consumer. They focus on creating value to the consumers. Whether it's opening a restaurant, a nearby mall, a movie theater, or housing, producers are always looking at the needs and wants of consumers and providing stuff to satisfy those needs and wants. Producers have to focus on their systems generating a profit with the borrowed money; otherwise, it will all backfires. Using borrowed money can turn around and hurt producers if they fail to turn a profit. That's why you see a bunch of Fortune 500 companies go bankrupt. It's funny they always tell you to borrow money but the #1 reason for Fortune 500 companies or small businesses going bankrupt is because the debt is too much for them to bear. The #1 reason that governments fail is because the debt is too much for them to bear. They borrowed too much money from too many people and they can't keep up. Many entrepreneurs go out of business within a few years because they lack the skills needed to build a business.

BANKER

Bankers, on the other hand, make the most money. They use borrowed money to lend out and tie up the borrower's collateral. They cover their downside and let the upside take care of itself. They are masters of shifting risk to the borrowers. If borrowers fail to pay, ties up enough collateral to make sure they make enough money. However, if the borrower is successful in paying back the banker, the banker still makes money because of interest. When you first get your mortgage they are a lot more lenient towards you in the beginning. Why? Because you owe them too much money. But towards the end, they got their money back so they are a lot more tough. They are a lot more tough towards the end. Why? Because they got their money and they know if they kick you out, they can do it all over again.

Either way, the banker wins. The best part of being the banker is that they recognize they don't need to have money to lend out. Through a combination of using borrowed money and "printing" money, they can make money, and lots of it. I'll explain that later. Every person on the planet fits into at least one of three teams (Producers and bankers, are, of course also consumers). There is no other choice. By default, people start as consumers, but producers and bankers become the rich. So when people say debt is good. I say if you do the math, it doesn't make sense to be in debt, especially consumer debt.

"Jake, what is that next level for you?"

My next level is a private equity or hedge fund where we buy out companies or lend to companies for a small period of time. That's going to be my play at age 45 or 50. At age 45 to 50, I'm using all the money I'm making in insurance and doing what I'm doing to become the lender and to buy out companies to sell it or leverage it as collateral to get more capital. That's my play to a billion dollars.

There are plenty of ways for us to get out of debt, I just want us to be smarter on how we do it so that we can climb and get there. The Bible says do not despise small beginnings – everyone wants to get to the end of the race before you have actually ran it yourself. So lets run it, lets start small and do what we can and eventually we will get to the point so we can be our own lenders and we can be our own boss. I want you all to start thinking, "You know what, I can do the exact same thing that they're telling me that I can't do." And if I go and start my own bank, I know starting a charter, I got to go through a bunch of discrimination that may not allow me to get the bank. But if I'm becoming interdependent inside of their system – that means I am using their system to become independent. I may not be fully independent but interdependent inside of their system functioning on my own. And that's exactly where you want to be.

CHAPTER 9: Two Type of Insurance Banks

You should be excited because we are going to be diving deep into the different types of insurance banks but most importantly we are going to take advantage of a white canvas and take advantage to create your lifestyle.
Your life, what you actually dream, and what you actually want.

You are missing life and the importance of it. Why would God allow you to be here on Earth if you believe in Heaven after this, why would God allow you to be here on Earth and go through turmoil all of your life and not get to see what Heaven looks like? God said that you would have heaven on Earth. The new Kingdom will be made on Earth. You can have it here. You can decide to be the bank, to be the business, to be the consumer, to have the cars, to have the lifestyle, you just got to have just a little bit of patience, and just a little bit of discipline. Even when things get tight, if you say you are going to start the bank with something no matter how tight it gets, you hold to it because guess what? Only through discipline and getting through tight and tough moments, can you be able to see the fruits of what your discipline manifests.

We will be stepping into the insurance banks and why we do what we do. I am going to be talking about why we are inside the insurance banks, and then I will break down the different types of insurance banks. I was recently talking to a business owner, a multi-millionaire, and he had about $6M in cash – some of it was in cryptocurrency, that equates to about $3M or $4M and he had about $2M in cash. And when I talked to him It took me 15 minutes to explain this concept to him, and he immediately said, if the banks are doing it, this literally makes sense, give me 48 hours and I want to put a plan in place. That's all it takes, it's only us that don't have a lot of income, got a lot debt, don't have a lot of cash flow, it's only us that try to pick and pull if you want to do $50 a month, $150 a month, $200 a month and you don't really understand.

This business owner said wait a minute, so you're telling me that just by me losing 40% of my liquidity, in 31 days I can get access to 60% of my cash flow that I put in and I can now have a forever system that's tax free that I can leverage? He said that's worth it any day. When I talk to people that are just like you and I that don't have that type of capital, that are head above their heels when it comes to debt, it's hard for us to even navigate that. So it's crazy the paradigm shift that some people have in comparison to others.

I didn't just say all that to impress you, but to show you how limited your thinking is stopping you from getting ahead. See you losing a little bit of that today to get more of it tomorrow, he literally saw as a business owner, you're looking at taxes. And he saw the banks use it as a tax shelter, he said, "Oh my gosh! You don't have to say nothing else to me!" "If the banks are using it and I am looking at their liabilities and assets ledger, and I'm seeing that they put seven times more, eight times more, even twelve times more money, inside of insurance cash reserves, than they actually put in the market, **THAT'S A NO BRAINER! Why wouldn't I do what the banks are doing?**

Welcome back to PBB and during this segment I am about to show you the difference in these banks and how you can literally fund your life, to fund your dreams, to fund your businesses and become the financier of your life.

Let's get started!

WHY INSURANCE? Why not any other cash pool or any other pool?

1. Because the banks are doing – Think about it, they say when in Rome do as Romans do. I say when trying to succeed and be successful in life do what billion dollars banks do. So versus me trying to pretend and act like I'm listening to a financial advisor who got a little bit of money but not really any money. Versus listening to these millionaires that are teaching financial literacy – they say success leaves clues and if you are really looking you will find a crumb trail. What we found in this system was the crumb trail. We looked at the **FDIC.gov** and we looked in the backside of it. For some people you got to see the Wells Fargo, you got to see the Chase Bank, you got to see these things. You're looking at these crumbs and they lead us to insurance.

2. Because of the protection of your assets – your most valuable assets, which are cash, and your meat suit. Once your meat suit expires, your ability to generate cash flow does too. What I typically like to say is, if it was hard to live life, why die cheap? "But I don't have any kids yet Jake." I mean, well, does that mean you don't progress your family in moving forward? Remember, you told your mom that you would retire her. And just because you passed away does that mean your promise falls to the ground? You told your father you would take care of him. And just because you passed away does that mean your promise falls to the ground? You told your wife that you were going to take care of her. You told the mother of your child that you were going to take care of her. You told your husband, the father of your children, that y'all were going to do it together. So just because you passed, does that mean you get to negate the promise?

3. Let's talk about the "meat suit" and why we are using insurance – why are we using insurance, for one it protects your meat suit. Life insurance is the only thing that you can put money into and it guarantees that your family will get paid out more than you put in. **What I'm saying is life insurance is the only thing that you can put your money into and it literally guarantees that it will pay out more than you put in.** Life already has too many variables that I cannot control. Life already has too many variables that are out of my hands. Life has too many variables that you would consider a risk. So the only thing that gives you confidence and walking this earth is to know that you have insurance and that are assured to have insurance to 0protect you no matter what happens to you, whether you live or you die.

So when we talk about insurance you got to understand the importance of it. A lot of us we believe in a life after this, whether you believe in Christ, whether you believe in Muhammad, Allah or whatever you believe in; you got to understand that if you believe in that, then there is some type of assurance that you have in the insurance of what you believe is actually true. And if that is true, that means you're believing in insurance without realizing it. See for us, we know that salvation through Jesus Christ, is our insurance. Through other people it may be Allah. Thought other people it may be the Universe. Through other people it may be the cosmos, reincarnation, or whatever your creed is, there is still some type of belief that you cannot back fully. So you have to have faith that the insurance plan that you have is going to come through when you want it to. Is that true? So, if I know that; that means that insurance is everything in life.

So just like I got insurance on my soul, I need to make sure I have insurance on my meat suit. I need to make sure I got insurance on my assets, to ensure that my assets continue to move forward with or without me. Because whether you understand it or not, if you have kids, you made a promise to your kids that you would take care of them. They didn't ask to be here. So, it is your job to ensure that whether you are here or not. Most of you wouldn't have made it on this Master Class if you did not have insurance, and if you don't have insurance you need to be calling us asap. Because what good is knowledge if you can't ensure the application of it? So I can't ensure this business that we're in will be passed down to my family but I can ensure cash flow and equity can be passed down, and that's why we use insurance. If I put cash flow inside of my bank account, my family will only get what I put in. If I die with money inside of my investment account, my family can only make money on what I put in. With life insurance my family is guaranteed to get more than what I put in no matter what. And that's the deal and that's what I like.

4. Cash – why do we use insurance for our cash? There are couple of things that we know that go against our cash. We use insurance to protect out cash. If we remember the Master Class PowerPoint, we know that insurance is to protect from financial loss. And there is one piece of loss that most of us do not take into account and it is called inflation. We have to understand that inflation does not care what color or creed you are. At one point in time ten dollars could fill your car tank. But today that same ten dollars doesn't fill up your tank of gas. You can barely chug along with ten dollars. That's what inflation does. If we don't understand how inflation works, what happens is the value of our money begins to eat itself. It begins to die! So, if I do not have my money in some type of vehicle, that beats inflation, I could have $100K inside a safe. In Dallas - Fort Worth I can look at a house that's $100K. If go to that safe twenty years from now, I can't go and buy that same house I was looking at why? The cost of inflation, the cost of goods, and that $100K won't buy what it can today. And a lot of us fail to realize that. So the value of your money, it eats away at itself if you don't pay attention. A loaf of bread used to cost less than what it does today. Which means you have to spend more money for the same item. We use insurance to protect us against inflation.

How can cash keep up with inflation when it is under valued medium? The reason why we using insurance is because inside the cash reserve we know that we are getting a guaranteed 4% of guaranteed money. We know that the average interest rate of inflation is 3%. So we already know off top the 4% that we are receiving annually, is beating inflation in itself. That's why when you keep your money in a safe or keep your money under your mattress, you are actually deadening your money. Let me give you an example. Your blood has to always be circulating. If your blood ever stops circulating, you're dead! Water has to always be circulating. If water were to ever stop circulating, no rain, no replenishment of itself, we all would die, the earth would die. Now if water works that way, if blood works that way, if the air that we breath works that way – carbon dioxide comes out; it goes through trees, they clean it and oxygen comes back in) everything in life that has life, has to be circulating or it dies.

So if my money is any place that is not growing above the cost of living, that means my money is going to what? DIE! That's exactly why we have to make sure that your currency, your money – flows like we talked about, is always going out and coming back in. Money does not serve us to just go and purchase something that increase in value and not do anything with it. So gold, yes you can purchase it and it grows in value. But the purpose of currency (remember the definition) is to be flowing consistently, running consistently. Which means the actual definition of currency is – it's supposed to be flowing!

117

Going out and coming back in – Going out and coming back in – Going out and coming back in! Leaving out – purifying – coming back in! That's supposed to be the flow of currency.

Just like the infinity sign,

5. **Capital Gains** – We use our cash for capital gains. So when we think about capital gains it is profit from a property or an investment. So Jake why do we use insurance for capital gains? Because we only deal with companies that pay dividends.
(A dividend is a sum of money paid regularly by a company to its shareholders out of it's profits or reserves.) Because we only deal with the mutual companies; mutual companies don't have shareholders, but the policy holders are considered partners with the mutual company. Which means by law, the mutual company has to share profits with us. So if I were to invest in the stocks, I would only invest in the stocks that paid dividends, me personally.

Jake, how do you know that we are going to be able to get dividends?

Well, the company can't promise dividends. But we only deal with companies that have more than 100 years of existence of paying dividends every year. Why? Because every company wants to be profitable. So why wouldn't the insurance company want to be profitable?

How are the dividends calculated? We do know that once you give your money to that reserve to the insurance company, they have to put your money to work. They have to grow your money in order to back up the promise of paying out your death benefit when you expire. So they have to put your money to work, for the cost of insurance, along with the money that is going into the reserve. They can't just take the $100 a month, leave it in a reserve and not grow it and expect to be able to pay out all of their death benefits.

What do insurance companies invest in? They invest in debts.

A) **Bonds** – both **commercial and government**
only invest in **triple A Bonds** – the highest tier of bonds (only invest in what we call triple A bonds) Either they are securing of assets or you're dealing with a company that has years of history of paying all their debt off.

*Why would an insurance company invest in a bond?

Because they need guarantees to get the money back. Because in this life it's about financing, so they're doing what the banks do. Well somebody said, "Well Jake, I can just put my own money in a bond. I don't need to use this system to do that." That is true, but then your money is locked for the entirety of that term of that bond. What we get to do, we get to use the leverage of our money growing with the bond, and still use our money the entire time.

Versus locking your money with a bond and not being able to use it. So typically there is a term period on the bond; five-year, ten-year, twenty-year, one year, that the bond has to be paid back in full. That's one way they invest their money.

B) **Real Estate** – And it's nor real estate like you think, it's not just about buying buildings, there are known insurance companies that invest in big huge areas of land, buildouts, and shopping centers. There are some that do that. But in real estate, most of them lend their money out to financing companies. So those companies that offer mortgages and they only lend mortgages – the majority of them buy blocks of cash from insurance companies and then the insurance companies charge a percentage of money and then that mortgage company charges you the difference. So they buy blocks of cash from insurance companies.

"Jake, what do you mean by blocks of cash?"

It's very simple, they look at cash as units. Say for instance I am a mortgage company and I told the insurance company I wanted to buy $500K worth of cash (borrow) from you at 5%. So the insurance company loans that money at 5% and then they go and charge 8-9% in arbitrage in the difference. A bunch of financing companies borrowing money.

Then you have residential and commercial. Jake, "I could invest my money in that myself." Yeah you could but your money wouldn't be liquid. You couldn't just put $100K in on a real estate or commercial property and use the $100K while getting the cashflow. You can't just do that right? So we are leveraging the expertise of them growing money while consistently using the cash on the way while benefiting from the wise investments.

C) **Stock Options** – but they only typically use about 3-4% of their portfolio to invest in stock options.

D) **Joint Ventures** – usually anywhere from about 5-15% of the portfolio for joint venture where the know they have a clear shoo-in to win.

All areas that we have just discussed, this is all your monies being invested in these entities. People usually ask me, "Jake when are you going to get into real estate?" I honestly tell them, I'm in real estate. My insurance is a fund, and its purchasing all this stuff in large portions. The only difference is with your funds versus my funds, I have guarantees and you don't. The only difference with your real estate plan versus mine, is when you give your $10K – your $10K is locked! When I put my $10K in I can use it!

✓ **I do have bonds.**

  ✓ **I do have real estate.**

    ✓ **I do have small stock options.**

      ✓ **I do have joint ventures on the highest level.**

The only difference is, I can still use my money when I gave it away. When I'm doing my deal and investing my money, they immediately make the money work for you. When we see that 40% going out for the cost of insurance, you got to understand that the cost of insurance is also helping manage your management account, which is why your cash reserve can grow at such a fast and rapid pace.

When you give your money to the insurance companies and the reason why they can give the guarantee and the dividends is because of this: **Bonds, Real Estate, Stock options, and Joint Ventures).** One thing you got to ask yourself, the more money that you have in an investment, is it not true that you will not get more dividends back? Is that true?

So when I look at these numbers here on his slide, I begin to see, "Oh! That's why Jake when I have more money in my cash reserve, I'm starting to see more and more dividends. As a mutual company and as a policyholder – you're a partner inside with the company.

SO YOU'RE A PARTNER WITH A BILLION DOLLAR COMPANY!
That gives you guarantees of death benefit and guarantees your money!
Why would you want to put your money anywhere else?

So notice here, the first ten years, I got about $6500 in dividends.

Age	End of Year	Contract Premium + Riders	Cash Value	Death Benefit	Contract Premium + Riders	Cash from Policy	Cash Outlay	Annual Dividend	Cash Value	Death Benefit
32	1	24,000	11,991	1,238,168	24,000	0	24,000	117	12,108	1,238,285
33	2	24,000	24,394	1,305,491	24,000	0	24,000	117	24,632	1,306,286
34	3	24,000	40,726	1,370,564	24,000	0	24,000	117	41,089	1,372,015
35	4	24,000	62,163	1,433,471	24,000	0	24,000	117	62,655	1,435,557
36	5	24,000	85,217	1,494,298	24,000	0	24,000	117	85,843	1,496,998
37	6	24,000	108,711	1,553,118	24,000	0	24,000	429	109,787	1,556,723
38	7	24,000	133,836	1,610,018	24,000	0	24,000	784	135,732	1,616,085
39	8	24,000	158,253	1,665,069	24,000	0	24,000	1,173	161,385	1,675,249
40	9	24,000	184,306	1,718,345	24,000	0	24,000	1,547	189,088	1,734,291
41	10	24,000	210,843	1,769,919	24,000	0	24,000	1,983	217,766	1,793,188
		240,000			240,000	0	240,000	6,501		

But as you can see the more and more money I have; the more and more money in dividends I'm getting paid out.

42	11	24,000	237,872	1,819,855	24,000	0	24,000	4,606	249,626	1,854,293
43	12	24,000	266,582	1,868,216	24,000	0	24,000	5,440	284,157	1,922,709
44	13	24,000	295,879	1,915,058	24,000	0	24,000	6,324	320,352	1,992,425
45	14	24,000	325,765	1,960,420	24,000	0	24,000	7,248	358,286	2,063,466
46	15	24,000	357,437	2,004,346	24,000	0	24,000	8,211	399,235	2,135,831
47	16	24,000	389,758	2,046,878	24,000	0	24,000	9,273	442,205	2,209,562
48	17	24,000	422,760	2,088,054	24,000	0	24,000	10,376	487,319	2,284,791
49	18	24,000	457,639	2,127,911	24,000	0	24,000	11,534	535,876	2,361,495
50	19	24,000	493,249	2,166,487	24,000	0	24,000	12,795	586,892	2,439,728
51	20	24,000	530,763	2,203,818	24,000	0	24,000	14,127	641,661	2,519,610
		480,000			480,000	0	480,000	96,436		

The more money you have in your cash reserve pot, the more money that they share with you, because they are using your additional cash to continue to push their portfolio forward. They are allowing you to participate in the growth of the company. Which is why you don't want to keep your money with the banks because they're growing your money and not giving you nothing back. My cash reserve is doing the exact same thing it would be doing in the bank.

42	11	24,000	237,872	1,819,855	24,000	0	24,000	4,606	249,626	1,854,293
43	12	24,000	266,582	1,868,216	24,000	0	24,000	5,440	284,157	1,922,709
44	13	24,000	295,879	1,915,058	24,000	0	24,000	6,324	320,352	1,992,425
45	14	24,000	325,765	1,960,420	24,000	0	24,000	7,248	358,286	2,063,466
46	15	24,000	357,437	2,004,346	24,000	0	24,000	8,211	399,235	2,135,831
47	16	24,000	389,758	2,046,878	24,000	0	24,000	9,273	442,205	2,209,562
48	17	24,000	422,760	2,088,054	24,000	0	24,000	10,376	487,319	2,284,791
49	18	24,000	457,639	2,127,911	24,000	0	24,000	11,534	535,876	2,361,495
50	19	24,000	493,249	2,166,487	24,000	0	24,000	12,795	586,892	2,439,728
51	20	24,000	530,763	2,203,818	24,000	0	24,000	14,127	641,661	2,519,610
		480,000			480,000	0	480,000	96,436		

The only difference is I have a bottom-line guarantee on this side, plus a guarantee of life insurance if anything happened to me no matter what. So it's a win-win! So that's why when I got entrepreneurs that are putting up big money to get inside their banks, I don't have the problems with them thinking I'm trying to get over on them or them, being scared with their money. Because they immediately see the value. Versus when I am talking with somebody who's not really confident with money, doesn't really got a lot of debt, got cash flow but they're scared, those are the ones that have all the questions. But we're changing that right?

52	21	24,000	569,017	2,239,941	24,000	0	24,000	15,289	698,907	2,600,933
53	22	24,000	608,000	2,274,898	24,000	0	24,000	15,620	757,831	2,682,342
54	23	24,000	648,923	2,308,729	24,000	0	24,000	15,972	819,704	2,762,126
55	24	24,000	690,594	2,341,473	24,000	0	24,000	16,323	883,344	2,840,351
56	25	24,000	734,189	2,373,168	24,000	0	24,000	16,685	949,962	2,917,054
57	26	24,000	778,549	2,403,855	24,000	0	24,000	17,048	1,018,420	2,992,288
58	27	24,000	824,837	2,433,570	24,000	0	24,000	17,433	1,089,922	3,066,105
59	28	24,000	871,876	2,462,352	24,000	0	24,000	17,819	1,163,307	3,138,572
60	29	24,000	919,647	2,490,237	24,000	0	24,000	18,337	1,238,693	3,209,853
61	30	24,000	968,140	2,517,262	24,000	0	24,000	19,012	1,316,242	3,280,317
		720,000			720,000	0	720,000	265,974		

So when we look at this, we begin to say, "Oh! This makes sense." So I am losing 40% of my liquidity so that I can have all of this working for me plus the basic cost of insurance.

Now do you understand why we're using insurance?

So we know we got to use insurance but what we got to understand is the reason why your first ten years is a completely different outcome than your next ten years, is because you put a total of $240K in. **(lets go back to the power point)**

37	6	24,000	108,711	1,553,118	24,000	0	24,000	429	109,787	1,556,723
38	7	24,000	133,836	1,610,018	24,000	0	24,000	784	135,732	1,616,085
39	8	24,000	158,253	1,665,069	24,000	0	24,000	1,173	161,385	1,675,249
40	9	24,000	184,306	1,718,345	24,000	0	24,000	1,547	189,088	1,734,291
41	10	24,000	210,843	1,769,919	24,000	0	24,000	1,983	217,766	1,793,188
		240,000			240,000	0	240,000	6,501		

60% of $240K went inside of your cash reserve. So that means **$144K** actually went inside of your cash reserves.

37	6	24,000	108,711	1,553,118	24,000	0	24,000	429	109,787	1,556,723
38	7	24,000	133,836	1,610,018	24,000	0	24,000	784	135,732	1,616,085
39	8	24,000	158,253	1,665,069	24,000	0	24,000	1,173	161,385	1,675,249
40	9	24,000	184,306	1,718,345	24,000	0	24,000	1,547	189,088	1,734,291
41	10	24,000	210,843	1,769,919	24,000	0	24,000	1,983	217,766	1,793,188
		240,000			240,000	0	240,000	6,501	$144K	

Which means you had a 60% internal rate of return on your money. So I put $144K actually went in my cash reserve and everything else was cost of insurance.

37	6	24,000	108,711	1,553,118	24,000	0	24,000	429	109,787	1,556,723
38	7	24,000	133,836	1,610,018	24,000	0	24,000	784	135,732	1,616,085
39	8	24,000	158,253	1,665,069	24,000	0	24,000	1,173	161,385	1,675,249
40	9	24,000	184,306	1,718,345	24,000	0	24,000	1,547	189,088	1,734,291
41	10	24,000	210,843	1,769,919	24,000	0	24,000	1,983	217,766	1,793,188
		240,000			240,000	0	240,000	6,501	$144K	

So that means on 60% of my money, not even 100% - but only in 60% of my money my cash reserve has almost caught up to the amount that I put in with only using 60% of my money. That lets you know that the internal rate of return inside of my policy is moving a lot faster than I can fathom.

37	6	24,000	108,711	1,553,118	24,000	0	24,000	429	109,787	1,556,723
38	7	24,000	133,836	1,610,018	24,000	0	24,000	784	135,732	1,616,085
39	8	24,000	158,253	1,665,069	24,000	0	24,000	1,173	161,385	1,675,249
40	9	24,000	184,306	1,718,345	24,000	0	24,000	1,547	189,088	1,734,291
41	10	24,000	210,843	1,769,919	24,000	0	24,000	1,983	217,766	1,793,188
		240,000			240,000	0	240,000	6,501		

The next ten years, it gets greater later.

42	11	24,000	237,872	1,819,855	24,000	0	24,000	4,606	249,626	1,854,293
43	12	24,000	266,582	1,868,216	24,000	0	24,000	5,440	284,157	1,922,709
44	13	24,000	295,879	1,915,058	24,000	0	24,000	6,324	320,352	1,992,425
45	14	24,000	325,765	1,960,420	24,000	0	24,000	7,248	358,286	2,063,466
46	15	24,000	357,437	2,004,346	24,000	0	24,000	8,211	399,235	2,135,831
47	16	24,000	389,758	2,046,878	24,000	0	24,000	9,273	442,205	2,209,562
48	17	24,000	422,760	2,088,054	24,000	0	24,000	10,376	487,319	2,284,791
49	18	24,000	457,639	2,127,911	24,000	0	24,000	11,534	535,876	2,361,495
50	19	24,000	493,249	2,166,487	24,000	0	24,000	12,795	586,892	2,439,728
51	20	24,000	530,763	2,203,818	24,000	0	24,000	14,127	641,661	2,519,610
		480,000			480,000	0	480,000	96,436		

I put a total of $480K in here. That paid for cost of insurance, management cost, price loads they do; plus the money went into my reserve.

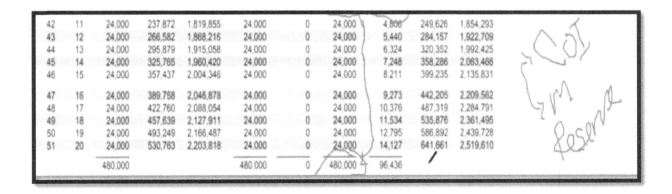

So only **$288K** of my own money I put inside of the cash reserve. But the cash reserve reflects how much? **$641K** – which means that I'm continuing around **50 – 60%** rate of return inside of my policy.

42	11	24,000	237,872	1,819,855	24,000	0	24,000	4,808	249,626	1,854,293
43	12	24,000	266,582	1,868,216	24,000	0	24,000	5,440	284,157	1,922,709
44	13	24,000	295,879	1,915,058	24,000	0	24,000	6,324	320,352	1,992,425
45	14	24,000	325,765	1,960,420	24,000	0	24,000	7,248	358,286	2,063,466
46	15	24,000	357,437	2,004,346	24,000	0	24,000	8,211	399,235	2,135,831
47	16	24,000	389,758	2,046,878	24,000	0	24,000	9,273	442,205	2,209,562
48	17	24,000	422,760	2,088,054	24,000	0	24,000	10,376	487,319	2,284,791
49	18	24,000	457,639	2,127,911	24,000	0	24,000	11,534	535,876	2,361,495
50	19	24,000	493,249	2,166,487	24,000	0	24,000	12,795	586,892	2,439,728
51	20	24,000	530,763	2,203,818	24,000	0	24,000	14,127	641,661	2,519,610

Thirty years later it begins to get better later. Why is it getting better later? I put only **$720k** in total income. I put **$432K** into my plan over a thirty-year period and I got **$1.3M** plus I got a guaranteed **$3.2M** death benefit, which more than triples what I put in for the entire plan. So what you are beginning to see is that with only using **60%** of your cash going into your reserve, it's outpacing the full **100%** of money that you put in for both insurance and the reserve. Does that make sense?

52	21	24,000	569,017	2,239,941	24,000	0	24,000	15,289	698,907	2,600,933
53	22	24,000	608,000	2,274,898	24,000	0	24,000	15,620	757,831	2,682,342
54	23	24,000	648,923	2,308,729	24,000	0	24,000	15,972	819,704	2,762,126
55	24	24,000	690,594	2,341,473	24,000	0	24,000	16,323	883,344	2,840,351
56	25	24,000	734,189	2,373,168	24,000	0	24,000	16,685	949,962	2,917,054
57	26	24,000	778,549	2,403,855	24,000	0	24,000	17,048	1,018,420	2,992,288
58	27	24,000	824,837	2,433,570	24,000	0	24,000	17,433	1,089,922	3,066,105
59	28	24,000	871,876	2,462,352	24,000	0	24,000	17,819	1,163,307	3,138,572
60	29	24,000	919,647	2,490,237	24,000	0	24,000	18,337	1,238,693	3,209,855
61	30	24,000	968,140	2,517,262	24,000	0	24,000	19,012	1,316,242	3,280,317
		720,000			720,000	0	720,000	265,974		

Question:

"Can I increase my policy?"

The problem that you have is (and you will see when I break down the difference between an index bank and a guaranteed bank) when you start a bank, you cannot change the rule set and the foundation of that bank. You have to get another one. You got to get another bank, which is no problem – I have eight!

Question:

"Jake, how can I have a plan that gets better later?" "How is that possible?"

Very simple – The less risk the insurance company takes the better the plan gets to work in your favor. **What do you mean by that Jake?** Well you only put $24K into the plan and if you died year one, your family would get $1.2M. Which is why in the beginning the cost of insurance is costing you more money than it will later.

Age	End of Year	Contract Premium + Riders	Cash Value	Death Benefit	Contract Premium + Riders	Cash from Policy	Cash Outlay	Annual Dividend	Cash Value	Death Benefit
32	1	24,000	11,991	1,238,168	24,000	0	24,000	117	12,108	1,238,285
33	2	24,000	24,394	1,305,491	24,000	0	24,000	117	24,632	1,308,286

The more money you build in your cash account, the less risk the insurance company is taking. The less risk the insurance company is taking, the more goes into your cash account.

Age	of Year	Premium + Riders	Cash Value	Death Benefit	Premium + Riders	from Policy	Cash Outlay	Annual Dividend	Cash Value	Death Benefit
32	1	24,000	11,991	1,238,168	24,000	0	24,000	117	12,108	1,238,285
33	2	24,000	24,394	1,305,491	24,000	0	24,000	117	24,632	1,308,286
34	3	24,000	40,726	1,370,564	24,000	0	24,000	117	41,089	1,372,015
35	4	24,000	62,163	1,433,471	24,000	0	24,000	117	62,655	1,435,557
36	5	24,000	85,217	1,494,298	24,000	0	24,000	117	85,843	1,496,998
37	6	24,000	108,711	1,553,118	24,000	0	24,000	429	109,787	1,556,723
38	7	24,000	133,836	1,610,018	24,000	0	24,000	784	135,732	1,616,085
39	8	24,000	158,253	1,665,069	24,000	0	24,000	1,173	161,385	1,675,249
40	9	24,000	184,306	1,718,345	24,000	0	24,000	1,547	189,088	1,734,291
41	10	24,000	210,843	1,769,919	24,000	0	24,000	1,983	217,766	1,793,188
		240,000			240,000	0	240,000	6,501		

The more money you have the less risk they take and the more goes in your reserve.

Age	of Year	Premium + Riders	Cash Value	Death Benefit	Premium + Riders	from Policy	Cash Outlay	Annual Dividend	Cash Value	Death Benefit
32	1	24,000	11,991	1,238,168	24,000	0	24,000	117	12,108	1,238,285
33	2	24,000	24,394	1,305,491	24,000	0	24,000	117	24,632	1,308,286
34	3	24,000	40,726	1,370,564	24,000	0	24,000	117	41,089	1,372,015
35	4	24,000	62,163	1,433,471	24,000	0	24,000	117	62,655	1,435,557
36	5	24,000	85,217	1,494,298	24,000	0	24,000	117	85,843	1,496,998
37	6	24,000	108,711	1,553,118	24,000	0	24,000	429	109,787	1,556,723
38	7	24,000	133,836	1,610,018	24,000	0	24,000	784	135,732	1,616,085
39	8	24,000	158,253	1,665,069	24,000	0	24,000	1,173	161,385	1,675,249
40	9	24,000	184,306	1,718,345	24,000	0	24,000	1,547	189,088	1,734,291
41	10	24,000	210,843	1,769,919	24,000	0	24,000	1,983	217,766	1,793,188
		240,000			240,000	0	240,000	6,501		
42	11	24,000	237,872	1,819,855	24,000	0	24,000	4,606	249,626	1,854,293
43	12	24,000	266,582	1,868,216	24,000	0	24,000	5,440	284,157	1,922,709
44	13	24,000	295,879	1,915,058	24,000	0	24,000	6,324	320,352	1,992,425
45	14	24,000	325,765	1,960,420	24,000	0	24,000	7,248	358,286	2,063,466
46	15	24,000	357,437	2,004,346	24,000	0	24,000	8,211	399,235	2,135,831
47	16	24,000	389,758	2,046,878	24,000	0	24,000	9,273	442,205	2,209,562
48	17	24,000	422,760	2,088,054	24,000	0	24,000	10,376	487,319	2,284,791
49	18	24,000	457,639	2,127,911	24,000	0	24,000	11,534	535,876	2,361,495
50	19	24,000	493,249	2,166,487	24,000	0	24,000	12,795	586,892	2,439,728
51	20	24,000	530,763	2,203,818	24,000	0	24,000	14,127	641,661	2,519,610
		480,000			480,000	0	480,000	96,436		

So in the beginning years you are high risk to them and they didn't get to make any money off of you.

But in the latter years, the plan works better because you have more what?

Cash reserve – **which means less risk and your plan begins to work better.**

Age	End of Year	Contract Premium + Riders	Cash Value	Death Benefit	Contract Premium + Riders	Cash from Policy	Cash Outlay	Annual Dividend	Cash Value	Death Benefit
32	1	24,000	11,991	1,238,168	24,000	0	24,000	117	12,108	1,238,286
33	2	24,000	24,394	1,305,491	24,000	0	24,000	117	24,632	1,306,296
34	3	24,000	40,726	1,370,564	24,000	0	24,000	117	41,089	1,372,015
35	4	24,000	62,163	1,433,471	24,000	0	24,000	117	62,665	1,435,557
36	5	24,000	86,217	1,494,298	24,000	0	24,000	117	86,843	1,496,668
37	6	24,000	108,711	1,553,118	24,000	0	24,000	429	109,787	1,566,723
38	7	24,000	133,836	1,610,018	24,000	0	24,000	784	135,732	1,616,085
39	8	24,000	158,253	1,665,099	24,000	0	24,000	1,173	161,385	1,675,249
40	9	24,000	184,308	1,718,345	24,000	0	24,000	1,547	189,088	1,734,291
41	10	24,000	210,643	1,769,919	24,000	0	24,000	1,963	217,706	1,793,188
		240,000			240,000	0	240,000	6,501		
42	11	24,000	237,672	1,819,855	24,000	0	24,000	4,606	249,626	1,854,293
43	12	24,000	266,562	1,868,216	24,000	0	24,000	5,440	284,157	1,922,709
44	13	24,000	295,879	1,915,053	24,000	0	24,000	6,324	320,352	1,992,425
45	14	24,000	325,766	1,960,420	24,000	0	24,000	7,248	358,299	2,063,466
46	15	24,000	357,437	2,004,346	24,000	0	24,000	8,211	399,295	2,136,801
47	16	24,000	389,756	2,046,878	24,000	0	24,000	9,273	442,205	2,209,562
48	17	24,000	422,760	2,088,094	24,000	0	24,000	10,376	487,319	2,284,791
49	18	24,000	457,839	2,127,911	24,000	0	24,000	11,534	535,876	2,361,495
50	19	24,000	493,249	2,166,487	24,000	0	24,000	12,795	588,862	2,439,728
51	20	24,000	530,763	2,203,814	24,000	0	24,000	14,127	641,661	2,519,610
		480,000			480,000	0	480,000	96,436		
52	21	24,000	569,017	2,239,941	24,000	0	24,000	15,289	698,307	2,600,933
53	22	24,000	608,000	2,274,898	24,000	0	24,000	15,620	757,831	2,682,342
54	23	24,000	648,923	2,308,729	24,000	0	24,000	15,972	819,704	2,762,126
55	24	24,000	690,594	2,341,473	24,000	0	24,000	16,323	883,344	2,840,351
56	25	24,000	734,189	2,373,168	24,000	0	24,000	16,685	949,982	2,917,064
57	26	24,000	778,549	2,403,693	24,000	0	24,000	17,048	1,018,420	2,992,288
58	27	24,000	824,837	2,433,570	24,000	0	24,000	17,433	1,089,922	3,066,105
59	28	24,000	871,876	2,462,352	24,000	0	24,000	17,819	1,163,307	3,130,572
60	29	24,000	919,647	2,490,237	24,000	0	24,000	18,337	1,238,693	3,209,863
61	30	24,000	966,140	2,517,262	24,000	0	24,000	19,012	1,316,242	3,280,317
		720,000			720,000	0	720,000	266,674		

That's why in the first ten years you do not see that reserve get going. The example I like to give is the airplane. When the airplane is on the ground, it's at its heaviest, because it has over 10K miles worth of fuel in it. But the moment the airplane can get off the ground, it takes a bunch of energy for the plane to get off the ground, depending on how heavy it is – and it flies 8K miles, it burns 8K miles worth of fuel, which means now the plane is lighter because it used 8K worth of fuel. And at the 8K mile mark the plane can work more efficiently because it is not as heavy.

Your bank is like a plane. The longer you have it in flight, the better it gets. That's the reason why, when you start the bank you can't stop. When you start the bank, say year four, you decide you do not want to do the bank anymore, and you want to cash out and be silly, because you have someone that has told you about a better investment. That's why in year four, you put $96K in and you are only going to get $62K from it.

That's why you can't stop it until the plan goes all the way through. The more in your cash reserve, the more efficient your plan gets. The less in your reserve, the more risk the plan takes. You got to see the difference in cash reserve to death benefit like fuel. The more they work together – the better the plan gets.

The difference between a guaranteed bank and an indexed bank:

Indexed Bank	Guaranteed Bank
➢ **0% Floor with a higher ceiling** **- Some 11 -13%**	➢ **4% -8% -- with a 2-4% Dividend**
➢ **Cost of Insurance is initially lower**	➢ **Cost of Insurance is higher**
➢ **Flexibility**	➢ **Access money within 31 days**
➢ **Don't have access to as much capital up front. Minimum of a year or 2 before you can access the funds.**	➢ **No Flexibility**

Nothing comes free in insurance. Everything comes with a cost. With a guaranteed bank, the cost of insurance costs a lot in the beginning but as the plan gets better it works better. With the indexed bank, the cost of insurance starts extremely low, so you have all that difference to dump in your reserve, but every year it has something attached to it called the annual renewal term, which means every year the cost of insurance goes up like a stepping ladder, every year that you are on the plan.

So, initially it works in your favor, but in the end you better had been funding the reserve how you were supposed to. If you over fund the reserve, like you are supposed to and you don't change the integrity of the plan, then it will work out in its favor. But, if you do not continue to pay into that plan and over fund it as you are supposed to – the biggest down fall is, the cost of insurance will eat away at your reserve.

Jake, what do you mean?

Use your **COI (cost of insurance)** and your **CR (cash reserve)** – you have $250 that is going in, some is going in, some is dripping out to pay your cost of insurance. But if your cost of insurance is increasing every year and you're still only paying the $250, if you over funded it the right way in the beginning years, this would be ok. The interest that you make plus the new money that you are putting into the plan, is beating the cost of insurance, so you are beating that cost – and it's working together.

But if you lower your payment or if you stop paying new money into it over time, the cost of insurance will start to eat away like the hungry hippo at your cash reserve and will begin to drain out the cash reserve. With the flexibility of the indexed bank, you can lower the payments, stop paying, increase the payments, lower the payments, change the death benefit, etc.. as the flexibility of changing to your lifestyle is in the indexed bank. But, the cost of insurance can eat up all those changes. So you are flexible and you can maneuver it to make it work with you.

With the guaranteed bank there is no flexibility, you can't change the payment, you can't drop the payment – you pay what you pay, every month or every year! Versus, the indexed has flexibility for lifestyle, but it comes with a cost of messing up the integrity of your plan. With guaranteed you pay what you pay, its straight and narrow, it's level, so the cost of insurance today will be the cost seventy years later. That's why you see the plan gets greater later.

Question:

"If I start with an indexed bank can I ever transfer my money to a guaranteed bank?"

When I see the cost of insurance increasing, the answer is yes! You can move one policy and I can do an internal transfer, which is called a 1035, tax free – into another insurance policy. When you do the internal transfer, you got access to that cash immediately. So if you had an indexed bank and you built it to $40K in the reserve, and then you want to move it to the guaranteed bank, when you transfer that money, that $40K will be available immediately.

Question:

"How many transfers are you allowed?"

You can transfer five policies into one bank. It' your money, but you just can't keep doing all that back and forth between because that doesn't make sense to do that, **(like transfers between savings and checking accounts)**, you will not be able do that. You can't go from IUL to Guaranteed bank and then back to IUL, because once you do the transfer, it cancels that policy out.

128

NOTES

CHAPTER 10: The Power in Owning my Debt

Welcome back to PBB Master Class. In this segment we are going to be talking about becoming the banker. Not only are we going to be talking about how to become the bank but how we can access this money and how we can lend to ourselves. And how we can be the ones to lend and get rid of our debt, we will also discuss debt consolidation. You got to believe that God's word is true. God said that we are supposed to be the lender and not the borrower. He said that you are the head and not the tail. That's what God said. God said that you're supposed to lend to nations and borrow from none. You got to believe it!

You have got to believe that when you move in the actions of God that he is going to give you the resources that you need to make what he said will happen. See we want to believe – but we want to do God's part. The apple can't be the sun. The seed can't be the sun. The seed has to believe that when I break ground, the sun is going to be there. The seed has to know it can't water itself. So if nobody comes and waters the seed, it has to know that something is going to come along and water it. The seed has to know and we all are the seed. But you got to know that you can be the banker.

You got to know there is a chance and a way for you. You got to know that this wicked way of the world, telling you that you can only make it from borrowing from these traditional institutions, and not giving you any control of your monetary system – you got to believe that you can make it out of it. It's only through belief that everything begins to work. When you put any plant seed, any flower seed, any apple seed, any fruit seed into the ground – you have to believe that something at some point will break ground. You got to believe it. These are things that are naturally out of our control and because of the universe it works. And when I tell you banking works this way, you got to believe it. If you're running a business and you're literally waiting for your big break – if you have not been doing things God's way; that's what's been stopping your growth. God doesn't respect persons because he knows we will not do right. He respects principle. It's the principle, that's why it says that wealth is stored up in the wicked's hand. Its stored up for the righteous but currently in the wicked's hands. it's in the wicked's hands. What does that mean? That means even asinine can be planted and grow.

Poison can be planted in the same fertile ground that fruit can be planted and still grow. So he respects no person, but he respects principle. If you apply his principles, it works. The reason why God tells you to give, because when you give, its reciprocity – it has to come back. When I do right by others, it has to come back. Loyalty comes back. When you do right by people, people do right by you. When you truly do right by the right people it happens. And that's what lending is, that's what banking is. Banking is a philosophy – a mentality. If there was another product that we could be using to give us the same results, we would be using it. The reason that we use insurance is because it allows for us to control the banking system. It allows for us to take heed and take control of that and that's what we are going to be talking about in this segment. I apologize for preaching to you guys – for some of you that didn't want to hear it, I promise you I won't be doing that for long. I just had to get that off my chest. Because some of you don't believe that you can become the bank. Some of you really truly think up to this point it takes a lot, it just takes one step at a time. It's commitment to know. If this were not true, I would not be doing a master class. I would've just sold you a product. I wouldn't have gone over and beyond to give you all a class if I did no work. You got to believe. That's the only way God can do the things he has for you – you have to believe.

In this segment we will be discussing banking and the functions thereof. How to borrow from yourself, the cost of borrowing, how to pay ourselves back, and how to become the debt collections / consolidation all in one. But you have to believe that you can be all of those things. There is not a if that – you can be and all! You have to be disciplined enough to do it.

Before we talked about how to become the bank, how to utilize the bank and how the bank functions and also insurance banks. The next question is how do the policies work? How do we borrow from ourselves and how do the loans work? What is that process so that we are able to know how it functions? So we got to go back to the traditional function which are our two circles:

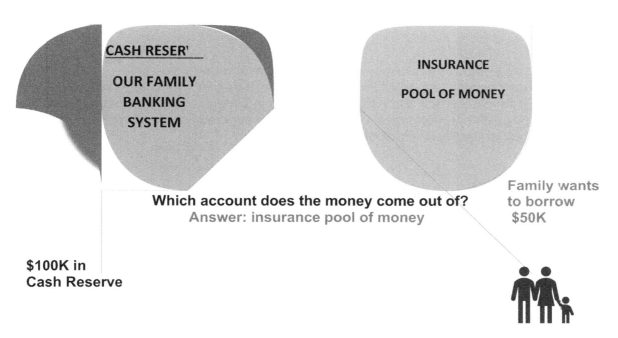

If we remember which account it comes out of which is the insurance pool of money. They check to see if we have it in our cash reserve and then it is loaned out to us via our pool of money.

Question:

They don't take the money out of our account but what do they do? They place a lien on our money. So if I wanted to take out $50K and they don't take it out but what the do is limit access to $50K. I have the $100K in there, I just can no longer access it. Lets say you use this $50K that you got from the insurance pool of money – the question is:

"Jake, where does the money go and how do I get it?"

When you fill out a loan paper, the ask you for your routing and account number for your checking account, and they literally deposit the money into your account. With a bank it takes 15 to 40 or more pages to sign to borrow the money. With an insurance company you have one

sheet you fill out the form with your account information, how much you want, you send it in. 48 to 78 hours they will deposit money into your checking account.
Question:

"What is still happening to the cash reserve even though you borrowed money from the insurance pool of money?" It is still growing and gaining interest.

So even though the cash reserve is not reflective of **$50K** you know the money was never taken. So you know the full **$100K** is still getting the interest and **4%** guaranteed plus the dividend.

So when I borrow money from myself, the question is, "Jake is that it?" "The company didn't charge me any interest?" NO, that's not it. The insurance company does charge you interest. They charge you 5% annual simple interest.

Question:

"Jake I thought we were using this so we wouldn't be charged any interest?"
The insurance company wouldn't be able to make any money if they did not charge you any interest. Notice I said simple interest and I didn't say compound interest. What we pay with our car notes, what we pay with our mortgages, what we pay with our credit cards, compound interest. Simple interest is literally 5% of $50K for the entire year.

In this scenario, how much interest would we be responsible for paying? $2500 of interest Are you really paying 5% if they are guaranteeing to give you 4% and they are charging you 5% - what's the difference between 5% minus 4%? **1%** - so what are you really being charged to use money? Typically you are only being charged **1%** to utilize money that's not even yours. Where can you go and borrow money like this at **1%** simple interest? That means you only pay **$500** to use **$50K**. Yes I am getting charged **1%** to use money but I am still getting dividends. So I am pretty much getting paid to borrow!

If I used this **$50K** to purchase a home that generates me **$2K** a month in passive income. Even if I die, my family gets what was deducted out of my policy, let's say **$1M** – my family would get **$950K** from the death benefit plus a $50K property that's probably up in value, in the **$2K** passive income even though I didn't pay it back to the pool of money. This function is called borrowing or a loan. You call your insurance company that we work with and you say, "I need he paperwork for a loan." They will email it to you and you fill it out. You will receive your funds between 45 – 72 hours.

Question:

"Do you have to pay it back in a year?"
No, this is your banking function, and you can set it up to pay it back in eight years if you like. You control the entire banking function and you are no longer subject to anybody's rules. You control your own rules. You are officially the bank, welcome to banking.

132

Question:

"Jake, how can I use this function to get rid of my debt?" First we must understand what debt consolidation is. Do we have a good understanding of what it is? Debt Consolidation is your way to get all the debts to be under one roof and pay a lower monthly amount combined rather than paying all debts separately. But there is one problem, the debt consolidation company does not go and buy all your debt at first. What the company tells you is to stop making all payments to all the debts you want to get rid of, except the ones that can ruin you, like mortgage. You wouldn't get rid of that running the risk of losing your home. You wouldn't do that to your car note or they will come take your car.

They look at your portfolio – look at credit cards, any payments that you are making on debts where they can't affect your pay like student loans – they typically don't accept student loans. If you stop paying the debts the only thing it will do is lower your credit score. They are not really worried about your credit score at the moment. I'm not really big on credit score because I don't borrow money anyway. But if you do borrow money you do need a good credit score, but I am going to show you how to do it.

When you pay off debts, it lowers your credit score. So for instance, you can tell the debt consolidation company that you pay a total of $800 a month for all debts. The company will say for $500 or $400 a month we will take care of all the debts for you. And you will reply with "if I pay $800 and you can get all my debts for $400 and all I got to do is pay you?" What will you say? "Ok. That makes sense and that frees my cash flow up $400" – depending on the time frame and how long you have to pay them. Typically five to ten years.

When you stop making payments on all debts, they tell you that your debt is going to default and your accounts are going to close, because you stopped making the monthly payments towards your debts and started making those monthly $400 payments to the debt consolidation company.

Question:

Have you ever been called by a collections company? Yes. What debt collections companies do; they buy your debt from whomever you owe for pennies on the dollar.

Question:

"What do you mean by that Jake?" What I mean is if you owe, say $1K to Macy's. The debt collections company will come to the people you owe and say, "Listen, you know that person is not going to pay no time soon." "It will be best if you just settle and I will pay you $400 for a debt that you know you are not going to collect. Give us the debt and we will own it – you're free clear and we will chase them for the rest of our money."

So what happens now is the debt collection company has bought your $1K debt for $400 and the company that you owed, settled because they knew they were not getting the money from you. Now what the debt collection company does, they call you and say that now you owe them, through Capital - One $1K – so they chase you down for the full $1K after they paid $400 for it,

133

that's how they make their spread. They call you threatening you, talking crazy, blowing up your phone, telling you that you owe Capital One and that they are going to sue you.

But in reality – Macy's nor Capital One can't sue you because they have already paid off your debt. They sold your debt to another entity and they are no longer involved.

Just because I don't believe in debt doesn't mean I didn't make stupid decisions of being in debt before I started actually practicing this stuff. I'm not the Lord, now! I am no perfect and all ye mighty! I can tell you what not to do based on what I have done, I did not build my business on debt. But did I have personal debt, yes. Did I have personal debt and credit cards before I started to build my business – **yes! Was I stupid – yes! Did I make bad decisions – yes!**

Question:

"If I pay cash on a debt, will I get that money back?" No. Why? Because I is a debt and my money went to something that died and its gone forever. However, it cash flowed for who I gave the debt to. The monthly payments that you are making towards those debts you can be putting it towards your insurance bank.

How to become both the Collections and Debt Consolidation Company

➢ **Stop paying debts**

➢ **Stopping the money from going to these accounts and transferring to your bank –** just like the consolidation company is holding your money and waiting until you got enough money in your escrow account to start bargaining your debts off, you're going to be hoarding your money the same way.

➢ **Jake what do you mean?** When a debt consolidation company is taking your $400 a month – that's $4800 a year that they are putting inside some type of escrow account and you better believe that they are growing it and is making some sort of percentage and income. When you have enough money in that account, they're going to start bargaining your debts off from smallest to largest the entire way.

➢ So they can't start buying and taking care of your debts until you have enough in your escrow account. So the same exact thing that they would do with your money – you're going to do with your bank.

➢ If you got $800 a month that you are paying in debt, and you are paying that to the creditors – you are going to stop the payment there and transfer that to your bank. Why? You can spend all your time in an escrow account – which is just a savings account or holding tank. When you fund your bank, you get a cash account plus a death benefit. Why? Because there are a lot of people who spend ten years paying off all debt, paying off all cash and guess what? They die and their family has nothing.

Question:

"Can you do debt consolidation with the indexed bank?" You can do debt consolidation with the indexed bank – it just takes a while for you to access it in comparison to guaranteed bank. No different, you will just have to pay attention to the rising cost that we talked about before to make sure you are keeping your eyes on your policy and keeping up with how it functions. And to make sure the policy is not getting eaten up by the cost of insurance.

Some of you will take everything that I say, and some of you will take pieces. But the biggest thing I want you to take is, that you have the ability to be the banker and you can be in control of your circumstances. If you are going to use the bank's money – which I don't recommend, put yourself in the seat where you are in control of it and they're not controlling you. Always remember that and pay yourself first and that God said you are supposed to be the lender and not the borrower.

CHAPTER 11: IT'S A FINANCING WORLD PART 1

Welcome back to PBB Master Class – Private Banking Blueprint Master Class, where I am forcing you to start to think like the bank, to start to become the banker, so that you can see that you can be in the system. In this segment we are going to be talking about how:

- ✓ "It's a Financing World Part 1 and Part 2
- ✓ The Power of the Banking Game
- ✓ The Importance of not Robbing yourself – the Bank!
- ✓ And to get you to start saying "I AM THE BANK" and it does force you to have to fund your bank and lend out your money.

But you want to get to the point to where you almost think it's ludacris to use a traditional banking system when you can control the banking system that you are in. we got to just talk about the history of the banking system and who's pushing the banking system. The Federal Reserve is pushing the banking system, and the federal reserve wasn't really in force and in play until after the great depression. During the great depression, Franklin D Roosevelt became the president, but there was a secret meeting that happened on an island, where on of the Rothschilds, and JP Morgan, sent two representatives – Bank of America had someone there, They met Franklin D Roosevelt at this island and they created what they wanted the new system that only benefited the banks. And one of the tricks and trades that they had to get Franklin Roosevelt to see, and said if we were to get you into office – can you get everyone off the gold reserve?

The gold reserve is, for every dollar that was out, you had a reserve – the banking had to have a reserve, whether silver or gold to be able to back up that dollar. And the formulation of the federal reserve and all of these traditional commercial banks – they had to get these gold reserve systems out of the way to ban it so they could print the money without having to back it to gold. They were able to get Franklin Roosevelt to sign off and he was voted as President of the United States. His first order of business didn't go through Congress, nor legislature, he used his power as the President to immediately ban the hoarding and trading of gold. From 1934 to 1964 there was absolutely no trading of gold, and then gold certificates were allowed to be traded again.

So, you guys can know that the entire banking system wasn't created for your benefit, it was only created for the federal reserve benefit. And the thing that Franklin D Roosevelt was able to receive was exactly what he wanted, to be President and to be in power, and they got him into the President's suite. This is public knowledge – it's not really private anymore. There was a woman in charge of the propaganda and marketing for Adolf Hitler – who said propaganda will always work – and the only way propaganda won't work is if you stop believing that it works and no one ever will. So, we really have to question the knowledge and the thinking we have before the 1930's. No one was really never really borrowing money from the bank like that. That wasn't a part of peoples natural everyday living. You lived together you typically bought your home out right. And it wasn't until the Federal Reserve, when they made that move, the Federal Reserve was a collection of banks that put their money together that created a system to where the entire system began to need it. And the Federal Reserve which controls all the private banks – it says Federal Reserve, but it's not a part of the Government, it's a private entity that the Government owes, because the Federal Reserve bought the debt of America to help them be able to wipe off their debt that they owed the majority of the country.

So, I'm giving you this history because they need us on their banking system. There was no need to know about it until now. Before then, banking used to be amongst households, amongst people who were broke. When you were broke, you were broke – and so, you couldn't lend and borrow. And there is another way to bring slavery about poor people, so it had nothing to do with color anymore, and they want us to believe it's about black and white, and some instances – it is. It's really about poverty and wealth. If you are poor and in the same class – now there are different tiers of poverty, we understand that but in truth there are other races in indentured servants along with us being slaves, but they were just above the slaves. When you move aside me being Black or that person being White or that person being Hispanic, you move that aside and you look at it, it's all to keep people in the same line – needing a system. And it is just a way for us to willfully give ourselves up to slavery.

So, you trying to stay in the banking system and trying to rationalize how it benefits you it's basically you just simply saying that you're ok with the fact that it was created, not for your benefit. It never was! And the more that we keep saying that I need the bank to fund my business and I need the bank to fund my property – and I want to pass these things down to our kids – truth be told, the majority of properties and businesses that are passed down to kids that owe or have a debt to it, the children sell it. The children sell the properties and takes whatever is left, and the banking system happens all over again. They convince us to do re-finances, they convince us to keep needing the systems and as long as you stay and want to be on it – that's why I tell you guys, I'm not a fan of paying minimums to keep up a credit score. If I want to get off the system, I don't need a credit score to do it, I fund it myself! A lot of us are pretty aware of this, but remember what we talked about, intelligence is the ability to acquire the information and apply It. And some people may say, "I'm using them like they using me." I mean, you're really not, they're still winning, and no matter what you think about them – you're still in that position to where you're not getting ahead.

And the only way to get ahead is if you decide – you make the decision that banking and getting in debt with the bank is literally putting yourself in slavery. Until you get to the point that you're tired of being somebody's slave, you're tired of that process; you will never be able to put yourself in a position to where you can get ahead, liked we talked about in the class. The number one reason that fortune 500 companies fall out of being a fortune 500 company and go bankrupt is because of DEBT! The number one reason that countries fall is because of DEBT! The number one reason why many people say that America is on its way down just like Rome was – Rome used to be that; it's because of DEBT! The more that you borrow, you're not getting wealthier. You're becoming more and more indentured slave serving the people that you owe. The more you borrow, the more you print, does not help it.

As we are learning the system, we talked about the Insurance Bank, and how to stop making payments one place and then start forcing money inside of your account and getting yourself out of debt that way – continuing and growing your system because I am on 100% committed to the information that I am teaching you for myself, and its key. And I think its very important for us to start to see how wicked the system is and you have to start believing that you are the lender and not the borrower. For some people that say, "Hey Jake, how do I make this work? I don't have a lot of money or a lot of this" But you have a brother, you have a sister, you have best friends, and you can create a contract amongst each other where each of you are the beneficiaries of the plan. Create a will in the contract and the agreement amongst you guys and you begin to use the policy like a banking system.

You can ask your mother if you can start a banking system with her as the matriarch or your father – and all the kids pay the premiums to boost up that cash account and each of you take turns to be able to borrow and pay back. These are all strategies you can be able to do if you were to truly, truly, submit yourself to getting off the system and control your own banking system. You're not stopping the flow because everybody in the world won't do it, But if you decide to do it; you stop borrowing from yourself, you stop borrowing from the bank, you start borrowing from yourself! In our strategy you are still using OPM – you're still using the Other People's Money, the insurances pool of money without losing the momentum growth of compound effect of your money.

The only difference is you're in control of the system, you're in control of the entire thing – you're not enslaved to the debt, when you pass away, the insurance company just takes the difference and gives your family the rest it's an easy formula, it's simple. We just make it difficult; we make it complicated, trying to make it more difficult than it has to be and we have to get to a point to where we don't do that. The more people I talk to that are of the higher wealth level that have the eight and nine figure businesses, they easily see it because it makes sense to them. I am paying twenty, thirty, forty thousand dollars a month to the bank for financing something I would have done myself if i knew there was another way.

So, me losing 40% of liquidity to get access to 60% of my money in a tax-free environment is a no brainer, we just make it more difficult than it has to be. I just wanted to say that so that we are all on the same page to know that the only way that this system will work for you is if you truly in your head believe that the only way you can take control of your life is if you have your own banking system. Because you have people that borrow money for their businesses, borrow money for their homes, borrow money for their properties, and you teach your kids to borrow money – so even if you paid off those properties, your kids are now engrained to borrow money to expand the family's business because that's what you taught them. You guys have come this far to leave this thinking that I can balance both. It's possible and you are only kidding yourself because you are always going to submit to the easier way.

CHAPTER 12:
IT'S A FINANCING WORLD PART 2

Before we get into this lesson, what we first have to understand is that this is a financing game that we're in, and everything we do is finance. Think about it, we are either:

There is no in between and when I understand that the world that we live in is a financing game, its easier for me to move forward and to progress inside the world that we live in. When I understand that I began to start looking at my vehicles to be able to determine which vehicle gives me the best leg up when it comes to mitigating through this financing world. The first vehicle that people typically like to choose is the **financing** vehicle. But we have to understand we are not financing. Financing means to borrow.

So, if I'm borrowing money, that means I'm –
(1) paying interest on the money I borrow
(2) losing inflation on that money that I'm paying back into this borrowing system.

> "Jake, what do you mean?" It's very simple. If I'm spending $500 a month on a car note – not only am I paying the interest of the car, but I'm also paying the interest of loss to potential income that I could've made.

> "What do you mean?" That money that I am paying every month in a car note versus it going to an investment account, it's going to a car that's depreciating. So, this investment account could be bringing me 6% but no, I put my money in something that is losing value. So, when I'm financing something, I am not only paying the interest, but I am also losing potential interest it could be gaining.

So, not only am I losing potential interest, I'm also losing interest because of inflation, because that money isn't growing to be able to beat the market. So, if I spend 90% of my income for the majority of my life financing cars and paying mortgage payments – I've spent my entire life paying my number one vehicle, my number one asset – is your income that comes out every single month, every single day and every single week. When I de-value that income in things that don't bring value back, meaning more money, that means I am what? I am losing on both accounts.

The next thing that we do, we talk about paying in cash. So when we think about paying in cash, I may not be paying anybody, but I am darn sure losing interest; because when I pay cash for something – remember its like the stair step, if this is the zero line and I am paying cash for something, I am spending all these years saving up my money and then I pay cash on a debt to end back at zero. And all that money that was gaining interest, I literally paid cash to lose all the interest on materials that don't generate a profit.

When I borrow money, I spend all these years paying back this money I borrowed and it never got to make interest and it never got me above zero. So, what I have to learn is that when I'm paying cash – it is better than financing, but I am losing interest – potential interest that the money could be earning, and also inflation which is 3.3%. Every single year my cost of money is diminishing, so when I am paying cash for something – I'm losing interest, which means I'm still paying interest. The fact that I am losing interest, which means potential interest that I could be making, if that money was in a vehicle or in an account that was growing interest; the moment I pay cash for something, I immediately lose all the interest that I could've made.

But when I am paying cash for something, I lost value on that, and then the rest of the time, that money could've been earning interest but I lost all of that because I paid cash. So, when think about the interest and the financing game; the biggest thing that I must understand is no, I am not paying interest – but I am for sure losing interest because it's not growing anywhere. When you understand that, the last thing you will think about is in our family banking strategy – not only do we beat inflation, which is our money is in an account and always growing interest anywhere from 4-%; our money is safe in an account. But I am also paying interest back to myself when I want to leverage the cash and leverage the money.

That's why we say it is a financing game!

> ➤ You got to determine what side of the game do you want to play?

> ➤ Do you want to always be at the lowest end of the stick, which is the financing?

> ➤ Or do you always want to stay at the second tier which is paying in cash?

> ➤ Or do you want to elevate to tier one – where you are leveraging your money, growing your money without ever losing the value of your money growing?

If you understand that and you can process that, everything in your life will switch, but you got to choose what side of the financing game that you want to be on.

CHAPTER 13:
The Power of the Banking Game: *Switch the Power in your Favor*

Continuation from last segment:

But you got all your body parts, which one would you choose? Would you choose to keep all your body parts and be their slaves, and subject to them – whatever they say or they'll kill you? Or they allow you to go free for your hand?

You have a choice to switch the power back to your hand, to your life, but it's going to take some level of discomfort and sacrifice in order for you to achieve that freedom again. So, when you have the ability to turn and switch over the power; when I tell you that you need to fight like hell for the next couple of years to fund your bank with as much money as you can, so you can finally switch the power over to yourself, there are going to be people who would prefer to keep their entire body parts to stay enslaved to the system.

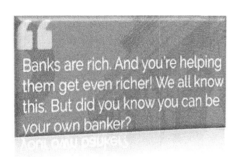

"Jake, what do you mean?"
What I mean is, you have the power to own your own bank! So, be your own banker! And it is going to take the sacrifice of somebody!

"Jake, what do you mean – sacrifice?"
I got an option – I can get my hand cut; I can go and have children, and they would never have to do the sacrifice of cutting off their hand to be free ever again.

Or, I can omit to not buckle down and do what it takes to be free and my kids will be born in the same system I despise.

So, it's funny, when it comes to us switching over the power, into our system, it's funny how most of us are wealth minded, passing stuff down to the generation to the generation, except you don't want to be the one to sacrifice it first. We don't want to be the ones to have to cut off our hand. But we say that we want our kids to be in an environment where they never know. You want them to be thinking – the way that y'all process is in the beginning, "*put money in insurance?*" You want them to think about that when it comes to borrowing money. *"Go to the bank?" "To borrow money?" "That doesn't make sense!"*
You want them to be telling people, **"explain to me how paying 40% in interest makes sense? Explain to me; y'all don't have y'all own family banking system?"**

See, If you want a certain lifestyle to be a norm, somebody has to sacrifice.
Let me give you an example:

Kobe Bryant, bless his soul, died. But his wife and his kids and their kids, will be able to live on the legacy of their father's sacrificing, spending time with them, to make sure that they don't have to worry about money again. So, he sacrificed his body and all the good years of his life, and he only spent four years of real freedom – so he sacrificed the majority of his life, to ensure, when he died, y'all, he left his family A BILLION in ASSETS! Because of a 20 to 30-year sacrifice.

So, the question is – are you willing to chop off your hand?

"Jake, what is the resemblance, or what is the correlation of chopping off the hand?"

- ✓ **Are you willing to stop eating out just for a little bit?**
- ✓ **Are you willing to stop buying stupid ass clothes and shoes?**
- ✓ **Just for a little bit? Are you wiling to put all your money that you can inside this banking reserve first, before you start trying to pay off debt with cash?**

Because you are more concerned with building your family's banking system than you are with trying to pay off debt to people that already wrote off the debt! You spend five years paying off debt, zero years starting your banking system and you got five years of debt paid off – you died the very next day you paid off your debt and left your family zero dollars of legacy and ensured the legacy of the people that you owe. You already owe them and the debt is already there. So, you have a choice to make. Why would I think about paying off something to somebody before I set up my own banking system? If the debt is closed why would I bash my head to try to pay off a debt for a credit score and your family's legacy score has not gone up?

So, when I think about a system of switching the light to transfer the power – if I have the ability to make sure my kids and kids are living the life of freedom – I'm not going to stay and say, "Hey master, I know I owe you ten more years – I am going to try to get free now! If the master has to come get me, my kids are free. So, what we got to understand is you have the ability to switch the power on. Now, I am not telling you if you have a mortgage and a car note, to switch that power – you better pay it or you will not have a place to live. But for the other stuff, that can easily be a write off for a company, they can send it to collections, don't act like it has not happened before.

You are not in jail for it, they were just blowing up your phone. Medical bills – they fall off too. Let's not act like we are saints and we are paying stuff off, it that's the case – then none of us have debt. Let's not act like we are **SAINTS!** Medical bills fall off after seven years, and that's a write off. The moment that the company feels that you are not going to pay, they write off the debt. **Why?** That's money they don't have to report as revenue, then they sell your debt to a collections agency and allow them to chase you down. They already made money on it. You will get yours if you stay around, but as of today – I am making a decision to think of my family first. Wealthy people go bankrupt all the time. **Why?** Because they don't want to pay the debt. **So, let's not be holier than thou now!**

So, I want to switch the power to my favor – and the only reason that this may not make sense for somebody is if they're still trying to use the banking system's theology. This makes sense to people that are trying to be their own bank.

The Power of the Banking Game:

1. **Switch the Power in Your Favor**

2. **I AM Never a SLAVE AGAIN**

I create my own rules, I create my own game, I set up my own pace. I'm shifting the control over. Now if you make $50K a year and only live only live on $30K, If you save $20K a year for

5 years you will have $100,000 in your banking system. If you run a business and make an additional $20K and put that into your banking system - $40K a year in your banking system, in 5 years you will have $200,000. Are you willing to cut off your hand to get there? Or do you want to live in comfort? You know freedom is not comfortable right?

3. You do know that to switch over to become the bank, there is a road that you have to take that most people don't want to get on. You know that right?

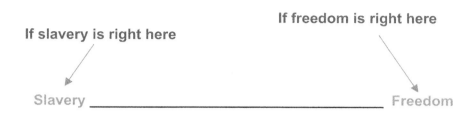

By Osmosis you can't be free – you have to take a journey that is going to challenge you but what keeps you going is the fact that freedom is around the corner.

So, the road to freedom is the part that we're scared of. We like the ideology of freedom. We like the ideology of funding our own bank. We like the ideology of funding our own businesses. We like the ideology of being the lender and not the borrower, but to actually get there, is the piece, that we don't want to take part on. And it's ok! Whatever side you want to be on, but I've never seen a story where somebody started off wanting to be free and decided to stop halfway through and say I want to be half free – half slave.

I never met a slave that said, I went to freedom, but when I saw what freedom was, I decided to stay in the middle, so I can go and be a slave half the time, and free the other half. My favorite book says, if you are lukewarm, I will spit you out – either be hot or be cold. If you don't know – you got to go. So, when I am trying to be free, there is a decision that has to be made. Am I willing to take the road to get there, or am I not? That goes to success in business. That goes to success in relationships. Am I willing to do the hard work – to get the result of a beautiful marriage? To get the result of a successful business? Or do I want to play the middle, and I never know what I get? I'm always lukewarm; I'm always indecisive; and I am never making a decision to be great. That's what we are talking about here, it's a decision. That means that you have to decide.

If we look at:

If you break the word down, DE means split, and CIDE means to kill off. CIDE is seen in genocide, pesticide, and homicide – to kill something completely off. I have to have a split decision to make. Split means half right? So, I am half free half slave, that person gets killed. I'm half boy or I'm half girl, and that person typically kills themselves. So, when I'm making a decision to decide, it's split, free or I'm not. Either way, I have to kill off one of the two – I can't be both.

You can't be half married and half not. You can't be half in a relationship and half not. You can't be half committed to your future and half not. You can't half want to graduate college and half don't. So, you have to decide – either I am going to kill off this ideology of being free or I am not. You cannot say that I'm going to start a bank but I am still going to use this system and think that both can flourish. One is not going to flourish like the other. Now if you are already in that system you got to work your way out, that's another thing – I'm not saying to make the decision and kill it off and be like, "Man, forget my business, forget my property, forget my car note," I'm not saying that – I am not saying to be crazy about it, but what I am saying is you have to have a made-up mind that says I'm going to fight like hell to never be the producer or the consumer only. I'm going to be the banker – that is a decision that you are going to have to make.

But, the power of the banking game is ultimate freedom! You have to associate – banking as freedom! How? A child has to ask their parents to do certain things. Correct? If I'm working a job, I have to ask my boss or my employer can I take a day off? Is that correct? So, are those two examples positions of power or inferiority? If I have to ask permission to do something? So, if I want to leverage money, borrow – do I have to go to the bank and ask them can I use their money? The answer probably is yes, you got to go ask them. Then they see how responsible you are. Let me see if you have been a good boy or a good girl, bring me your report card. I'll only trust you if you have a certain grade level – **only a B+…. TO GET A NO!**

The system I am teaching you – you call the insurance company and you tell them, send me my loan paperwork, you fill it in, you send it to them, they send it to you – no asking, people got to ask you to borrow your money! That's a position of power – that's a switch. And the God I serve is a God of power. He said with my tongue I can create – have the power of life and death within me. I can create whatever I want and it to be into existence. That doesn't sound like I am asking anything. My favorite book tells me to command it – so I am either going to believe in the world's system or I am going to believe in… nooo I am going to believe in the system I like to tend created the entire world.

Which system am I going to depend on? And with that system, you got to make the decision – who do you believe most? Do you believe the world's system that was created by wicked men? You think that they created systems to benefit you most? Now there are exceptions to the rules – people that made it out, people that were unscathed, that can live to tell the story, but you do not take exceptions and make them the rule. YOU DON'T TAKE EXCEPTIONS AND MAKE THEM THE RULE! And everybody thinks they are the exception, but everybody's not.

So, that's the power of the banking game, it's an ideology switch – that's all it is.

144

CHAPTER 14:

DON'T ROB THE BANK

(Why paying yourself back is important)

In this segment we are going to be talking about the importance of not robbing your bank. And the biggest thing we have to understand when it comes to not robbing our bank is because it would be easy to. Let me ask you a question – How does the bank money? Lending, right? They make money off of lending money out and making interest on it. Can the bank survive?

So, the bank make money off of lending and interest. Your money is always supposed to be flowing, right. So, can the bank be profitable or survive if the borrowers never paid back their debt; can the banking system survive if the borrowers never paid back their debt? The answer is no. So, what happens is because you are in control of your banking system and you are building up your banking system – the easiest downfall to having control of your banking system is because you will be the first to steal from it. Because in your head you are saying, "Well, I own the bank, I own the property, and I am going to live off the cash flow of the property and then – "Well, you know Jake said in the class, nobody is ever going to come after me on this debt, they can just get it when I die." But what you're doing is – robbing the system. How are you robbing the system? Because the money is not flowing back to the banking system. See your banking system gets better the more you borrow from it and pay it back. It enhances the system – so you don't even get to enjoy the growth and compound effect of you borrowing and paying yourself back and even lending and paying yourself back. If you were lending your own money you would hate if somebody were to steal from it. So, the one thing you have to be disciplined on is paying yourself back.

One of the examples that **Nelson Nash has in the book _Becoming Your Own Banker_,** he talks about how if a person owns a grocery store, and he knew how much it costs for peas, if he allowed his wife, and his family to pay wholesale price – which is what he got it for, or nothing at all for the groceries, he would end up losing his business. (Nelson Nash created a system called the Infinite Banking System – which is what we teach today. He was a man that completely got off the banking system – he was off the banking system for years. His entire family, none of them ever used banks. They only used insurance policies.)

The purpose of this is when you're using your banking system and not paying it back, you're not doing it any justice. You cannot rob yourself, because if that's the case, you will end up just like a lot of these charter banks that start and the owner of these charter banks – start the bank, and borrow from themselves, and never pay the interest back to the bank. The bank then falls upside down. Why? Because money is made in banking with lending and interest and you should be excited – matter of fact, you should be elated when it comes to this! But when you think about business owners, the majority you steal from your business. You know that there is a specific cost for a book, but when you give that book out to somebody, you don't pay out of your own money back for the book. You're stealing from yourself. And there is a reason why a lot of minority businesses can't get ahead, is because we give too much out – even to yourself. We don't know how to separate the entity from our personal gain. So, if I owned a shoe company, the average person that owned a shoe company, when they purchased the shoes for the low they would just buy it for the low. You really robbed your business because your business bought it, but you decided as the person, the owner, and CEO of the company to go and take the shoes. Now let me ask you a question – if you were the chairman of that same

145

company and you hired a CEO and your CEO was stealing shoes, would you be mad at the CEO? Would you be trying to fire the CEO because the CEO was taking the shoes, for the lowest cost and wasn't paying the full value for it?

Would you try to fire your CEO if you found out that CEO was letting his family eat or get shoes for the same price that you get them for and you putting up your money that he bought his shoes and he was giving out shoes at that price to his family and friends? Well if it makes sense that you would try to fire the CEO, what should you be doing to yourself as the business owner? You're stealing time away from the job for your business, and you are stealing your own products. You should be happy to pay full price for your products. You should be happy to pay $20 for your jug of juice, because it is just going back into your entity. But we don't know how to separate ourselves from the entity. We think that we are the entity – NO! You're separate from your entity; you are just in control of both. When we adopt this mentality – **I AM THE BANK** – We will be just fine! The I AM THE BANK Mentality! When we adopt the I AM THE Bank mentality.

Scenario:

Let's look at this business owner Marquise, who owns Frootkaves, and if I told him, "Hey listen, do you support other PH balanced lemonade companies that are just like yours?" Marquise would probably laugh at me and say, "Why would I give money to their company and not pay myself for the lemonade?"

If you owned a shoe company but you're patronizing other people's shoes? None of us would ever trust a Mercedes dealership owner that only drives Toyota. You would be like, "Wait, so you selling me Benz and you're selling me Toyota? So, you don't even buy your own products?"

You will never trust an owner of a company that don't buy their own products or use their own products. Is that correct? So, what sense does it make to be ready and geared up to start your own bank and you don't use your own product? You just let the product sit, the money sit – you just let the money sit. You have no purpose for it.

You got to put a system in place to where you understand –

- **I AM THE BANK!**
- **I AM THE BANK!**
- **I AM THE BANK!**

Why would I ever go and borrow from that bank and I need to be spending all my time and all my money building my bank? Why would I go borrow from Chase and pay Chase when I need to be borrowing from myself and paying myself the interest until I got enough money in my bank to do big deals? It doesn't make sense. "Well, Jake all I got is $500 to $1000 in my bank account." Well that means you probably need to be loaning to somebody."

That means you need to be multiplying your money. You need to be doing some title lending – where somebody gives you the title to their car and you lend them money from your banking system, and when they pay you back in interest, you release the title. If not, you take the title and go sell the car and you make your money back. No loss! Y'all thought that I wasn't going to show you how to make money from your bank? You really thought that? But, I can't show you how to make money from your bank if you are still thinking that you can do both. There is no purpose of us even getting there if I can't show you how to make money off of your bank! I'm not going to tell you guys how to be your own bank just so you can be your own lender to yourself. I mean, that makes sense but there are other ways for you to do it.

The biggest reason why you can't do both is because it's confusing. To believe in two ideologies at that same time will lead you to nowhere. It's kind of like when you are driving and you are confused on what road to take, you stop and then you go here and then you say was I supposed to go there, and you never get anywhere. We act like we are broke and your number one money making tool that you have is your income. Some of us are bringing in forty, fifty, sixty thousand a year – and if you just live like a little monk for 24 to 36 months or go find a way to make more money. Find another gig or sell something, and then use all the money that when you are selling something to just dump into your cash reserve.

I'm telling you – faster than you realize it you will be out your situation! We act like we're broke – we're not broke! We just got broke habits. We are talking about starting something new for our generations – breaking curses. And the person that breaks the curse doesn't really get to enjoy the blessings as much as somebody receiving it. We can go based on a bunch of other stuff. There are people who sacrificed themselves so that we can have the life that we have. A lot of us, we talk about it, but when it comes to actually doing it, you don't really want to do it. The hardest thing is you find the road to freedom and then going back to convince people that there is a such thing. If we just simplify – make it simple and stop trying to complicate it, it makes sense. When you simplify it. I'm putting money in the cash reserve and it's also paying for a debt benefit. So, the legacy is there regardless. It just makes sense, versus me paying 30 to 40% in taxes, 30 to 40% is paying for my death benefit legacy. So, the same money that would've been taken is going towards your legacy. You get two for one! The system is simple, how to do it is simple. That's why we spend so much time on just the mindset of it. When you get past that and realize that it is not that complex, this is no different than any other system.

You Can Be the Bank

It has been a pleasure – it has been my pleasure to be a part of taking y'all through the other side of finances, taking y'all though the other side of re-educating you on money. Taking y'all through so that you guys can be able to see what life is like. Some of you are still on the fence, of making the decision that this is something that you want to do. Listen, I get it, and I understand why you would still at this moment still be like – " ahhhh I don't know." Because to get off the grid, to get off the entire system that we've been taught on, which was to need the bank, to use credit.

Let me ask you a question – If there was no credit, if there was no debt, if there was no borrowing money, how would you be successful? How would you be able to do what you wanted to do? How would you be able to do that? What we teach brings a heavy word and we are bringing the truth of God inside of learning how to become your own bank and inside of that is going to teach you how to do it. But you just got to make the decision that you want this to be a part of your life. Now let me tell you, on limited income, on a regular job, it will usually take about fifteen to twenty years to be completely off of the grid without ever having to use traditional banking again. If you already have like a mortgage or already have stuff you can put plans in place to get you off it in nine or ten – but it will take maybe fifteen to twenty years for you to really feel like ok, my entire world – even my kids, kids, are using the OPM (Other People's Money) through our insurance policies.

For people that are more serious, that are moving a lot faster, with limited income, their goal is to be completely self-funded and self-financed in five to eight years.

I think it's very important for you to make the decision on what side it is you want to be on. And in this course you guys will never hear me say borrowing money from a bank is cool. You will never hear me say it. I don't care if the bank offers me $200,000,000 – they can offer me a BILLION DOLLARS to start teaching people on how to borrow money. I can't be sold! Because once you have tasted freedom and once you know that freedom is out there, It's a total different world to know that you don't have to depend on the system that was created to literally suck the life out of you. If you were in our last course, you know that the system that we are currently in that we depend on – you don't think that they created it for us to depend on it? You don't think they created a game for us to be able to look at our credit scores and be like – ooohh I got 20 more points! If I get 20 more points, I can get this card, and this card, and I can do this, and I can leverage that money, and I can do banking and I can do all this!

You don't think that they are smart enough to create a world where you need to depend on them? You don't think so? And when you think about it and you understand it in its full totality and you begin to realize – wait a minute; this world is a little sick. Yeah it is sick, and I been in this like – world that is hard for me to get out of and I want out. And it is going to be hard as hell for you to get out. But you got to want to get out. You got to cut them arms off, you got to cut them legs off, whatever it takes, to get out! Because once you are out, like is FREE! When you start to think about the access to life, access to lifestyle, versus wanting to go get an $800 car, you will start paying $500 to $800 a month for somebody to clean your house. You will start to think about dang, I don't want a car, I want an easier lifestyle. Then you start realizing, my house is clean – I don't clean my house. I want somebody to cook my food, and then you begin to realize the importance of time, and you have access to more capital and you are leveraging more. That's a trap – to want you to buy things that you can't afford.

THAT IS A TRAP! To want you to get stuck in homes for 30 years in a city that you don't want to be in for the rest of your life. You haven't even explored the world; you haven't explored the country, but you're stuck in a city and now you are tied and anchored to that city, paying property tax, paying mortgage, and paying all this stuff and you have not explored where you want to be – where God called you to be. What if God tells you tomorrow to move to Minnesota but you got a home and all this debt tied to you? How can you move? The only way to get out of the rat game is if you learn the game of the rats – the masters who created the rat game and then you reproduce what they did to you – you do it **FOR** you! Versus looking at it and saying, "man, forget them man, they got us enslaved man!" Rather than getting mad at them, study them and do it to where it benefits you. Do it to where you're in control.

What would you rather pay money for? Would you rather pay money for a better lifestyle and not having to think about things of life? Or, would you rather have to be worried about paying a car that you are not going to keep up? You really don't even like the car – because if you had the money to choose another car, all of us got a better car that you would choose. All of us have a better house that you would choose.

It's crazy how much we settle. It's crazy how much we ask God for something but we will settle for something else. I'm praying to God that we have so much overflow that I can hire a driver – because of the amount of money that rich people spend on leasing; I would rather pay someone for driving so I can put food on their table for their family. That's what I am talking about – **OVERFLOW!** When you begin to think about becoming the banker, you begin to think about overflow.

When I begin to think about overflow, I don't just think about my family being good; I don't just think about the people here at the home office being good – I think about overflow because when the Bible says that your cup will runneth over, and your jars will never be full – I want the jars of everyone around me to just be overflowing where you got to help other people.
You got to literally pour into everybody else's cup. So, when you think about it, I'd rather have lifestyle, I'm ok with driving a used car. I'm cool with it. If it means that my wife doesn't have to worry about cooking, that's the next thing. I want somebody to cook for us. We don't have to worry about cooking, we are making enough money here at the office that my staff doesn't have to worry about those things either.

Do you know how much better the home office will be if your executives had people that came and cleaned, people that came and cooked for them and all they can do is focus on the mission of the Kingdom, the mission and vision of the company, and what God gave you? Do you know how much sharper their mindsets will be? I tell my guys don't get caught up in the material things, because just like the material things, everything comes from dust and it goes back to dust. It's gong to be a new Lamborghini, it's gong to be a new Benz, its going to be a new house, a new car, more pools, another jacuzzi – there will be a bunch of these things.
You will always be re-creating, pro-creating, and breaking down and building again, looking at something new. There will always be another version of a jet, there is always going to be another version of a car, but when you begin to think about these things – there will never be another version of you impacting other people.

See, me taking $300,000 and pouring it into somebody for ten years, giving them a stable income, you can't reproduce that. **That's a lasting impact!** See when I think about cutting my grass, I don't think about saving money, I say God I need more – I need an overpour of abundance. Because I want to hire somebody so that I can bless them to be able to cut our grass so that when we can keep the money growing within our Kingdom, within our family – and within your people God! I need overflow like that! That's what I think about overflow – not so that I feel like I'm bigger than somebody – I'm thinking like a banker because I don't want to have to deal with the small things, I want to deal with the God things – things that are bigger, I don't want to have to deal with small things every day.

> ✔ I want to think about how can I progress God's kingdom forward?
>
> ✔ How can I move us forward?
>
> ✔ How can I move our people forward?

I can't do that if I am thinking like a consumer, because I get caught up in the stuff that don't matter. I get caught up in the stuff that doesn't matter – and if I'm not speaking the truth, let me know! I feel that I am supposed to be talking directly to you – like I'm supposed to be hitting you right in the heart, like I'm supposed to be hitting you right in the soul. We're going to hit you right in the spirit because I want you to think bigger. See, the ideology of becoming the banker is for you to think bigger, **to know that God IS BIGGER – He's bigger than you can imagine!**

It's not about you finding a little cubby hole, with a little curbside yard, it's about thinking that God is bigger. He created the Universe, there's an existence for you, bigger than you can imagine. Stop trying to penny pinch or borrow to penny pinch. So, when I think about debt, I literally think about – "ok Faith is to expect something even though I don't see it."

"Debt is to want something even though he told me it's done." So, if I think about debt, and I go and get it against his will of saying it's already done. So, me going to get debt is me basically telling God I don't believe what you said that you would do for me; so I'm going to go do it myself and I rather enslave myself to have it today than to have it clear and free to get it tomorrow. So, when I think about the ideology of the two, I'm thinking like man, debt is adverse over what faith is, debt is adverse to what God told me. Debt is adverse of walking by faith and not by sight. Debt says I know what you told me God – I know you told me that I can have a big vision, bigger than what I imagined. I know You told me that doors I walk through will never be closed. I know that You told me that I would be able to be a blessing to other people. But because I can't see it, my credit score tells me I can go get it today and I hope and pray that you bless me even though I go and get it without you.

You don't think that enemy creates devices? See, the enemy can't create what God does, but he can create carbon copies. So, God says he can create things that don't even exist to happen for you. And the enemy says I can give you stuff that does exist so he can have them for you. God says I want you to swipe my Mastercard; the enemy says I want you to swipe a physical Master Card, but the only deal is it just comes with the fact that you are going to be will be enslaved to me for thirty or forty years. And even if you are that person that says, "Listen Jake, I'm disciplined enough to get out in five to ten years."

 Listen, it's the drug, it's the hit, it's the fact that you say I can get out in five years and you do and then you feel like well I can do it again. It's the drug – it's the hit – it's the addiction, it's your feeling that I can get out and I can maneuver out. That's what happens with sin, you can get in, you can't get out but it's the added compound effect of you thinking you can stop when you choose. That's how addiction happens!

Debt is adverse of God's plan. I have never received something from God that had thirty pages of things I had to sign. The building that we are in today, I called the guy – and Connie can be my witness; I called the guy and the guy said meet me – I said what do you need for this building? He said all I need is first and last month's rent. I said, "I don't have to sign nothing? He said oh yeah, you have to sign this one paper. I said you don't need nothing else? You don't need to check our business credit – you don't need to check our revenue? He said nope, that's all we need." Our business started to grow. Partnerships began to align – Brother Ben' and I's partnership, there is no paperwork, there is no signed contract, just **GOD ORDAINED!**

Everything that comes from God doesn't come with a side thing attached to it. There is no yeah,….. but! There is no yeah, I'll give you $500,000 but …. I need assets of your home. There is no yeah, I will give you this business … but I need you to sign forty years to doing this or I will take it back. There is none! I'm sorry if you call yourself not being extremely religious, but I really don't care if you are extremely religious or not, because I just taught you all the stuff about how to be a bank and you can just listen to me rant for a little bit – lol! Because I would not be where I am if I were not swiping the Master's Card! Swipe – Master's Card – the Master's Card. Not the MasterCard that comes with a little …. It's kind of like the apples we eat from the grocery store – never rots. So what happens is the enemy creates carbon copies but there are side effects to it that end up affecting you in a worse condition later on in life. Things that are God made; they have a cycle, they don't hurt you – they're pure to you, they work with you, they don't work against you.

So, when I think about debt, excuse me – that I don't say there are people who get in and get out – but they stay in. Whether they can get in or get out; whether they feel like they have control, they still go back. That's what their drug is, especially when you feel like you have control. So, the question that you got to ask yourself is: AM I REALLY THE BANK? Because, for you to say that I am the bank, that means that you must know that your creator is the Federal Reserve. See, every bank has a Federal Reserve that has a bigger bank backing it.

- **Chase – Federal Reserve**
- **Bank of America – Federal Reserve**
- **Wells Fargo – Federal Reserve**

See my bank, I'm the bank, and what backs my bank – **IS GOD!** I don't owe no debt, don't owe no man. And I would rather rock that way. Proverbs 13:11 (ESV) says, "Wealth gained hastily you lose it just as fast, but wealth gathered little by little grows over time." No matter what your belief is, that is true for every belief. Wealth gained fast, you lose it just as fast, but wealth gathered little by little grows over time. A house built too fast will crumble just as fast as it is built. But a house built to perfection will last for a long time. That's no different and it's in every aspect of our life! When we use debt, we want it fast and it just comes with something that's attached to it. I appreciate you guys for letting me rant because I felt like somebody needed it. Because this thing doesn't work until you believe that it can. That's just like you got to understand that hard work and discipline is not enough to get over the edge. See, there is an element of faith and there is only so much that you can do. The other portion takes a supernatural force to bring it to pass.

Jake, what do you mean? I can put a seed into the ground and I can do my due diligence on that seed but it's other things that I cannot control that it takes in order for that seed to be able to grow like it's supposed to. And it is my faith to know that if I do my part, the supernatural will do HIS part! What you got to understand that when it comes to breaking from the curse, breaking from the chain, becoming free forever, it's not just banking and money I'm talking about, I'm talking about every aspect of your life. You got to do your part, but there is a supernatural faith and belief that comes with you got to believe that God is going to do the other piece.

See, that's where you get supernatural growth, that's when you get supernatural success, that's when you began to have things happen in your life that you cannot explain. I can't explain to you how our business is right now. I can't explain to you how I got somebody as committed as Connie when I couldn't pay her in the past. She stayed as if I was paying her. I can't explain to you how I met my wife and she was down and we were rebuilding the business and she stayed! I can't explain to you the partnerships and alliances – the only thing I can tell you is that I did my part but there is another element that takes your belief that God will do his.

There is another element, so when it comes to banking and for me to believe that I can't survive off of debt without using debt, that is basically you saying – listen, I got faith but I got to see it in order to believe it, and that's opposite of faith. My faith says listen, I am not going to no bank to get it, so I already know God told me it's going to happen so it has to come from somewhere. And you don't know that you are one person away from God changing your life, but because you decided to go get debt – you chose that road and he took that person away and gave him to somebody else that he made $100M on!

We don't want to stay, we don't want to develop, we don't want to build up these skill sets that require for us. See I built up so much restraint, so much discipline, so much belief in the supernatural – what God can do, that I began to expect things and it happens.

God says to expect things as though they are and I'm going to expect it as if it's already happening. Because I know I did my part, and I plant a seed into the ground, I don't question if an apple tree is going to grow up – I'm expecting for a tree to grow up. And if a tree don't grow up – I'm not blaming my efforts; I'm looking at the fertile ground. And I can't be mad at God because it's bad ground – I should've checked the fertile ground. But if it's fertile ground, if it's the right seed, and I have applied my effort, I'm expecting that a healthy tree is going to grow. I'm expecting it! We all talk about the truth and your fruit from the tree. Do you know that it takes an apple seed six to ten years to be able to grow before it has its first bushel of apples? It takes an apple tree six to ten years before it has its first fruits – the first bushel! Did you know the first bushel are not it's best! It takes six years for the apples to be seen! What if the apple says, "Hey yo listen, it's not happening quick enough so what I'm going to do, I'm going to the bank and they going to put apples on my branches. When people come and buy these apples off my branches, then I will pay the bank for fronting me." And you don't know that you are literally one, two, three years away from producing your own fruit for the rest of your life, without the anchor of being indebted to somebody else.

I told God I will wait my time. I will drive my used car. I will live today like no one else so I can live tomorrow like no one else. I'll put in my six years, I'll put in my ten years. I will put in my twenty years because I know that the amount of time that I put in its not equivalent to the overflow that I get. Becoming the banker is a different mindset to believing that there is more to offer you out there other than what you can tangibly see. What is more out there than what you can tangibly see? See right now I'm talking to you. I can see my house without physically being there. Why? Because I know it's there, I've been there before. See that' what happens with visions that God gives us. You got to see it and know it's there even if you are not physically in that location yet. OH – I'm talking to SOMEBODY!!!

I'm going to Arizona tomorrow, and I can see myself in Arizona before I take off the plane. I'm expecting a safe landing. I see it before I get there. I know where I'm going, I'm not getting on a plane and questioning what my destination is. Even though I got on the plane I'm not in Arizona yet but I'm willing to take the ride so that it gets me to my destination, when I'm supposed to be there, right on time. And a lot of us, we have become indebted, we put on our own shackles!

You know the sickest thing? The sickest thing is that – WE PUT OUR OWN SHACKLES ON OURSELVES! Because we are impatient – we shackle and enslave OURSELVES!
And do you know the craziest part about it for some of you – I give my heart to you and you're still going to decide to be in a maze. You're going to say, "Jake I understand, I get it, but"…
You can never say I didn't teach you and you were never taught. "Jake I can't grow my business without debt." You're a liar, sell products. You know business is not about finding funding. Business is about serving. My favorite book says, (y'all know my favorite book) It says, **"the greatest among ye shall be a servant of all."**

The greatest businessperson on this planet – all of them are really good at serving the multitude. You want to make a billion dollars? Serve a billion people – add value to a billion people, it's the easiest way. The more people you add value to, the more money you make.

152

The more people you provide a service to, the more money you make. That doesn't sound like you need funding to me. I mean think about it, take away debt, what do you need funding for? How much money do you really need to survive annually? Take the debt away!

If you really take debt away – how much money do you think you really need to survive annually? If you went into a foreign land right now, are you going to go to the Mercedes lot or are you going to do whatever you can to survive? Whatever your bare minimum is to survive because you are trying to build? You need to have an international's mindset. When internationals come to America, they are not thinking about borrowing.
They are thinking about puling up their sleeves and getting to it, saving money, sticking to it, staying to their core, staying small because they don't want to go back where they came from. So when we think about it we just need enough for food, clothing, shelter, and a little transportation. Everything else is overflow, it's just overflow. You live today like no one else, so you can live tomorrow like no one else. It's going to be a lot of people that's going to be surprised that five years from now – we think five years is a long time – a lot of us; but twenty, thirty, forty years pass just like that!

So five years from now there are going to be people that will be looking at you like, "Man, I wish – Man you so lucky!" And you are going to be like, "Girl… Dude… you have no idea what I've been through. You have no idea the sacrifices I took in order for me to be in the position where I owe nobody." Do you know how it will feel for you not to owe nobody? Think about it – how would it feel for you not to owe nobody? You don't have to cut nobody a check if you don't want to. How would if feel if you are not thinking about a credit score every day? What would life look like for you? How would you feel if you didn't have to worry about none of that? You could just focus on doing what you know you do best.

I was talking on social media today and I said it's funny, because God got a sense of humor. I used to get whippings when I was a kid for talking too much. My teachers told me that talking too much would be my downfall. I'm a brilliant kid but I don't know when to shut up. But we built a million-dollar company soon to be nine figure company off of me talking! **You can't tell me that ain't God!** You can't tell me that ain't God to take us from just crossing seven figures and about to jump us pass eight to nine. Skip smooth over eight to nine! **From TALKING!** All because I just waited on God to do his part and I just kept doing mine – I was just running my mouth! You know there are some people out there that make millions of dollars just listening to people. They don't like to talk but they are really observant and they just love to listen. There are some people that get paid millions of dollars just by thinking problems through – Engineers. You know a doctor is nothing but an engineer of the body. A mechanic is nothing but an engineer of the car. An airplane mechanic is nothing but an engineer of the airplane. They're all doctors, just in different fields. All because they have the creative minds to find solutions to problems. You don't have to go into debt to do that. Just believe that God is going to cut the check when you need it most.

Somebody out there needed to hear this – you are more than enough, do your part, don't look left, don't look right, don't look because they are moving faster. Do you know how many millionaires and billionaires fall straight on their face as fast as they climb?

I had a friend, he made a $100K in a month before me, like three years before me. He was stunting, went and bought an I8, and had a driver, he had a whole entourage, a penthouse, and I'm talking about living. I never got envious, and I said when it is supposed to be mine, its going to be mine. A couple of months later, six months to be exact, he got kicked out of his penthouse. And then he told everybody it was because he wanted to move into a house. He moved into the house and two months later he was evicted. His I8 – he bought it for $100K, he had to sell it for $40K because he needed quick cash. His Tahoe that he had his entire team in – repoed! You know what he's doing today? Selling courses, hustling people, getting them to pay him $10K for a course on what he did, not what he's doing. You know what God is doing for us here? Steady climbing! You know what we have? $100K a month – regularly! You know what we don't have? No debt, nobody coming and trying to knock on our door, nobody coming and trying to repo us. What I used to dream to do, we've done it in the first half of the month. I used to just want to make $30K in a month. Never would have thought it in a million years. I'm not trying to brag because that's nothing to what God is going to do for all of us. But what I am trying to tell you is I did that all without debt. Because I banked on the bank of Judah, the bank of Yahweh – I banked on my Master's bank! That's what I did. Most of us are fearful of the things that are unseen because we recognize the unseen as a place of darkness. A seed cannot grow if it is covered in darkness. Your dreams do not manifest until you're covered in darkness.

God does not bring your visions until its dark and your eyes are closed and then that's when he sends your visions to you! See, the most beautiful things happen through darkness – because when the light hits, it's typically after something went through the dark. See, if I wanted to be free, and I was fighting an oppressor, I can't just walk in mid-day and work myself free. The easiest road to get to my freedom is through darkness, through the places of fear, its walking with faith, that one day I am going to see light and when the light hits me it's going to be at the right time, at the right moment, and I want be scared anymore because I will be free.

So, when you think about the most beautiful things that emerged happened through darkness. It's crazy because I have been teaching financial literacy for seven years – and the apple tree doesn't really start to have its first bushel of apples until between the sixth and tenth year, usually the seventh year. And what we are receiving in our seventh year is so much overflow it made up for all the years before when I felt like I was underpaid. When you feel like you are underpaid, you got to keep moving because when God opens the door for you that overflow is going to make up for every day that you felt like you weren't getting paid what you should've been getting paid.

This class was to empower, uplift and set you free. Your soul was bound because you were still living by the ideology of the wicked person, the people of the entity that want you to be oppressed. See God is not an oppressive God, he's not a God that is going to want you to always be in shackles, he wants you to be free. So, anything that comes with a burden is probably not of God. God brings responsibility with a plan – the enemy brings burden with none. So, when I think about the burden, I think about the sleepless nights and you got to ask yourself was this really a blessing from God ? Or is this something I created with the enemy?

154

CHAPTER 15:

I AM THE BANK (Snow Balling Debt)

You can use your bank to snowball your debt away. We talked about debt consolidation and how we can literally stop paying all our debt to everyone that we owe and just start dumping money into our policies. But the biggest thing that I want us to understand is the simple fact that it is possible for you to be able to snowball your debt away and be successful at doing it.
Here is the deal: We are going to be talking about snowballing your debt away and we will also talk about how to fund your business, how to fund equipment. Listen, its going to take about maybe fifteen to twenty years – for some of you guys that are serious; about seven to ten years, for you to get completely off of the traditional system. Let's be honest, some of us are knee deep in It, and it's going to be hard to kind of get out.
One of the biggest things I want you to understand is that every single thing that is not an asset – you should be putting it on your banking system's credit system that we have. We will learn how to do that in this segment.
The biggest thing that I want to talk about is I know that some of us were a bit overwhelmed when we discussed the debt consolidation route. But the truth is the reason why I brought up the debt consolidation route was because there are some people who are drastic like me that don't care about the credit game.

But also too I do know there are some people that say, "Listen Jake, I have spent all my life trying to fight to try and get my credit score where it should be. And I know I am not supposed to be using credit, but I'm not willing to risk all this hard work that I've done to get me here." And I'm ok with that. **What's the use of good credit if you are not going to use it borrow money?** But, either way – *tomayto, tomahto* – I'm here for all of it and I want to make sure I can be able to show you this. The key is, as you guys get used to this banking system, I want you to be able to use your imagination on how far this banking system can go. There are so many things that you can do, in order to make sure that you can capture as much wealth as you can inside your banking system. It's not just this or just that – I'm giving you guys so many different scenarios so that you can be able to determine what you want to use your bank for. You may never want to use your bank for debt, you may use your bank for debt consolidation, you may use your bank only for cars, you may use your bank only for houses. I don't know what you would use your bank for but what I'm saying is – you **CAN** use your bank and I will show you how to do it. So here it goes!

I will now show you how policy buildout works. I am going to show you $2K a month and if you're paying $500 a month, the system still works the same. You just have to learn how to utilize the system with whatever money that you are using.

Scenario:

In year 1, this person was putting $24K into their system. We know that Inside of their **CR (cash reserve)** – they're only going to be able to have access to **$11,**

Age	End of Year	Contract Premium + Riders	Cash Value	Death Benefit	Contract Premium + Riders
32	1	24,000	11,991	1,238,168	24,000

991 at the end of the year. *All of us have these numbers in our illustrations, if you have a bank.

If you started your bank, received your policy and have not looked at your illustration, its important that you do, so that you are able to see what I am talking about.

We know that this person put $24K in and they have access to $11,991 year one. So, we divide $11,991 from year one by 12 months - because when you look at your illustration, it only shows you in terms annually **(see below)**

Age	End of Year	Contract Premium + Riders	Cash Value	Death Benefit	Contract Premium + Riders	Cash from Policy	Cash Outlay	Annual Dividend	Cash Value	Death Benefit
32	1	24,000	11,991	1,238,168	24,000	0	24,000	117	12,108	1,238,285
33	2	24,000	24,394	1,305,491	24,000	0	24,000	117	24,632	1,306,286

The illustration breaks down annually – not monthly – so you will have to take the $12,108 per month and divide that by **12 months** and that will let you know how much a month you have access to as far as capital.

You know that this person is putting **$24K** into a system and he has access to year one about **$12,108**. If I wanted to know how much access I have monthly to this plan. I would divide **$12,108 / 12 (months)** and that will let me know that I have **$1,009** available after every time I spend **$2K** into this plan my first year. I'm showing you this so you can see how to play the debt elimination game.

How do we play the debt elimination game? It's very simple – let's say for an example I have a credit card that has **$3K** of debt on it and my monthly payment is **$50** per month. So, when I'm doing my debt snowball, I know that I want to take care of the smallest debt that I have. So, let's say this **$3K** was the smallest debt that I have. Well if I know for every **$2K** that I put into the bank; I have access to **$1,009** – **How many months would it take for me to be able to have money in my cash reserve to take out this credit card?**

How many months would it take for me to be able to pay off this credit card for the full $3K? Because I know that for every **$2K** I put into the plan, they will give me access to **$1,009**.

If I take **$1,009 x 3 (months)** – I know that's **$3,027** that I have available to use inside of my cash reserve. So, now If I want to play the debt snowball game and I wouldn't want to do what we call debt consolidation, where we teach to stop paying the **$50** a month and start reverting that back to your policy – IMMEDIATELY! But, say we didn't do that, we didn't want to keep a good credit score, what you will continue to do you would still pay the minimum but you would not pay anything above it. Why? Because we are trying to build up enough money in our cash reserve – so that when we have enough in our cash reserve we can literally take care of this debt and no longer have to pay the $50 a month for that credit card. And we can start reverting that $50 a month into a segregate account to start saving outside of our plan for now.

Now that we understand that, let me explain to you what I teach when it comes to paying off a debt. So, what do we know about saving money to pay off debt? Typically they teach us to save cash and pay off your debt using cash – correct? Is that what they teach us; to pay off our debt using cash? Ok. Let's say we did that.

Scenario:

Let's say we are saving $1000 a month into a savings account and we had a $3,000 debt with a credit card company. How many months would it take for us to save $1000 a month to get to $3,000 to eliminate the credit card? Three – that's simple right? Why? Because $1,000 x 3 months equals $3,000.

Now what do when we have the money if we're paying cash? You take the $3,000 and pay off the credit card, and eliminate this debt – is that true? If this $3,000 was in a savings account, we will take this $3,000 and pay it on the debt, it eliminates the debt, then we cut the card up. That's what we teach. But If I only had $3,000 in my savings account and I use all that money to pay off a debt what does that leave me in my savings account? ZERO! So how many months would it take me to build up the $3000 again to pay off the next debt? It will take three months for me to build up $3,000. But we see one process that's not really working – I'm literally growing money to dump it at debt and it's not benefiting me more than me eliminating debt. Because I'm literally growing $3,000 and then spending $3,000 on debt and repeatedly repeating this process.

So, with the system that I just showed you, what is the difference when you do that inside your insurance bank? Every time you pay off a debt – you still got to build up your savings account again. The only difference is when I use this **$3,000** to pay off that debt, I still have **$3,027** in my account, I just don't have access to it. So for the three months that I spend in building the account back up, now I'm paying the debt, I'm saving money again, to pay off the debt, I'm saving the **$3,000** over again. I take three months to save it again, they release the lien on my money – the only difference is I have the interest that is accumulated over the three months while I use the money.

Now that I have freed up **$50** that was going to a credit card, that **$50** is now free a month that you can use to add to the **$1000** that you're paying a month into your savings account, that's typically what people do when they snowball debt. So, now that's **$50 + $1000** which is **$1,050** and then they save this money for a period time to get to a certain amount to take care of another debt. We're doing the same strategy; the only difference is we're using our bank – we stopped using our credit cards during this process. The only thing that you're doing is you are paying your credit card's minimum.

Let's look at an example:

Say I have credit cards and I am paying:

- **$120 a month and I owe $4000**
- **$50 a month and I owe $2,000**
- **$100 a month and I owe $500**

Typically, people have three credit cards – the above example is **$6,500** of debt. But in total the monthly payments are **$270** that you are spending toward the debt, which will take you forever to pay off – about five or six years to pay off the credit card debt. So, what we do – we find the free money. We revert that money and put that it into your insurance bank. So, say we found like in the previous example, **$2,000** a month which ended up being **$1,009** going inside your insurance bank every month. Well, we know with **$1,009** of access that in month one, which debt can we take care of with **$1,009**? Which debt can we take care of month one?

157

Absolutely right! The $500 debt. So what do we do? We borrow $500 from our self, which doesn't take from this money still growing in interest. We take that money and go tackle the debt, and you no longer owe the credit card company $500. How much more money a month did you free up? $100. So we take the $100, and usually if you owe $2,000 or whatever you would have a higher monthly payment. So I am going to do $250 to make it more realistic.

$250 a month and you owe $2,000

So you free up $100 – so where else would the $100 a month go? If you don't spend it, you use it to pay off the debt that you borrowed. So how many months of paying $100 a month would it take you to make back the $500 that you borrowed? Five months. So you take the same $100 that you were paying to the credit card, now you take that $100 because you no longer have the debt, and you take that $100 and put toward the debt that you borrowed to pay it off. So it takes five months. You paid off that debt, correct?
Simultaneously, for five months you were still putting $1,009 in your insurance bank, so at this moment $1,009 x 5 you have how much available? You have about $5,045 available inside your insurance bank to go and tackle whichever one you like. I hope this is making more sense.

So when you do this is what you have to realize is you are freeing up money while I take care of the next debt, and the next debt, and the next debt – while I'm paying myself back every three, five, six months until I have enough money to go and take care of the mortgage.

So, now let's use a mortgage as our next example.

Age	End of Year	Contract Premium + Riders	Cash Value	Death Benefit	Contract Premium + Riders	Cash from Policy	Cash Outlay	Annual Dividend	Cash Value	Death Benefit
32	1	24,000	11,991	1,238,168	24,000	0	24,000	117	12,108	1,238,285
33	2	24,000	24,394	1,305,491	24,000	0	24,000	117	24,632	1,306,286
34	3	24,000	40,726	1,370,564	24,000	0	24,000	117	41,089	1,372,015
35	4	24,000	62,163	1,433,471	24,000	0	24,000	117	62,655	1,435,557
36	5	24,000	85,217	1,494,298	24,000	0	24,000	117	85,843	1,496,998
37	6	24,000	108,711	1,553,118	24,000	0	24,000	429	109,787	1,556,723
38	7	24,000	133,836	1,610,018	24,000	0	24,000	784	135,732	1,616,085
39	8	24,000	158,253	1,665,069	24,000	0	24,000	1,173	161,385	1,675,249
40	9	24,000	184,306	1,718,345	24,000	0	24,000	1,547	189,068	1,734,291
41	10	24,000	210,843	1,769,919	24,000	0	24,000	1,983	217,766	1,793,188
		240,000			240,000	0	240,000	6,501		

So the entire time that we are building money inside of our account we're paying off debt the entire time – paying it off , paying ourselves back, paying it off, paying ourselves back. Because in the tenth year we want to completely get rid of the mortgage with the bank. So you're using your money the entire time getting rid of debt and paying yourself back, and you will still have $217K or more in your cash reserve to get rid of a mortgage.

Let's say I have a mortgage, I'm in year one. I got a $200,000 mortgage and I know after 30 years I would end up paying around $343K into a home or to the bank. And I'm trying to stop this. So, if I am paying $2,000 a month, I know that in year ten, based on this plan (see above) you will have $217K inside of your insurance bank.

158

So, the entire way to get rid of the final debt that you owe you literally were borrowing money paying off debt, paying it back, borrowing money, paying off debt, paying it back, all using the same money while getting rid of all your debt, to get to the final day that you are getting rid of your mortgage from the bank forever.

Age	of Year	Premium + Riders	Cash Value	Death Benefit	Premium + Riders	from - Policy	= Cash Outlay	Annual Dividend	Cash Value	Death Benefit
32	1	24,000	11,991	1,238,168	24,000	0	24,000	117	12,108	1,238,285
33	2	24,000	24,394	1,305,491	24,000	0	24,000	117	24,632	1,306,286
34	3	24,000	40,726	1,370,564	24,000	0	24,000	117	41,088	1,372,015
35	4	24,000	62,163	1,433,471	24,000	0	24,000	117	62,655	1,435,547
36	5	24,000	85,217	1,494,298	24,000	0	24,000	117	85,843	1,496,998
37	6	24,000	108,711	1,553,118	24,000	0	24,000	429	109,787	1,556,723
38	7	24,000	133,836	1,610,018	24,000	0	24,000	784	135,732	1,616,085
39	8	24,000	158,253	1,665,069	24,000	0	24,000	1,173	161,385	1,675,249
40	9	24,000	184,306	1,718,345	24,000	0	24,000	1,547	189,028	1,734,291
41	10	24,000	210,843	1,769,919	24,000	0	24,000	1,983	217,766	1,793,188
		240,000			240,000	0	240,000	6,501		

So I know I have $217K in the bank by year ten. I was on a 30-year mortgage and in ten years – I pay off my mortgage using my bank. Let's say I am paying $1500 (mortgage payment) a month into all of the costs for this home. So, in ten years I have $217K in my bank and I got rid of every debt on my way to this big moment. I'm paying off my house twenty years faster than I would have if I stayed using the bank. I use all of my $217k to pay off the rest of the home the same exact way that I paid off every other debt.

At this moment, I have paid off a car, I've paid off my credit cards. So with the credit cards I know that it was:

$ 100.00	Credit Card
$ 120.00	Credit Card
$ 250.00	Credit Card
$ 615.00	Car Note
$ 1,085.00	

So we know that we have freed up $1085 a month and we are about to free up the $1500 a month debt.

Year ten, you take all of the $217K and you do what with it?

$1,085.00
$1,500.00
$2,585.00

You borrow $200K from yourself and then you do what? You go to that bank with pride, with joy, and you say what? You say, "I need the deed to this house, because you are no longer my master!" So you take this $200K ($217K - $200K) – they are only going to give you access to $17K, but we know in the full account you still got $217K growing 4% to 8% interest. You just only have access to $17K. So you take the $200K and you go and pay off your mortgage **in year ten.** Mortgage is completely paid – you own the DEED! Year ten you own the deed, you don't owe nobody and now all you're doing is, you have $1,085 a month that you have freed up. If you add how much you were paying in mortgage, which was $1500…

159

You know that you just freed up $2,585 a month that you were paying to a bank! You just freed up for yourself.
The $1085 came from the car and the credit cards. The $1500 a month came from you home mortgage. So if you add it all up – that's how you freed up the $2585 a month that you are no longer paying the bank!

So if you follow the same method that we've been doing with borrowing money, paying a debt, paying it back, what are you now going to do with this $2585 a month? We are now going to take the $2585 and start paying back the $200K that you borrowed from you bank. You saved yourself $143K to $200K of interest that you would've paid a bank that now you have taken care of paying it back to yourself. What you borrow from your bank, you put it back inside your bank. You cannot steal from your bank or else you will be stealing from your legacy.
The best part about is if you lost your job, and if things got tight, you control your monthly payments. So, you can stop paying for a couple of months – get yourself together and get back right on track. But the best part is I had $217K in my account year ten, when I borrowed the $200K that left me access to $17K but I was still getting the full interest $217K. Every time I paid $2585 to my banking system, it increased how much access I had. So, if I was putting $31K (which is $2585 x 12), that means I am putting $31,020 back inside and I am paying off the debt. Once I pay off that debt, they're going to be releasing more and more of my access. So, $31K a year of access, is going to be allotted back to me, like paying off a credit card. The more money you pay on a credit card, the more access you have. So $31K year one you have $48K of access, $31K added again (year 2) from you paying that, you got $59K of access. So as you are paying yourself back, you are getting more and more, and more of access. Which means that if anything ever came up you can still utilize the money you have access to – to be able to make moves and plays without ever jeopardizing the growth of your money. Everybody say: "CHESS NOT CHECKERS!"

So when I tell people it is ludacris for somebody to feel like they need the bank. The bank is like said before, it is a drug. They give you a little bit of it and you get out. It is no different than having unprotected sex. You have sex one time and you are clear and free. You say, "Well as long as I do this I'm good. And you keep dong unprotected sex, but then you find yourself doing a bunch of unmarried, unprotected sex and then you find yourself with a STD or with a baby because you kept playing with fire. That is no different than taking a drug. I take a drug and I feel, Oh I ain't addicted, - take it again and you feel like, I can stop at any time. Before you realize it, that drug has become a part of your life. And you literally think that you can stop at anytime but you never do. Which means that you are and have became an addict. This is how debt works.

How much do I have to invest in my bank before I can borrow to pay my debts?
That has everything to do with what you decide to put in. If I know that I will have 50 to 60% of access, if I only put in a $100 a month that means I am only going to have $50 of access. Which is why I tell people you may as well buy a term with that and wait until you get more money to do more banks. So when people start a bank with $200 to $300 a month because of their fear, they don't really realize they are jeopardizing the growth of their money because of that phobia. You are only giving yourself access to $150 to $200 a month when you do $300 a month.
Yes, a Debt Addict! **Are you understanding how to control and move your entire system?**
If you are on a fixed income you just can't do it, but you're getting the knowledge first. It's ok if you are not ready right now it is about getting the knowledge so that when you are ready, you can make the right decision, knowing you are making the right move.

Can you increase your monthly contribution? Unfortunately like I said, when you get started with a specific type of plan, you are stuck to the parameters of the plan you started and you would have to get another bank. Which is not a big deal, I have eight. I think of banks like credit cards. Most of us before you came into knowledge, you had three or four credit cards, right? Most of us got three or four banks. You got Chase, Bank of America, a Credit Union – so you can have six or seven banks, it doesn't matter. Every bank doesn't get the majority of your money, some banks only got a little, some credit cards you got a $1000 limit. Some credit card you have a $10K limit or a $15K limit, your banking system can work the same way.

What type of insurance do you offer? We do both **Term and Whole Life**. We tell people if you can't afford the whole life dividend banking policy that we teach, it's just simple to get a term policy and get as much coverage as you want for a cheap amount so that you can have more money to be able to build in your bank.

How to Build your Bank to purchase a Car:

Let's say this person had no debt and in the third year they wanted to purchase a car. So they would have how much money in their third year? How much access would they have? Say this person wanted to get he and his wife a car for $20K a piece. So what they would do, $20K a piece means $40K. So he wants to borrow $40K for two cars, so what he would do is set up monthly payments based on a payment plan that the bank would give him to purchase the two cars. So if the bank would have given him, let's say $789 a month for two car payments and you did this for months. Let's say you have $41,089 and you borrow $40K, you will only have access to $1089 and of course it will keep growing as you pay into. So let's say in year three you borrow to purchase the two cars, you make those $789 monthly payments for 72 months, which will end up being $56,808. You make the $789 a month payment back to your banking system where you borrowed the $40K.

"What are you saying Jake?"

The same way you borrowed money from the bank, you need to be paying that same money back to your banking system or it does not work. And you do this process for everything. So for anything that you know that does not generate you cash flow per say – you use your bank. If you want to use cash to invest into a business or into something you know is going to generate you cash flow – you can mitigate using the bank if you choose because you know it's going to generate you cash flow. You don't have to borrow from your bank but I would, only for things that you know are cash flow, but for things you know that are liabilities, clothes, vacations, cars, borrow from your bank and purchase this stuff like you would on your credit card, pay yourself back the interest and now you have an entire banking system.

What I'm trying to show you guys is not to look at this as an investment. This should be a lifestyle.

Question: "If I paid the bank cash total, how does one come up with the monthly payment to pay yourself back?"

Well if you paid the money out your bank, you still have your income from your job that you would use if you borrowed money from a bank. Let's not make it over complicated.

161

If I'm paying $2K a month into my banking system – say I paid off all my debt, my cars, originally, I free up $1K a month, of stuff that I was paying for such as debt, credit cards and all that. That is a total of $3K a month for total income. If somebody makes $4900 a year, you still got $1900, let's not over complicate it.

Question: "How do you come up with the amount?"

What you would do is go to car financing calculator, or home mortgage calculator, and whatever the bank would charge you, you may walk into your banking institution and ask them what they would charge you a month to borrow $40K and then you say, "OK." "They then ask do you want an application?" You reply, "NO ma'am. NO Sir." And you know how much to charge yourself based on what the bank would charge you. That keeps you equitable with the banking institutions and it keeps you from robbing yourself. Because you need to be paying yourself back in finance charges.

You are pretty much getting paid to borrow from you.

CHAPTER 16: The Last Call: BECOME THE LENDER

We talked about how to become a banker, how to build a Kingdom, we talked about how to budget, where to find money, and how to find money. We've talked about all of these things. We've talked about the mentality of a banker, we've talked the mentality of the consumer, we've talked about the mentality of a producer, we've talked about how to eliminate debt within the banking system. We talked about how to become the banker mentally in some strategies that we use, we talked about consolidation, we talked about snowballing, but in this very last segment, we are going to be talking about how to become the lender.

How to use your banking system to become the lender!

What we got to understand is that bankers want their money to be moving constantly. They always want loans, they always want their money to be moving however, they want to make sure that depositors don't move their money on them, so they ask the depositors to keep their money idle in the savings accounts or certificates of deposit because this allows for the banker to move dead money. Because they know that money that does not move is dead money. Which is why they teach us to keep out money in places and reserves that do not move to our benefit so that they can move it for us.

So that's exactly why they want us to put our money in CD's, that's exactly why they want us to put our money in savings accounts, because what we what we're talking about is not using the insurance banking system, like it's the best investment in the world, what we're talking about is – that it's the best reserve in the world. So we are completely interchanging the banking system, and we're not trying to compare it to the stock market or to real estate or to a business in the growth that a business or real estate or the stock market can have.

We know that. We are just comparing apples to apples, banking to banking. And what the banks know is that the banks need borrowers to borrow their money so that they can continue to grow it.

> They work with the customers using other people's money who trusts them. It's no different than a hedge or investment fund, or other entities that were created to use other people's money to leverage it – to grow it. All of this will begin to make sense later but we got to realize we need to understand one thing – **the bankers make the rules!**

There are a few things that we got to understand, we got to be able to decipher between an investor's mindset and a banker's mindset. They are two total different mindsets. Unfortunately most of us think that investing and banking is the same thing. What we will begin to realize is that they are not the same, but most importantly when we begin to talk about those things you will begin to see Warren Buffett, and the people that you admire the most that have the hedge funds, the investment funds, you will begin to see that they don't have an investor's mentality – they actually have a banker's mentality.

The difference between winning big and losing big is adopting the banker's mindset.

What we got to do is break it down: When we are looking at this, there are two types of mindset.

The Investor's Mindset	The Banker's Mindset
✓ Wants to hang on to Equity to show net worth	✓ Want investors to keep their equity because it makes the bankers shift more risk to the investor and less to the banker and less to the banker
✓ Own properties	✓ Use properties as collateral to ensure cashflow ✓ Hate Owning Properties
✓ Land lording Business	✓ Money Business
✓ Gain Cash Flow by using the banker's money and owning property	✓ Make money by using the consumer's money and collateralizing the mortgages they get when lending the money out
✓ Asset Rich but cash flow poor	✓ Asset Rich and cash flow rich
✓ Investors need good credit and financials in order to secure loans	✓ Do not need either - good credit or financials to lend you money

So the bankers need the protective equity that the investors brag about to protect their loan to value when they loan the money. **So Jake what do you mean by that?** It's very simple. The more that investors brag about their equity, the more equity that the banker (the loaner) can tie up to make their investments (their loans) safer to the investor.

Let's say for an example, if somebody wanted **$100K** to borrow from me, if I were to do **a150%** loan to value; and if they wanted a **$100K** to borrow from me, I can potentially tie up **$150K** to **$200K** of their equity. If they default in paying me back, I make more money by taking their equity because they have more to offer. So investors think about equity and bankers think about taking the investors equity. They leverage and use it as collateral.

I talk about properties, not because I hate real estate – I actually love real estate. I talk about properties because that's what Americans typically understand when it comes to borrowing money to leverage it. Because Americans know and they look at debt as a way to gain property – that's what is talked about most when it comes to leveraging. I tell anyone, that later on in my life I am not interested in becoming a landlord. I am interested later on in my life, lending to people who want to be landlords. Because if I was to lend to somebody who wants to be a landlord, I'm getting paid to front the money for the work that they would do. See, if I was a landlord, that means I got to deal with the people. As a banker all I need is the money.

164

The landlord has to deal with the management team, the maintenance team, the development team, the rehab team, and the renters.

The banker deals with one person – the landlord, whose responsible for all of the property development. So it's funny how there is two sides to making money, the only side that we hear about is the investor's side. When you think about it, we thought the investor took less risk. But it's really the banker who takes less risk. Why? Because the investor needs the banker's money in order to produce cash flow and own properties. The banker needs the consumer's money in collateralizing the mortgages of the consumer or the investor to protect what they are lending out.

So if you guys had a choice (leave the opinions of what you used to know behind you) who would you rather be, the investor or the banker?

Investors are asset rich and cash flow poor and bankers are asset rich and cash flow rich. Now, you may say, "well Jake, I don't consider that to be a fact." Well, let's take a look at it. Typically investors have a bunch in assets, but they're limited in cash flow when it's comparative to what they control. Let me give you an example. I was watching Dave Ramsey today, because I watch all of my competitors, and Dave Ramsey had a caller call in, that had $5.8M of property assets, the loan to value asset of that property was only $1.7M but they controlled $5.8M of property. They had 12 units only making $7K a month. That person is asset rich but cash flow poor in comparison to what he actually controls.

How does the bank get asset rich and cash flow rich? Because they own assets that they don't have to manage, such as mortgages. And they are cash flow rich because they're making passive income from the monthly payments plus interests that the people mortgaging from them have to pay. Bankers don't need good credit or financials to lend you money and make money passively. If you had $10K right now and somebody needed $1K – you could literally charge them 25% and make passive income monthly to maybe having them pay you out for three months. But you could make passive income without ever showing your credit. But as an investor needing debt, in order to make money, I need to show good credit and a good credit portfolio, because I want to prove to the banker, that I'm responsible.

So what we have to understand is that when we look at either or, we have to make a decision. Now the best part about being the banker, (because you can be the banker and the investor) but it's very hard for the investor to assume the banker's mentality because the bank has done such an amazing job at making you think that you need them in order to survive. Think about it, if the banks only waited to make money *is* by lending you money; wouldn't you, if you were the bank, make the producers and the consumers think that the only way to go through them, the only way you can have what you have, is by borrowing? **Wouldn't you make the consumer and producer think that?**

Let's look at an example:

You have a house, and the homeowner decides to buy at $100K. 80% is a loan and you put 20% down. They get a loan from the lender for 80% of the property on $100K house which means they only needed how much of a loan. They only borrowed $80K which s 82% - whose money is at a higher risk, the homeowner or the lender?

165

If the homeowner bought the house today and the had to sell it tomorrow, the truth will be the homeowner. But here is the reason why. (You need to be able to calculate it) If the homeowner bought the property today and had to sell it tomorrow without putting any money down on the property – they would be at risk! Why? Because when they sell the home, the bank has to get how much of the money first?

$80K first to the bank from that property. And because of closing costs and commission that the homeowner, who is the seller would have to pay, that would leave them $10K to $12K left to walk out of the house with. So they put $20K down, but they left with $10K to $12K and the bank got their money first, which means what? The bank was not in as much risk as the homeowner was. The down payment is in a higher risk factor than the bank and the earlier parts of a mortgage. **I'm telling you this so you can see how to become the banker.**

So when we look at the 2000's – let's see what happened during that time:

During the 2000's era there was a mortgage burst. The lending industry was literally giving homes with no money down, which shifted all risks to the lenders, and the homeowner had no money in the deal, so it was easier for them to walk away. So in this case all the risk was shifted to the lender and the homeowner had no value in the deal. That lead to the mortgage burst. They had absolutely nothing to lose. When we begin to think about why the banks don't like to lend money or borrowing doesn't make sense or most in most accounts or usually people say its because I'm a minority and I can't get funding – the truth is you can, if you bring more to the table. If you are able to eliminate more of the banker's risk.

Why? Because the bankers are not in the business of putting themselves at risk with nothing to hold on to or assets to hold. Which is why they are big on finding people who already have assets and giving them more money, Which is why you saw extremely wealthy people who don't have debt looking at the people who are borrowing money and looking like they were rich in the 2000's because they were overleveraging themselves just because they had good credit, and you are literally just waiting on one burst to happen – and everybody who looks wealthy because they borrowed to get their wealth will literally have everything collapsed. Especially when you are taking ninety-day loans for flips and you get that note on the ninetieth day called on you – you can literally lose everything. We have to understand that the banker is really good at shifting the risks to the borrower. There is always a risk in relationships, but what the bank is looking to do is get as much money out of you up front, as they can for a down payment.

The perfect scenario is a 35% / 65% relationship where you are able to put 35% down and the bank gives you a 65% loan and they collateralize the whole entire deal. Why would the bank prefer that position?

Less risk. If the homeowner decides to bounce on the property, after they have spent a couple of years paying down this risk, guess what? That puts the lender in a better position to what? Collateralize and make it a profit on the full property. So that's why you see a lot of people, that the banks really do not mess with when you are not paying your mortgage. They are willing to work with you in your first fifteen years. But it's after the fifteen years that they want to collateralize your full property. They want to foreclose you so fast, better than you can believe. Because they are able to make more money from you foreclosing a property because they already got their money out of the deal.

So the investor says let me find a property that's distressed. The investor says let me get the bank's money because I see a property that I can get that's worth $75K. If I fix it up right now I know that the property is worth $100K. How many of you know real estate professionals that teach you how to find distressed properties? If I borrow $80K from the bank that gives me $5K to do what? Use the remaining $5K to fix up the home. An investor says, I can pay them $75K, it's worth $100K right now but if I borrow $80K from the bank, and I put $5K into the property, I raise the value of the property to now worth $150K.

So in their heads, they're thinking, I really need this money, and I can generate a good profit off of this. I wish this banker knew how good this deal was, because I've done great deals just like this. He should lend me the money. NO question. So this person goes to the banker and you know what the banker says?

I know you need $80K and this property looks like a good deal, but are there any other assets that you have? Are there any other assets, or something besides the home that you are willing to use as collateral? So the banker is thinking, he has good financials, this property looks good, but I wan to tie up everything he has. The property looks good, but I want to tie up as much as I can outside of the property to see if I can get more out of the deal than he's giving me. The investor is thinking if I can just get this $80K – I will let him tie up whatever. How many of you literally used to think like that? Be honest.

The banker says what else do you have? The investor says I put it in my financials, I own a rental property, that is free and clear and worth $120K – no debt. In the investor's mind he is thinking like, that should do it. I told him about my investment property, if he really saw how good a deal this was, everything is going to work great. I just need his $80K and he can tie up my investment property because all things are going to work out perfectly. What is happening is the banker and the investor are going back at it, and the investor is thinking if I pledge $120K all I need is $80K – I just need to get the $80K so I can buy the property for $75K and then fix it up for $5K with bank and it will be worth $150K and then I'm good.

So the banker says Ok, if you are willing to tie up this asset worth $120K and I'm willing to give you $68,300 for this property, you can use all money for this property and it's a deal. The investor says. "No I need at least $75K." **Why?** Because the property is worth $75K.So the investor in their head is saying I need to find a contractor, I can make this deal work. I got to have the deal. So the investor comes back to the banker and says. "For $75K you got a deal." What do you all think happened? Of course the banker can't let the investor get the best of him. So the banker says, "I will give you $72,400 at 8% not a cent more, not a cent less or you can walk away." That investor needs that money like yesterday. So what do you think the investor says? He says, "Deal! I can find the other $2,600." The investor says, "Man, I just won!"

They both go home and get on Instagram. The investor says I just went to the bank and walked out with $72,400 on a property and I just got to do a little rehab to it. It's going to be worth $150K. The banker goes to his boss and says, "Listen, I just had the steal of a lifetime. This borrower came in here thinking they were going to flex. You know what I tied up? I tied up a $120K property free and clear. I also tied up a $150K property that he is going to fix up with his own money, and I only gave him $72K to tie up $270K." Who do you think was the winner? The banker or the homeowner? The lender or the borrower? Who do you think won that game? Do you think God created this world without having a reason why we're supposed to be the lender and not the borrower? No it's not messed up – that's the game.

167

And when you decide to cut yourself short, by only playing the game on one side, you don't realize what you are giving up, al because you wanted to borrow and didn't want to be the lender. When you think about it in truth and you look at the numbers – you will say, I wish I knew Jake sooner because my life would be totally different. If I understood the game, my life would be so much different."

That's why I'm telling you the Bible says to be the lender and not the borrower. Because we see an opportunity and we want to pounce on the opportunity and leverage the bank's money and not realizing what you're giving up. We have to understand that we gave up a few things.

The bankers are the masters at shifting risk. They teach us to be risky. How many of you have heard some type of investment advice from a mentor that said investments are supposed to be risky? **So why does Warren Buffet say, "Rule No 1: Don't lose money. Rule No 2: Don't forget Rule No 1."** A true banker understands risks and tries to shift the risk from them and more on you.

That's why they tell us to put up 100% of our money and take 100% of the risk while they get a 2% maintenance fee. Management fee on the fund while they get a 20% gain without offering no guarantees in between. That's what they tell us. So when you really think about making a move – when I talked to you in the very beginning, during the first Master Class, I told you it goes from:

There is a reason why I have lent and not invested. Because when you begin to look at all investments, from a banker's eyes, you are going to look at all investments as a lend, not an investment. And you are going to start being careful with your money and start mitigating and analyzing all risks to put all favor more in your hands than in risks hands.

Bankers are focused on covering all of the downside, and letting the upside take care of itself. What happens is they teach us to be so engrained about the upside, then we look at more of the upside than the downside. We look at more of the potential than we do of the risk. We are literally playing Russian roulette with the only resources that can give us true financial freedom which is our income. We are so much into gambling and thinking about potential, that we never think like a banker.

We never ask ourselves can I be the house? Can I be Wall Street? Can I be the Casino Company? Can I mitigate risks? Why do you think the Casino company allows for people to make money and allows for people to gamble? You don't think the house always wins in the end?

They are going to let somebody win $1M. They are going to let someone walk away with $2M. If that means that it's going to encourage you to keep spending so they can make $10M for every $2M they give out. That's why God told us not to gamble. Not because he doesn't want you to have fruits of life, because he knows what will happen with the addictive spirit if you win one time. You begin to consider that to be the standard and not the exception. Just because you got out of debt one time and you leveraged the bank's money one time and you won, don't make that exception the standard. That was the exception!

The down payment on a property is in higher risk position than the lender. It's crazy how people give us real estate advice and say, "If you put $20K down, the bank really at risk. Think about it." "If you only put $20K down, they gave you $100K .. I mean, they gave you $80K but you only put $20K. Think about it." And the bank is thinking, they gave me $20K, I gave them $80K but I own a property that is really valued at $150K plus I have collateral of other assets that they have. While you are bragging at your position the bank is laughing at you bragging, and they gave you a dum dum sucker out the door and told you to come on back for more. What bankers understand is – for every $1 that I have, I can tie up an asset and get interest on it. What an investor thinks about is – for every $1 that I have; I can get into debt to make cash flow.

Bankers see money as a little salesperson that is going to go and make them more money. Bankers say "Hey little soldier, for every $1 I want you to go and tie up an asset and bring me back more money. An investor says, "Hey little soldier, I want you to go collect debt, then I want you to generate cash flow off of the debt. Which one makes more sense? Collect collateral and cash flow or collect debt and cash flow?

We have to understand that everybody has a role to play. So just because people don't understand or agree with your stance for becoming the banker you got to know there has to be borrowers, there has to be consumers for this economic system to flow. But you making the decision to become the banker, it's what's going to set your family free, whether people around you agree with it or not. It's not up to you to convince them. It's just up to you to say listen, "I'm becoming the banker and this is how we are doing it." If they say, no I believe in borrowing. Listen, you need them. Why? When your bank gets full, you want those borrowers. You want to see what their credit looks like. You want to keep encouraging them – keep getting good credit.

Guys that was the end of the PBB Master School, where I have literally taught you how to become the banker, by taking you from consumer to banker, and it's up to you to decide on what you need to do next for you and your family.

COACH'S CORNER

RECAP: Welcome to Kingdom Banking

* Coach Jake's Final Thoughts

Welcome to banking, I pray that you received everything you needed from this playbook. At this time if you are thinking clearly you are now the banker. You have the tools needed to take your family's finances to the next level. As I said before, Welcome to banking.

If you need help putting a privatized banking system in place, please do not hesitate to reach out to our office. You can set an appointment at kbappointments.com, or give us a call at 214.412.3092.

NOTES

PRIVATE BANKING BLUEPRINT: BUSINESS EDITION

- **Welcome to the OTHER SIDE**

- **3 Teams, What side you on?**

- **Remember Why Banking is Key**

- **How to make 6 figures lending**

- **Real Estate Developer vs Lending Company**

- **Real Estate Developer vs Lending Company (Part 2)**

- **Secured Lending**

- **Lending with your Insurance Reserve**

- **Unsecured Promissory Notes**

- **Secured Promissory Note (How to Guide)**

- **Do's and Don'ts**

- **Promissory Note Breakdown**

- **Becoming A Private Lender**

- **Interview With My Dad On How He Was Making $3K To $5K A Month Lending**

CREATOR & FOUNDER – JAKE TAYLER JACOBS

Jake has been educating families and college students on the topic of financial literacy since 2012. Though he was passionate about teaching on the topics of legacy building and financial freedom Jake never thought in a million years he would build a business in the financial industry especially since he went to school to be a PE Teacher. Clearly, God had other plans for him, because Jake's break in the entrepreneurial world came in 2016 when he built his financial firm on 7 napkins in a local Applebee's. Since then, the company has evolved to a brokerage vastly exceeding 100+ licensed brokers in 7 states and counting. He and his team of superheroes are building one of the fastest growing minority-owned financial firms in the country and are dead set on growing it to 2600 independent agents putting 260,000 plans in place by 2029.

Seeing a huge disparity and misrepresentation of diversity in the financial services industry, Jake has made it his mission to change the face of the industry by having an organization that is reflective of the communities they serve. Jake is also the author of a phenomenal financial awareness book: "We are Sick: Surviving Financial Cancer" a phenomenal financial transformation book! Jake's passion for transforming and developing the lives of anyone searching for purpose is second to none. He feels it's his calling to help as many people become truly free; free of financial struggles, free of negative peer pressure, free from self-doubt and worry and most importantly free from living a life of underachieving. Jake created PBB MasterSchool to continue his teaching legacy by helping students become successful. Jake has a passion for helping anyone and this platform proves just that! PBB MasterSchool will help students continue to help their families and help change communities. His work has touched the lives of entertainers, business leaders, youth, and future college grads. He believes that the millennials will impact this world like never before!

Jake is a loving son, brother, devoted husband, and father. He wants to use his platform to not only impact people around the world but be the biggest hero in his family's eyes. Poverty knows his family all too well and he is on a mission to single-handedly propel his family to prosperity and financial peace. Jake lives in Dallas, Texas with his wife AJ and their daughter Tayler.

Welcome to the OTHER SIDE

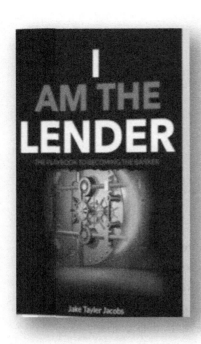

What's going on family! This is **Jake Tayler Jacobs** – *(MR. BE THE BANK)* and I am excited that you finally transitioned over from our **PRIVATE BANKING BLUEPRINT Masterclass** to now learning how to become the bank – how to become the lender. Now putting yourself in the position so that you can now become a lending source to the same very people that need your money in order to be successful. But before we can get there, we kind of have to do a recap in this segment, so that we can be able to fully transition on how we can actually take what we have just learned to where we can actually make money.

I know it's very important for us to understand how to make money and become the banker, not only just lending to ourselves but also being able to lend to other people making money. And I am going to share with you stories about my father and how he lent money. I am going to show you how I lent money to my best friend and he is paying every single month. He's going to be paying me for a very long time but, this is passive income that you can be able to produce for yourself, for your future so that you can be in a position to take advantage of the blessings of being the banker. So with that being said, everything that you will see on the inside of this segment and inside of this module and learning how to turn your new banking knowledge into a business and into income, we will be sharing with you and how to do that.

Welcome to the OTHER SIDE!

3 Teams, What Side You On?

Now that we are on the other side, let's recap some things to make sure we have some things in mind as we begin to start to think about we can make money with this new found knowledge. So what we have to remember is that there are three teams. How you position yourself on these teams will determine what your future will look like and what it will be as we move forward. With these three always remember that:

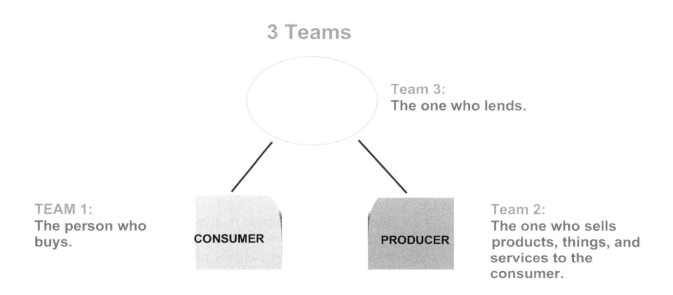

We want to position ourselves to not only to where we become the banker, but we want to be the banker for everything we purchase, we want to be the banker for all the businesses we create. This is a way of life and a way of being. We have to learn and see that it's more beneficial for us to become the banker than it is for us just to settle in these three areas.

When you realize as successful people began to get older and they begin to make more money – they began to start thinking about ways for them to be able to get the most out of the dollars that they earned. And typically what happens is you have somebody that builds a successful business, they then begin to open up and become public and they begin to start taking other people's money so they can put themselves in the position of being the so-called banker.

Remember:
- ✓ **The Producer is the entrepreneur.**
- ✓ **The Producer is the business owner.**
- ✓ **The Producer is the real estate developer.**

These are the ones who make the houses, who flip the houses, sells the houses, and develops the houses. All these things are important!

When it comes to the banker, we have to remember the banker is the only one who wins on both sides. Why is that? Because the consumer is taught to what? **Buy, buy, buy, buy, buy!** And because the consumer is taught to buy, to finance, why spend your money when you can borrow from the bank and then slowly trickle it away. So this is exactly what the banker typically teaches and wants to get the producer and consumer to want to come and borrow money from the bank.

So remember what happens, like clockwork, the consumer asks for money from the bank, the bank gives money to the consumer and the consumer has to pay the money back. The same thing with the producer, the producer asks for money from the bank, the bank lends the money and the producer has to pay the money back. So in this case, this transaction is happening every single time, the producer, which is the business owner, the entrepreneur, feels like they are getting ahead, and they feel like they won the lottery because they are using the bank's money, to sell to the consumer and for the consumer to pay back the money to the producer.

So this product happens over and over again. The entrepreneur borrows money from the bank to make a product, sell a book, to make investing in real estate, to get properties, and the entrepreneur then sells those products to the consumer and the consumer buys those products from the producer and in return the bank is making money – **remember** … *on both sides*.

When it comes to the positioning and where you want to be – a lot of people get stuck right here on being the **producer**. Remember we talked about that. A lot of people get stuck being the producer, as the entrepreneur, and they are ok with paying whatever percentage back to the bank. Because they are like, yo, "I'm going to keep doing it, I am going to keep feeding them." But if you ever look at the biggest buildings or the wealthiest families – those families came from somehow becoming the banker, and those hedge funds.

People talk about Warren Buffett, and they talk about Jeff Bezos, and all of those people have become the bank. They borrowed or used other people's money at a low risk, without any real guarantees and they grow that money and build their businesses off that money. So some people like the producer, they say, "Oh, I did become the bank. I'm using other people's money to make a product and sell it. So I am making the difference in between."

But what I am telling you is, there is life after producer. There is life after entrepreneur, and that you want to become the actual banking entity. So just imagine for a second if this was your family bank. So whatever your family's name is
(Family Bank: _____).

So this is your family bank that lends to your family business.

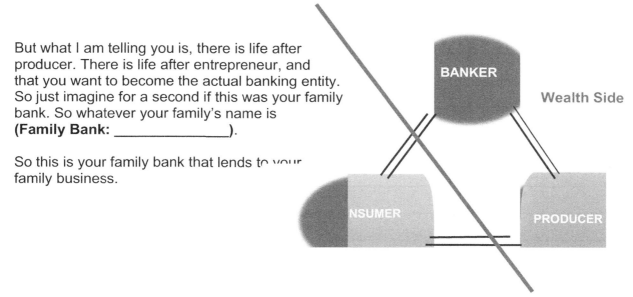

The family business then creates a product and it sells to the consumer, the consumer pays the family business back and in return the family business pays the family bank back so that the family bank continues to grow and more people can utilize this banking function. Imagine if you were to corner wealth on this side **(Producer side)** Imagine if you had the opportunity to corner wealth? I call this the wealth triangle, where you have the consumer, producer, and the banker. And everybody wants to become on the best side of the wealth triangle which is typically at the top. And with this wealth triangle you want to corner the best versions of this triangle, which is the producer side, which is the entrepreneur, and also the banker side. When we are able to do that, we put ourselves in position to where we can actually, literally see wealth stay within our system so much longer.

When you are selling a product and some of that money – 6% to 28% of that money that you make is going to the bank every single month, every single year, and every single quarter, for twenty, thirty and forty years, and what you are going to start to realize is that so much roughage you could've obtained – if you decided to learn how to become the banker. I think it is very important that we understand what team we need to be on because when we decide to be on the banker's side, some things in life may not make sense.

People will be talking, and though they are making money as entrepreneurs, as a banker you have to start to think long-term, so that you can always position your family to be in the driver's seat of money so that you can become the banker.

This concludes this module of the first segment of this side, *the money side.*

Welcome to Becoming the Bank!

NOTES

Remember Why Banking is Key

To fully understand how to become the banker you have to understand from the point of view of the banker and the point of view of producers, why consumers get the (s**** end) of the stick because the truth is if you think about the bank as a business you wouldn't be so mad at the bank and you would actually want to become the bank because what else would the bank do? So think about it. Let's look at the consumer.

Team 1: Consumer

- The consumer's train of thought is to always buy.
  We have to understand when we are dealing with the consumer, it is typically what happens is, wealth for the most part – money is not created, it's transferred. Only the Federal Reserve actually prints money. When it comes to the traditional banking institutions, banks don't even print money. So for the most part, banks use other people's money.

Actually before we continue, let me just show you what the banks do.

- **The question is how do banks get money?**
- **What is the bank's real job?**
  o I am going to answer the second question first and then I will answer how does the bank get money. To answer the second question – what and why do banks exist and what is the bank's main job?

The bank's main job is to manage money. They're a part of money management and how money management works is: Because you (the bank) can't manage or protect your money in the best fashion, or function, we will house the money for you, we will place insurance of $250K on that money so that it's protected and in a safe place and we will incentivize somebody and pay them 1% to allow us to manage their money and borrow their money to grow their money.

So back in the day, think about warehouses, and think about where money is typically stored. If you think about Lot and Abram, who is known as Abraham in the Bible – they had land but the majority of their **"quote on quote"** money was in their livestock. And because their money was in their livestock, the bartering system was slowed down. You have to imagine where that livestock or those animals were housed. **Stay with me** – because you got to think about housing, those animals just weren't allowed to just roam freely, they had to be housed and had to be counted every single day.

So of course the larger your land, the larger your money, the more service – or the more people that you hire, to be able to help you keep track of the resources that you have. So typically these animals were housed in a warehouse, or housed in barns, or housed in shelters – places where they can be counted every single day or utilized to be able to help generate money for the family.

Well as things began to transpire, remember how we talked about how money actually grew earlier in the course, as things began to transpire, gold and silver began to be the easiest way to exchange. **Why?** Because it was hard to barter animals. So for an example, if you wanted my sheep and the only thing I did was sell guns and I didn't want guns but you wanted my sheep, there is no way that we could barter because I don't want what you have. So the money or currency, or silver or gold, was created as an I.O.U. so that we could exchange. So if I wanted your sheep and you wanted my guns, I could give you gold or silver that you could go and trade for it at my bank or at the place that I'm housing. So anytime I wanted a gun, I could just go to your shelter and go get the guns.

So when it comes to the function of banks, the banks *hold!* People begin to amass so much wealth when it came to gold and silver – you're used to turning your gold and silver in to these managing centers, i.e. goldsmiths, silversmiths, which is housed to hold your money. They will create armor or hire army people who can literally manage or protect your resources, day, and night when you didn't have to.

And what they gave to transfer from gold – you turn your gold in and they gave you slips, or I.O.U. papers. They gave you these papers or slips based off what was on your slips or receipts that you got printed. That let anybody know how much gold and silver you had at this warehouse. So if I were to give you my receipt that said 10 gold coins for exchange of something you had, you could go to my bank and pick up those ten gold coins and then keep it at your house or whatever.

But what will begin to happen is the banks were managing money. These were people. Banks used to be people managing other people's money or managing other people's gold and silver in exchange for receipts.

So what happened is banking institutions and people began to say, "**wait a minute, they rarely ever come back to come get their gold – so if we print more receipts, *fraudulently*, and hand people more receipts where they can lend and borrow from us that is how we will do it.**"

So when it comes to banks you have to understand that the bank's main identity and main goal is to house and manage our money. So when it comes to that you have to understand the bank's function – **they house our money!** That's their main purpose – managing.

So they give us 1% - we used to have to pay them to manage our money because they didn't take anything else, but now they pay us 1% and they entice us to pay the 1% so they can go out and make money selling and lending our money. So we want to adopt that mentality, and become our own goldsmith, or silversmith, or money managers of our own money and we want to do the exact same thing the banks are doing – which will allow for us to amass much more wealth and understand the functions of how and why we do what we do. So now we got to figure out how the banks manage money, so how do they get their money?

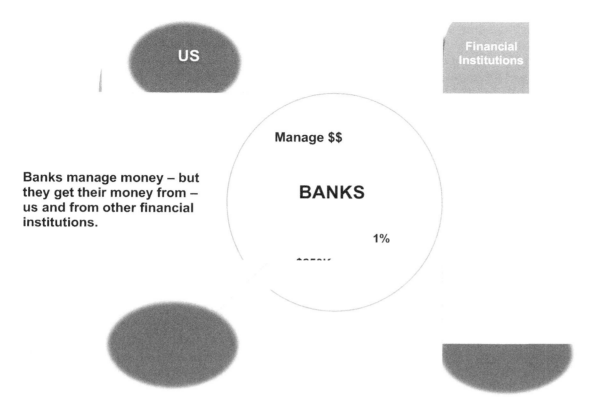

Banks manage money – but they get their money from – us and from other financial institutions.

Very simple, [...] omes in they entice us to ho[...] them. And because we agree to house our money with them – they say ok we will give you .08% to 1% on your savings account to house your money with us. So we will house your money and we're going to pay you 1% to use your money so that we can lend to other people. That's what we agreed to. And then from the other financial instituions, they borrow money at .5% to .25% and up to .5% so that they can lend money to consumers and producers.

"Jake, why are you going back over this?" I think it is very important if we go back over this so that you can understand the banker's mentality because it will go right back to the point I was trying to make. When it comes to the banks's main job and how they make money, managing money, and lending money, that's how they make money, So wouldn't it be in the bank's best interest to create campaigns, get behind people, to pay peoople, to get more people to house more money with them, so they can lend more money out? Wouldn't that make sense?

So it's the same exact way that the producer creates marketing ads and marketing campaigns to get consumers to buy and to market to this consumer so that the consumer feels like it's a safe bet to buy or utilize the product or service.

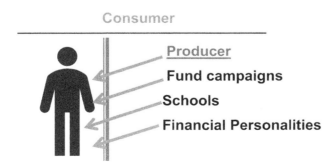

Well the bank does the same thing. The bank creates money from getting us to give the money and then in the very same breath, they lend that money out, **10 times more actually** – called **fractional lending**, they lend that money out to other people, so remember when I told you how back in the day you put your gold there and they gave receipts? So what happened was – you took your gold to this place – say 10 gold coins, they in return give you ten receipts. Ten separate receipts that are a repesentation of each gold coin that you have housed in my bank. So you can always come and redeem your gold coins.

So what they would do is go out and talk to other people and buy their products in exchange and the only thing they exchanged were these receipts that were widely accepted because the receipts identified that they had gold or silver coins in their bank. So this person could always go and redeem those gold and silver coins. So what the bank does, for every dollar that you put inside the bank, they print ten receipts that never existed before, and lend to the consumer. Well, becase we can't print receipts, we want to practice in the same function and practicing the same function just simply means, I want to use the same money from entities, i.e. my business. i.e. myself, and I want to fund my own reserve, so that I can do the same exact thing that the banks are doing.

And when I understand the mentality – if the banks never got the conumer to believe in the power of borrowing, the banks would be out of business, i.e. which is why they teach us to continually borrow day in and day out. So in order for us to undestand that mentality, we got to understand how we are being targeted as consumers to keep us on the right team. Because you will hear people on social media, you will hear people on YouTube, you will hear people on FaceBook, and you will read books that get you to being here (as the consumer) or being here (the producer) thinking that this is all that life is cracked up to be! They'll teach you that being the producer or the consumer is like being in heaven.

BUT NO ONE IS TEACHING YOU HOW TO BE HERE ➡ **BANK**

So we have to understand the psychology of why bankers exist? What's the purpose of the banks? And why consumers are targeted so much? So that we can understand the psychology of why certain marketing tactics and certain books are written and certain people are getting us to continuously borrow money from this system, so that we can continue to be enslaved into this system that we can actually mimmick and create the same freedom for ourselves. So I think it's very important that we understand the functions of why; the psychologies of why, so that when we see it in the marketplace – we don't become a victim to good marketing, we can analyze it and give credit of where credit is due and not participate in these functions because it will cause for us to stay as the consumer or stay on the producer side of things and that's not where we want to be. So we want to understand the psychology but not participate in the games because we want to stay the bankers!

 "You want to be the wealth money manager for youir family! You want to create that system for yourself and you don't have time nor should you play in the games when people are teaching you to stay as producer and consumer – when there is so much more freedom as the banker!"

*Jake Tayler Jacobs

I will prove it to you as I show you how money is made by becoming the lender.

182

NOTES

How to make 6 figures lending

Now it's time to get into the meat of things, which is simple: How to make money, and lending money as a banker. The truth is it's extremely simple.

How to generate 6 figures lending – it's very simple, it's just a function of doing one thing over and over again. This is exactly how my father made $2K to $3K a month passive while he was working for the Dallas Morning News. He was lending money to people who needed it because they lived over their means. So my father used the money he was not spending over his means to lend to other people that were living above their means and had some type of gap protection in between their last job and their next pay check. So it's just literally as simple as this, one person creating a promissory note – the promissory note is the money they are promising to pay you back. There are two types of **promissory notes:**

Unsecured Promissory Notes – you are trusting or believing a person's credibility, and they are somebody that has high integrity, someone that you have been knowing for a long time, somebody that you believe that their word is good enough. Much like a credit score at a bank. What the banks do for unsecured loans, which are credit cards, they typically look at how much money you make and your credit score. When it is an unsecured loan, the interest rates are a little higher – with secured the interest rates are a little bit lower.

Secured Promissory Notes is accompanied by other documentation that pledges collateral. The borrower pledges this collateral in the event he can no longer pay and the loan is declared in default.

With a promissory note you can literally create a fortune for yourself as passive income, the same way my father used additional income to be able to get him through his working period. The same way that we have done here at ABS in lending money out and to be able to do it. So its very simple, with this promissory note you literally find somebody who wants to borrow money to utilize it. So the best type of people to lend money to are people who are successful business persons, or people who are really good with integrity and you have known them for a really long time and that will make due on their word. I wouldn't necessarily lend to people that you really don't know. What we are doing here is learning how to become a private lender and learning how to make passive income literally lending to other people. It's very simple, with the promissory note you will be able to manage and create your own lending relationships and partnerships with other people.

You have your promissory note and you literally go out and you find someone who is eligible or that you deemed worthy of lending your money to. And this type of person is a business professional – those are the best. Or somebody you know that has high or extreme integrity or that made a purchase and this is just a rough spot for them, something came up, the car had to be fixed and they just didn't have the money, something like that – they're typically good with their money but some stuff just kind of happened, where it forced them. So you have a working professional that's extremely trustworthy. Remember there are two types of ways that you can create a promissory note, which can be unsecured or secured and we will talk more in detail about that on the latter portions of this segment and training. I just wanted to give you the glimpse of the understanding so you can see. What happens is they borrow money from you and they borrow money from the promissory note, and sign their name agreeing to whatever requirements or terms that you have for them and they use your money and then they pay you back your principal plus interest. Literally with the interest and principal – you make money! Its just that simple. This transaction over and over again, will literally make you a fortune, and I'm going to show you – let's use a real estate professional as an example.

You have $10,000 that you want to work with – so your lending capability is $10K. This is the amount that you have ready and you are willing to lend and of course you find someone who wants to borrow it. You create your terms, of the promissory note, and they sign their name. If your terms were they pay interest of 12% on the money and the term is six months, and within six months they have to pay you back the entire deal. There are a couple of ways that you can do it – you can let them borrow the money and only pay you interest for the six months and on the last month they can actually pay you the full principal.

If we were to do the math right here it would be $10,000 X 12% = $1200 in interest that you will make over the six months. If they were to pay you interest for six months; they would be paying you passively $200 a month for six months – and then on the sixth month they pay you the full $10,000 back. If you look at it, this $10,000 would have been sitting in the savings account or sitting somewhere not making you any money, but what you did was create an asset out of a piece of paper. They needed the money and because they needed the money, they went out and worked, and you literally took money that was sitting, you created an asset – a piece of paper, they signed the paper, and they paid you $200 a month for six months, and you made this money passive!
PASSIVE FOR SIX MONTHS!

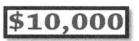

Promissory Note

12% for Six-month Term

There are some people who rent real estate that don't even make $200 passive from their real estate property. And you had no headaches, you got into no debt, you did none of that, you know why? Because the only thing you did was literally lend money from a piece of paper. So the last six months they have to pay you the full $10,000 and you made $1200 of interest on that money for six months plus you've got your $10,000 back. Now this is the natural function of how the lending works. There is a difference of unsecured, which is typically somebody who doesn't have assets, so usually you will use a higher percentage to loan them money by taking more of a risk and secured is when you use an asset. We will talk about both and how they function but this is just the function of it all. So lets just play the numbers game ok?

Let's just say you did this times (5) – which will be $50,000 that you lend out. Well if you did this times (5) – 200 times 5 people that you lent $10,000 - you would be making $1,000 a month passive. And if you did that for 12 months, that's $12,000 of interest you would be able to make passively for that year. So if you think about it as you gradually take that interest versus spending that money, you are putting it back into the pot. We will go more into that, but if you did not understand how this functions, go back and review this section again and we will go more in depth because this is literally the play on $100,000 passive. And there are people, I promise you family, who have real estate that don't even make $1,000 a month passive, or make $12,000 passive – and you have less headache, you have no property, you have nobody you owe debt, and you have none of those things and you are still able to generate income passively if you utilize this function.

I will see you all on the next lesson.

NOTES

Real Estate Developer vs Lending Company

Hey Family welcome back to **PRIVATE BANKING BLUEPRINT**, this is *Jake Tayler Jacobs*, (*MR BE THE BANK*) and in this segment we already talked about the three teams, when it comes to where you want to be – consumer, producer, or banker. We've already talked about how you can actually make money passively. On this segment I want to talk about how the producers make money, how the entrepreneurs make money and I'm going to actually break down real estate. The only reason I am going to break down real estate is because a lot of people are actually talking about real estate right now and passive income through real estate. The big purpose of the **PRIVATE BANKING BLUEPRINT** course is to show you that there are many other ways for you to create passive income without having to take on the burden of borrowing money from the bank in order to get a certain level of passive income.

There are a lot of people who think I am just talking negatively about real estate, but there are other ways for you to be able to participate in this thing that we call passive income, if you really understood the value in how numbers actually work. So I am just trying to show you how to create passive income that you want to replace with your income and add value to your household's income without taking all of the risks that come with borrowing money from the bank to mortgage properties Because if you think about companies that fail, those are typically companies and people that go bankrupt. Why do they go bankrupt? They go bankrupt because they overleverage and they borrow too much money from the bank and the bank comes and collateralizes and takes that asset that they collateralize. So what I am going to show you are the numbers of a real estate property and then I am going to show you the numbers that you can actually make passive income lending money. Next, I am going to show you the difference of the two and move in the same regard of how it pertains to the money that we are utilizing when it comes to that.

ENTREPRENUER

Let's talk about the producer. Typically when it comes to real estate, what do they tell us to do? The producer is the entrepreneur right?

Typically the entrepreneur is taught to use OPM (*Other People's Money*) in order to grow their wealth. When it comes to an entrepreneur using other people's money to grow their wealth, one of the biggest things they teach us is to borrow money from the bank. When it comes to that, why are we borrowing money from the bank? Because we want to purchase a house to create passive income.

Home is worth $250,000 – when you look at this house and we do our numbers at a 4% mortgage rate

Mortgage calculator		
Monthly cost		Maximum loan
Mortgage amount	Interest rate (%)	Mortgage period (years)
$ 250,000	4.1	30
Total cost of mortgage		$434,879
Monthly payments		$1,208

✓ This is your typical 3 BR / 2 BA Home

✓ Lets' Google the Mortgage Calculator

✓ We see that this is our mortgage at 4.1%

✓ Monthly mortgage will be $1208

So this is a real estate property – and a property that we make money on, so we have to calculate family, we have to calculate your monthly maintenance costs. Your maintenance rate on a home is 1.25% on your monthly mortgage. So if we do the calculations on our calculator:

$1208 **(Mortgage)** 1.25% **(Maintenance Fee) X = $1,510**
(Yearly Maintenance on property)

$1,510 ÷ 12 **(months) =** $125.83 **(**
Monthly Maintenance should not exceed $125.83**)**

**IF it is above that you know that you have bought a bad property or you got someone that is not taking care of the property.

Next we need to add our mortgage insurance – on average the rate is 1.75% **on the actual total cost of the home.

**So if I have a $250,000 home at 1.75% that will tell me what my yearly average mortgage will be – which is:

$250,000 X 1.75% = $4,375

$4,375 ÷ 12 **(months) =** $364.58 **(Monthly Mortgage Insurance on home)**

So If I were to add the full cost of the real estate property it would be:

$1208 + $125.83 + $364.58 = $1,698.41
(Total Responsibility for this Rental Property)

Remember: I am showing you the difference between a rental property and you actually lending and making the same passive income being the lender than someone who actually has a rental property. So your total cost when it comes to your hard cost on this 3 BR / 2 BA rental property that you now have, your hard cost is going to be $1,698.41

So lets say for an example – you rent this property at $2,000 a month. Well at $2,000 a month when you rent this property that means your net income on this one property – (I rounded $1698.41 up to $1700) and if I want to be exact, that's $301.50 – you make this in net passive income for one property.

So I have a $250,000 property **3BR / 2 BA home** – my hard cost on this real estate property is going to be $1,698.41 if they take care of my property and everything goes well and everything is fine. I rent out this property at $2,000 a month, my passive income from this one house is going to be $301.50

$301.50 – **that's my passive income off this one property!**

The biggest thing that I see when it comes to actually being in real estate, you're on the ringer for $250,000 with the bank. So you got all this responsibility and all of this heat, only to make $301.50 passive versus becoming the lender.

So say for an example you are the actual lender, you are the bank. So remember what we talked about – when you are the lender, the one lending the money, the passive income to somebody. Now remember what happens, all you need is a piece of paper called a promissory note, which discloses how much money you are lending them. You take that same real estate developer and they need to borrow $15,000 from you to get this property. So you lend it so they can get the property.

Now there are two types of promissory notes like we talked about, there are unsecured and secured promissory notes. For this example we are just going to say promissory note, I will get more in detail with the differences between unsecured and secured. In this case if we are lending to somebody whose in real estate – we probably will get a secured promissory note. Which means that we can actually collateralize and take ownership of their property. So they go do all the work., we take ownership of the property and we control the deed until they pay us off, but we will go in more detail of that on our next segment.

So with only $15,000 we lend to this person at 12% for **six months**. So the terms of this agreement is you pay me interest only. This is a six-month term with a clause that says you will pay me interest only for six months and on the seventh month I want my entire $15,000 back. So let's pay the numbers.

If I were to do $1500 X 12% = $1800 – that's $1800 passive that you earned in six months. Well if **I divide** $1800 **by six months, my passive income is** $300 **a month for those six months, plus I get my** $15,000 **back.**

Now let's go back and compare. The real estate investor went and borrowed $250,000 from the bank, and they got a renter in the house, what's the risk of that? They can beat up your property, you got to put more money into it, you got to do all those things. Let's say for an example, you got to do all those things to keep up the property, they have to pay you your rent, they have to pay you on time, or they can leave and leave you stuck with not only your mortgage, but the mortgage of the property.

189

So say for an example, with this house, this real estate investor, they're making $300 passive with $250,000 of debt on the line. I just showed you an example how just with $15,000 of your money – you can lend money to somebody at 12% with just a promissory note.

You can literally sit at your house with a cup of whiskey, you can sit at your house watching television and this $300 a month is going to come in passively every single month without taking a $250,000 risk like the real estate investor did.

And we wonder why the banks are actually making more money, living a much better quality of life, than people who are actually out there borrowing money from the bank and then doing whatever they got to do with the money to be able to pay them back. **Because guess what?** At the end of the day I made my $300 passive every month lending my money out to somebody and I got my $15,000 back on the seventh month.

Look at the numbers: if I were to do that for the entire year, $300 (a month) X 12 = $3600 – that is passive money I made lending money out without ever having to leave my house.

Now let me ask you a question:

> **Which side of the spectrum would you want to be?**

- ✓ **Do you want to be the producer, the entrepreneur or real estate investor that has to seize control of this property?**

- ✓ **Take 100% of the risks?**

- ✓ **Get in debt $250,000 only to make $300 passive from renting out that property?**

- ✓ **Or Would you rather be the person who literally just created a contract?**

You lent money to somebody off of a contract and makes $300 a month passive income every single month – just from lending money!

- ✓ **Which side of the spectrum do you want to be?**

- ✓ **Do you want to be the entrepreneur or do you want to be the bank?**

That's why I tell you I'm **MR. BE THE BANK** and I want to teach you in this course as you guys have been seeing this entire time, the whole spectrum is to get you to become the banker. And we wonder why the banks make so much money. Because they just do this process over and over again. Lending money, lending money, lending money............over and over and over again. Making what we made at work and doing the work, while never leaving the house. They have a black box full of promissory notes that they're getting passive income from just by lending their money out. When you change your perspective, you can change your bank account!

That's all for this segment and when we go into the next segment we will talk about actually securing assets with the promissory note putting you in a much better position than somebody borrowing money from you.

I will see you on the next lesson!

NOTES

_____

_____

_____

_____

_____

_____

_____

_____

Real Estate Developer vs Lending Company (Part 2)

Welcome back inside the course **PRIVATE BANKING BLUEPRINT** inside the **Business Edition** and in this course we are going to talk about the bank versus the real estate developer. Because remember I'm trying to get you to see that there is much more power to get you to be the banker than it is to be the producer, the entrepreneur or even the consumer. We've already kicked out that being the consumer is the actual worst position – the second position is the producer, which is the real estate developer, this is your entrepreneur, this is your business owner, and a lot of us as I have said, countless amounts of time, **we get stuck on the entrepreneur portion**.

So I'm going to show you the power of learning to become the banker, while leveraging and taking less risk than somebody who is actually a real estate developer. And what I 'm going to do to be fair – I'm going to use a real estate developer who has a multi-unit property – which is a four-unit property, versus you the bank lending money.

I want to show you that it doesn't take having millions of dollars and it doesn't take hundreds and thousands of dollars of risk to make the same passive income as someone who has a multi-unit property. And if you understood exactly how it works you could put yourself into position to being able to literally uproot and uplift your family to transitioning to becoming the banker.

So what we are going to do right now is draw a multi-unit property that has four units. So what most real estate investors tell you to do – they say get a multi-unit property, live in one unit, and rent out the other three. **Correct?** Isn't that that what people typically say? Let's examine the **Bank vs the Real Estate Developer:**

REAL ESTATE DEVELOPER

192

- $600,00 **Four Multi-Unit Home**
- 4.1% **Interest rate**
- $2,899 **Mortgage Payment**
- **Maintenance Fee** $301.97
- **Mortgage Insurance** $1000
- **Total Raw Monthly Cost** $4200.97

Live in one and rent out the other three. So what we are going to do, we are going to do exactly what real estate developers tell us to do. We found this multi four-unit property – let's say for $600,000 at a rate between 4.1% to 4.3% mortgage, lets 4.1% and we know your mortgage on this property for a multi-unit for $600,000 your monthly mortgage is going to be $2,899. Now don't forget we have to also include the maintenance rate. So at $2,899 X 1.25% maintenance rate divided by 12 (months) – we know that your maintenance costs on this property per month should be around $301.97

The maintenance fee is $2,899 + $301.97 = $3,200.97

And we know that when it comes to mortgage insurance if we were to do one mortgaged home – it's about $364 a month for your mortgage insurance.

We can come to the conclusion if we multiplied $364 times all four units that your costs for mortgage insurance will be pretty much up – so we will multiply $364 X 4 units, we know that the insurance will be anywhere from $800 to $1400 a month– we will just do the latter and say $1000 per month for mortgage insurance for this multi-unit real estate property.

$2,899 + $301.97 + $1000 = $4,200.97 (raw monthly costs for this four multi-unit property)

Let's just say that each one of these units had **2 BR / 2 BA** and you were able to rent each of the rooms for $1800. So you live in one and you rent the other three for $1800 each month for this property. Well we know our raw costs every month are expenses of $4200
We are going to multiply $1800 X 3 (units) that are paying rent.

Why only three Jake?

- ❖ Because you are living in one. This is what most real estate professionals teach you to do – live in one unit and rent out the other three. So I have $1800 a month on three units, which will equal $5400 that you make renting out the three other units.

193

So you made $5400 as you live in one and rent out the other three units on the property. So let's do the math:

$5400 (rent) - $4200.97 (for this property) which means your net income for renting out this multi-unit would be $1200.97

So you got a real estate developer with three units he or she is renting out and the mortgage is about $2,899 with maintenance fee of $301.97 and mortgage insurance is $1000 and your hard costs for this property are $4200

What are the risks? You have three big risks.

➢ You have three renters that you depend on to help you pay down this mortgage.

➢ This entire mortgage is now dependent upon you.

➢ Most people don't tell you that the average unit is being rented out and every year and a half every unit goes ninety days to six months of being vacant before it gets refilled and replaced.

Why? Because most landlords have a hard time and are not good at finding good people to come and stay inside their units and they usually wait until the last minute.

Yes this real estate developer is getting $1800 a unit but after the full cost of the actual property he's only netting about $300 a month on the property that they have.

Now let's become the banker and see how much money you can make if you lent money out.

BANK

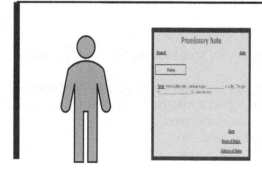

- $50,000
- **12%** on the $50,000
- Six-month term

- $6,000 passive over the six-month term

So let's say for an example, this is you, and you created a promissory note. You lent out $50,000 to a real estate developer. You charged this real estate developer because this real estate developer allowed you to latch on to an asset. Lets say you charge this real estate developer 12% on the $50,000 and you gave them a six-month term.
What's the six-month term? The six-month term says you are going to pay me my interest and all of my money back within six months.

194

So what's $50,000 X 12% = $6,000

That means you will make $6,000 passive over the six months just on interest alone. Well if they pay six months of interest – that is only $1000 a month that you make lending out $50,000 at 12% - and at the sixth or seventh month, they give you your entire $50,000 back, that's called short term lending. Let's say for an example you did that twice. You did this exact example above twice, well that means its full twelve months.

If I did $1000 a month times 12 months, that's $12,000 I made passive income lending money to a real estate developer versus taking all the responsibility of going to go get a property and then getting this property and then what? I rent out three units, I stay in one, and I only make $300 passive.

Now lets do **$300 a month times 12 = $3600** that year that you made in passive income from this three unit multi property versus $12,000 that you made in passive income never having to look after renters – never having to take the $600,000 risk, you literally lent $50,000 out on a promissory note to a real estate developer and you charged them 12% interest to lend the money to them – you did two terms of six months, and made $12,000 passive just by lending your money out!

Now let me ask you a question family – What side of the spectrum would you want to be?

- ❖ Do you want to be the real estate developer that took $600,000 of risk?
- ❖ You're in risk of these renters bailing on you and now you have got to take the hit of the $4200?

I'm just saying in a perfect world, everyone paid their rent for the entire year – you've made $300 passive on this property and this property made you $3600 that year versus taking $50,000 and lending the money out for the year and doing the same thing.

Ok Jake, I don't have $50,000. Ok, let's say you lend $20,000.

> $20,000 X 12% = $2400 – if you did a six-month term
> ($2400 / 6 = $400 passive you make on $20,000)

$400 a month lending $20,000 out to an entrepreneur or real estate developer at 12% -
You made $400 still which is a $100 difference than somebody borrowing money from the bank and renting out three units. You made more money passively lending out $20,000 at 12% to a real estate developer or entrepreneur to a $100 more money than somebody taking the entire risk.

Now over a **12 month period, $400 times 12 months is $4800**. The other person made $3600 – that's a $1200 difference and you made more money passively being the banker by taking less risk.

So when I tell you guys, and when I am teaching you guys, that it's important for you to understand the psychology of learning to become the banker – its very important!

Why? Because the banker always wins, the banker always makes the most money, the banker has the better quality of life, the banker has the biggest building, the nicest buildings, the best setup because they make money on both sides of the spectrum. You took less risk and made more money.

Why? You understood the importance of that passive income and you made your money work for you without having to get into debt. I'm not telling you not to get into real estate and I'm not telling you to buy properties. But what I am telling you is if the end goal is passive monthly income – there are much better ways for you to generate passive monthly income without having to take the majorty of the risks and putting yourself in debt to these banks that's going to make more money off of you than you think you are making off of them. I'm telling you guys right now, if you understand this game – your entire life wil be changed. And on the very next segment I am going to be showing you guys, exactly how to lock in an asset with seured lending that will put you in the position of being the person in power versus the one who is taking the majority of the risks. Which is why when you lend money you are actually putting yourself in a position play than somebody else.

See you on the next lesson!

NOTES

Secured Lending

Welcome back to the **PRIVATE BANKING BLUEPRINT Business Edition**, this is *Jake Tayler Jacobs, (MR BE THE BANK)* and as you guys can see I get so excited when we come to actually learning how to build out this banking system and learning how to become the lender. It's a mind switch and like I told you originally in the beginning of this course, and **Master Class** I showed you it's going to be extremely hard to transition your mind set to believe that you can become the banker. But I have always said, and you guys are going to hear me repeat this probably until I die, is the fact that I believe in the word of God. And the word of God told me that the wealthy will always rule over the poor and the borrower will always be slave to the lender. I think it is very crazy how in that same scripture and sentence he says the wealthy will always rule over the poor and the borrower will always be slave over the lender, giving me the perception and understanding to believe that the wealthy are the lenders. It also tells us in God's word, we will be lending to many nations and borrowing from none.

However how it comes to the psychology of building wealth, a lot of us think that the only way to amass wealth is to borrow and leverage debt in order to get there. My only point and my only notion that I am trying to prove to you is that is further from the truth and it's not an absolute fact. I'm just wanting to build up a nation of people who believe and want to stand on God's word that they too can be the lender and they can put themselves into positions where they can actually be able to create the passive income that they desire and need without having to leverage and use so much as a burden or as much debt or leverage or risks in order to accomplish those same goals. So I think its very important that you guys stay with me because in this business edition of **PRIVATE BANKING BLUEPRINT** – I want to be able to give you all of the tools needed and required of you to be able to put yourself into a position to become the lender and to stay away from being the borrower. I will show you guys with just small amounts of money that you can create tremendous passive income just by leveraging the money that you have. Which is why it's very important for you to live under your means so you can have more money at the end of the month to be able to utilize like the bank.

Why? Because the banks don't just allow your money to sit there. Matter of fact, plenty of banks put billions of dollars in insurance reserves, because that money is allowed to sit there but make money. But the point of it is that the banks move money faster than you can blink. As soon as you put that money in, that money is going out and being utilized – so we got to get used to doing the same thing when it comes to us, if not we will always be a slave to the very people who are lending us the money and we will never be put into the position of power to becoming the actual banker. When you look at the scope of life and you look at the scope of learning how to become and build wealth, you got to understand the Bible also says, do not despise small beginnings. Don't allow anybody to take you off your track in becoming the banker because you are not a millionaire or you don't make six figures yet. You don't build a house with big pieces at a time – you build a house one brick at a time and eventually you will have the exact house that you want. So if you want to become successful, you have to learn how to build that success with as little to no debt as possible which is why I'm teaching you how to become the lender because you can start one piece at a time, and be able to position yourself to move in a position of power so you can take advantage of the gift that God gave you. Which is the ability to re-utilize resources in a way that can grow the resources that God bestows upon you and use good stewardship and discernment to be able to do that without any risks.

So in this lesson that we are about to talk about right now, I'm going to show you how to become the lender and take as little risk as possible putting yourself into the powerplay.

198

So when it comes to lending money to entrepreneurs and real estate developers and even other people, remember there are two types of ways that you can lend money – **unsecured or secured.**

Unsecured is more built off of trust and in the banking world or the credit world, it's called the credit score, but when you're the lender, you can look at somebody's credit score if you choose or it can be somebody that you trust and you believe have good integrity and a good job but they are just in a tight spot. At the end of this business edition, you are going to see an actual interview with my father. While he was working, before he got sick and before he got laid off, he was making an additional **$2K - $3K** a month lending money to people at his job. What you have to understand when it comes to the unsecured route, it's a much riskier way for you to try to leverage and lend your money.

Why? Because the only thing that you are going on is the word of mouth, or bond and typically what happens to people who don't have high integrity or their word is not good, when it comes to you lending money to them you find yourself in the position that most people do when we lend money. You're hounding them – you're calling them and you feel like you're the collection agency, and their ducking and dodging you – not paying you back and that's the position that we want to stay away from. You want to put yourself in the equity or assets position so that you can get the bank for your buck! When people think about pawn shops, they think about they can go there and get money. But what you're failing to realize when you go there, they ask you are you selling your items or are you pawning? If you are selling that means you don't want to get it back, if you're pawning – that's the word they use to say you are just getting a loan because I'm going to come back and get this asset because I value it.

The pawn shop is nothing but a **smaller version of asset lending**. They take your electronics. They take your gaming systems. They take your TV's. They take your guns. They take all things you can quote on quote pawn that they see as an asset and lend you money at an interest rate and if you want the item back, you make payments back to it and that's how they are able to make money. So the pawn shop is nothing but a mere lending facility that you just didn't understand the value of it. When it comes to things of that nature we have to put our self into position to be able to make sure that it's a lending business – because that's what I'm teaching you, I want to put you in as much of the power positions as I can so that you can eliminate risks and put yourself in positions so that you can be able to make that passive income and also secure the income that you're lending. But the only way that we can do that is if we move with secured lending versus unsecured lending.

When it comes to secured lending, there are a few things that we want to do.

Warren Buffet says:

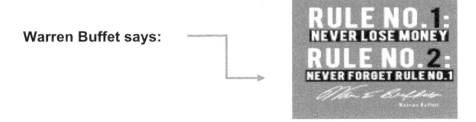

So that means we have to be extremely keen on looking and make sure we are eliminating our risks as we are a lending business. Why? Because you make money on lending. There are a few things you want to think about when you're doing secured lending.

199

Real Estate Investor   **SECURED**

How does it work? It's the same as we know, you have a person who has money and they want to lend that money to make passive income. How do they do that? They literally create a paper called a promissory note with words on it that typically have the dollar amount that this person promises to pay back. Well if there is someone that you don't really know or fully trust them, things of that nature, you got to make sure that they are someone that you are willing to invest in and it's no different than real estate. When you find someone to rent in your property, you just don't want to rent to anybody. You have to do some sort of verification, some sort of credibility check – something to let you know they are a good renter. That's the same with a lending business. You want to know that there is someone that is going to be good with their word, or that you can at least take on their asset.

So when it comes to a promissory note we want to do what? We want to make sure that we are eliminating risks as much as possible. So we want to do secured lending. So I've already shown you how being a lender you can make more passive income taking less risk than people in the real estate industry. And honestly a lot of people that are in other industries making passive income doing all the extra work that they don't have to do to make just the same amount of money passively. Because we already know that and you've been in my **PRIVATE BANKING BLUEPRINT Master Class** long enough to know that this is something that's possible.

Why? Because not only do I do it but - I literally saw my father do it for over a decade, which lead me to believe that this function actually works. So when it comes to the promissory note, there are a few things that you want to do on the promissory note.

This is typically the asset. You have the money that they owe you – and the asset that you are assuming control of. When you go to a bank they teach you how to use a **HELOC** (*Home Equity Line of Credit*) you use your home as an asset, where you are borrowing against your home, you're using your home as collateral, borrowing money from the bank. But what we don't know is that it is actually the more preferred route that lenders like to go because they want to lock up the asset that gives them more bang for their buck if anything. And typically what happens the banks and other institutions like to borrow or collateralize and lend money when there is an asset more than **150%** more than what they are allowing you to borrow.

So when it comes to lending – my rule of thumb, I only like to lend to high income earning working professionals. **Why?** Because they make enough money to pay me back.
Or I like to lend to people who are entrepreneurs, or real estate developers who need money, such as short-term sales, and I see a way for me to lock up their asset with this promissory note. **So what happens?** With this promissory note I have literally a piece of paper that I lend to real estate developers. This real estate developer is going to make money but they need money to do it.

Why? Because that's their whole notion, leveraging other people's money to lock up the deal. So in my promissory note, dealing with someone like a real estate developer, I would want to become the first lienholder or first lender or title lien or the first person that they owe, when it comes to the order of the house. **What do I mean by that?** Because as a secured promissory I want to lock up ownership of the house. **Why is that?** When people say I borrow money from the bank or I used or mortgaged money from the bank, so that they can buy my house, but I own the house. That's not true. The person who paid for the house, owns the house. So as the lender I want to put myself into position to where I am controlling the asset. So what the real estate developer would do – they will come to me with the deal and say, "Hey Jake, or hey Susan, or Hey Ben, Hey Kim, or whomever you are – I have a house, that I want to do a fix and flip, or I have a house that I am trying to get.

Now what I want to do with this home Jake, it is a house that I am getting undervalued. The house is selling for **$40,000** because the mom died or this is a property that they don't want and I know that if I buy it for **$40,000** – they don't know the real value of the home and they're trying to sell it quick and trying to get rid of it. If I buy it for **$40,000** I know, based on equity in the home, based on the neighborhood, that this **$40,000** home is actually worth **$80,000**. I know that this is home I worth **$80,000** and because they need access to this money fast, they're trying to sell the house fast or something happened where it was an emergency. They're doing what's called a **fire sale**. In a fire sale, they're trying to get rid of the property as soon as possible.

The real estate developer says, "Hey Jake I want to borrow **$40,000** from you. I (or you) may say ok, what are you lending the money for. They say I have a property and I can buy it for **$40,000** and I am going to borrow **$40,000** from you because I am going to immediately put it up for **$80,000** because they don't know the true value of the house – because they don't know the actual true value of the house which is actually **$80,000**. Which means that this house has equity value of **$40,000**. How is it equity value of **$40,000**? Because they are selling it for **$40,000** but the market will buy it for **$80,000** which means there is **$40,000** of equity inside of this property.

So I say ok, I'm going to lend you **$40,000** at a **12%** interest rate. And I am going to lend it to you for three months. The person will say – "Ok Jake, I got three months because it is a **short sale,** so I am going to borrow from you and flip it in 90 days. And I will respond, "OK this is a three-month lease or a three-month note that I am putting on the house, so I'm going to agree to give them **$40,000** and he is going to agree to **12%** plus the three months.

Now watch this family: $40,000 X 12% = $4800

So in interest, I have already made **$4800** lending money to this person and the agreement that I give them, I say you're going to pay me interest only for three months, and on the third month, the property needs to be sold or I am going to call the note, and I will foreclose the property. So three months of **$4800** is **$1600** a month. They are going to pay you **$1600** a month passive! A lot of people may say, "Jake, **$1600** a month passive just lending money to somebody?" "**YES!**"

This is why I tell you that you don't need to borrow money from the bank to get into real estate to make strong passive income. You can become the lending source to these real estate developers until you have accumulated enough income to be able to get into real estate without

201

having to utilize the bank's money in order to do it. This is why I teach you the power in becoming the lender.

Now there are a couple of things that I just did.

I lent this person **$40,000** but because I am the first lienholder and I bought the property, when the property is done, I'm not going to give the **$40,000** directly to them, we're going to use a title company, because when you use a title company you have everything on the books twice. Not only do we have a promissory note, but the title company has a book of records. The title company will make sure that you as the lienholder – **will get paid first!**

My next step is to send the **$40,000** to the title company and the real estate developer is going to get the money from the title company that I paid to him or her. Now, the real estate developer is going to leave the title company and they are going to do a video blog, or brag on how they got the funds using somebody else's money to purchase this property and make money on the property. They are very excited about doing that but watch what I just did:

The only thing I did was had the money, created a contract, went through a title company and that's all the work I've done. And by doing that, the real estate developer just put into my possession a house worth, **$80,000** and I only lent them **$40,000** – so not only am I getting passive income of **$1600** a month, plus I am going to get my entire **$40,000** when they sell the home, I am also collateralized and I have a secured asset – a home and property that I never had to do the work on.

So why is this important? Because if this person doesn't sell the property, and I call the note and they cannot pay me back, I can foreclose the home and can seize full control of the home – **Why?** Because I own the deed! **And why do I own the deed?** Because I am the first lienholder. I get paid first. I can foreclose the property, can completely kick them out if they don't pay me up. I made **$1600** a month for however long I could. Say I made **$1600** a month for three months, and I made my **$4800** and they bailed on the deal or they couldn't sell the deal and got out because real estate people say if it's on your credit you can just do that or do another LLC and we got some crooks like that. They bailed on the property.

So not only did I make **$1600** passive, I now own a property out right and I can sell this secured asset to some other person. Let's say at **$60,000** and I not only made **$4800** in passive interest I made on lending the money, I have also made **$20,000** – why is that? Because I lent **$40,000** out and I sold the home that I didn't want for **$60,000**, which meant I made **$20,000** positive from lending money and not doing the work. This is something that banks do time, and time and time again. Which is why they keep lending money to overzealous real estate developers. Why? Because they're looking and analyzing how much liquidity and assets can they lock up to secure their money.

What did I just do? I lent out **$40,000** and the house is only worth $80,000. That's **100** times the value of the money I lent, which means I can have **100% gain** if I sold it for $80,000 – I can get **100%** gain on my money which is the full **$40,000** back of positive profitability plus the **$4800** I made in interest payments being paid to me. And this is why I say the banks always win. And this is why you want to use secured assets.

202

For example, cars, if someone has a paid off a car, you can use the car as an asset. You can lend them money, they don't pay it, you got the title for the car, and you go and seize ownership of the car, and then you can use the car to leverage the loss of getting you back to what you lent to them. You can use other assets like the pawn shops do. This is just a way for you to learn how to secure. So when I'm looking at deals or I'm looking at lending money – the very first thing that I'm looking at is what can I do to eliminate as much risk as possible?

How can I put myself in a win win situation? I can do that by dealing with overzealous real estate developers and I have a promissory note that locks in that contract and then on top of that I can foreclose the home if they do not uphold their part of the deal, and I get the passive income by lending the money to them the entire way. Say for instance, they sold the home and did exactly what they said they were going to do and they paid me my **$40,000** back and say I only made **$4800** on the deal, that was for three months. If I did that four times throughout the year (every three months), **$4800 X 4 = $19,200**

That's **$19,200** passively using the same **$40,000** over and over again, every three months lending to real estate developers. You can make **$19,200** passive. The only thing you have to do is pay capital gains tax on the money because you are lending the money and what they pay you back is your principal money. You just pay the interest on the interest that you actually gained. That is exactly how you secure the assets and you can utilize this. This is how you can lock up people's businesses, you can lock up equity in their home. You can lock up all these things that they go to the bank to collateralize – you can collateralize the same very things. You can collateralize the cash value inside their insurance policies, anything that has an asset that can bring you control to eliminate your risks, you have the ability to generate passive income eliminating risks. But if I were to compare that to a real estate developer, which is taking all this passive income but encompassing so much risk. They are encompassing the risk of the money borrowed. They are encompassing risk of somebody bailing on them, the renter, they are encompassing so much risk but by putting yourself in the bankers position you are allowing yourself to really take advantage of the fact that you can create passive wealth income for the majority of your life. If you did that for ten years, **$19,200 X 10 = $192,000** that you can make literally working a job while lending money to people while you keep the roof over your head.

Because being a banker is a lot sexier and I like my hands clean and I don't like to do the dirty work. I would love to lend to people that actually got it and so what I say to you is that when you start a lending business, you can become the lending source for your family. You can become the lending source for your own business. If you think in terms of that, think about how much money we pay the bank in interest? If you had a family banking system, like we teach you in **PRIVATE BANKING BLUEPRINT Master Class**, with that family banking system, you can literally lock up all that interest that you would be paying somebody else's family bank, and you could actually put that in your own banking system. Therefore creating generational wealth that will allow for your family and your kids, kids to be able to participate in this thing that we call wealth transfer.

Become the banker because when you do, your life will change. Let me tell you this is just getting good, we got more in the course after this segment.

I will see you on the next lesson.

NOTES

Lending with your Insurance Reserve

Hey Family, this is when it gets fun. I think its very important that we understand and that we feel that we actually can become the banker. But it gets really fun when you actually indoctrinate your insurance reserve inside this lending practice of becoming the banker, because you are just double anchoring down and you're doubling down on the security of you lending. And on your lending practice of you becoming a private lender, the best part about using this is because typically when you use a savings account or you use your safe or wherever you put your money – you're liquidating that account to lend that money out with the risk of possibility what? Taking on a loss and potentially using your money no matter if you have leveraged assets or not. Because in most and some cases you will take losses – that's the business.

But when you're doubling down on security and you want to put yourselves in position that's a win, win, as much as possible leaving out risk like almost minuscule. So when we use the insurance reserve, there a couple of things that we have to look at. The first part of the insurance reserve is what we all know. We all know that guaranteed inside this reserve, we get a guaranteed 4% inside this reserve any day plus we get to participate in the profitability of the company and get dividends of 2% to 4% every year.

LENDING WITH INSURANCE RESERVE

Promissory Note

Lender

Borrower

Borrows $20K @ 12%
Six Month Term

- **Insurance Reserve**
- 4%
- 2% to 4% **Dividends – every year**
- **sliding scale of** 4% to 8%
- $20,000

Assets

DIRECT DEPOSIT

- $20,000 from Ins Reserve
$20,000 still in bank making interest

Which means we have a sliding scale as much going into this reserve that our money is going to make 4% to 8% anyway no matter what regarding the economy, regarding the system no matter what it is. This is why banks actually house their money inside of insurance reserves,

205

because while that money is sitting and it's not being lent out anywhere and not being grown by lending, they go sit the money inside the insurance reserve.

Which is why we showed you in the very first **Master Class** how banks are literally making drones and drones of money that they are putting in insurance reserves because that is the best place they can actually house and sit your money. So let's say you have $20,000 in your insurance reserve. In a typical function, we know for a fact, that the strategies that I showed you – using the money, lending the money and leveraging the money out and we have the promissory note to lock up assets and then also to be able to get a legally binding contract between you and the borrower so that you can be able to confiscate and get back what is owed to you if something bad were to happen.

So what we are doing right here, the borrower is coming to you and I told you that typically I like to lend money out – my father lent money out. My father did more unsecured and I've done unsecured but I like secured lending – things I know I can at least get my money back for. Some type of trade in, some type of asset that I can hold and potentially get my money back if you decide to bail on me, I at least want to be able to make that.

Now lets look at the borrower, they are going to tell me what they are bringing to the table, they're going to tell me the asset that I am going to be able to collateralize. An asset can be a home, a car, it can be anything that has liquidity that you can sell fairly easy to be able to at least recoup the losses. The point of locking in assets is to be able to recoup your losses. It is really just a waste of time but you are trying to secure your leveraging to make sure that you're protected on the back end. The beautiful thing about using the insurance reserve is, remember when we borrow money against our policy, we're not actually using the money.

Let's say for an example this person needed $20,000 and not only do we lock in the asset they have, for an example - a house or a car – we lock up the assets. Not only is that in the contract but with the car we go through a title company and as well as with the home. They both work because you want a middle person keeping account of the record and I would pay a title company to help me manage this versus me doing it on my own. Unless you just feel confident with the person that you're going through and that's just an agreement that you both have and you have to make that decision for yourself.

** See Illustration on previous page:

Let's say for an example this person is going to borrow $20,000 and then sign their name to the contract and upon signing their name, we go to a title company or you give them the money directly, when you collect the promissory note. My father used to go by the asset used which was your name. So what happens here, is that when using insurance reserve, we know that in insurance even if I borrow money on my policy, I may not be able to get access to that money, but that money is still there making interest.

So what do I do? In this agreement they agreed that I could charge them 12% and of course you create the terms, it could be three months, six months, nine months, or twelve months. You create the terms. But in this case we do a six-month term. They pay us not only the interest but they pay on the principal every month. Here is how we come up with that:

$20,000 X 12% = $2400 (this is the interest that they owe you). So if you add $2400 (interest) to $20,000 to add the principal plus the interest payments, you can do that or you can go to an amortization schedule or use a calculator to quickly add up those numbers to see what is the monthly payment you should receive.

We are currently trying to add that function or tool so it can be quickly be an available resource for you. But you can put in **Google** *(amortization calculator)* and input the numbers and it will tell you exactly how much someone will pay you over the term period that you have. So this term / contract is for six months and we are going to do: $2400 + $20,000 = $22,400 (that they will have to pay) – we want them to pay that over six months, so $22,400 / 6 = $3,733 a month – so you lent money out and now you're making a passive income. They agree to the terms and sign their name.

Now let's get you the money. So we go and borrow the money from our insurance policies. Remember when we borrow the $20,000 from our insurance reserve, we are actually at $20,000 still.

**Please note that if this is something that your mind is kind of lost on, you need to go back and review the previous courses and classes so that you can get refreshed on how this works.

So this $20,000 is still making interest, we just lose access to the $20,000 until the $20,000 is paid back. **Does that make sense?** When it comes to the $20,000 that we borrowed, they send us the money to our direct deposit, and then we send the money to the borrower.

**See pictured Illustration on previous page.

So I lent $20,000 out and I am making 12% but on my $20,000 I am still making 4% to 8% even while I lent out $20,000. We went from making guaranteed 4% to 8% to adding 12% - which is now 16% to 20% annual on that same $20,000 by leveraging your insurance reserve. By doing this is what you have to see is that this $20,000 when it gets paid back, then you can have access to the $20,000 plus the interest that you earned along the way.

So, the question is, Ok, Jake, remember the insurance company charged me 5% to utilize the money? $20,000 X 5% = $1,000

So the insurance company is going to charge 5% against your policy, which will be only $1,000 that you will have to pay the insurance company in interest to get back full access of your $20,000. So you will only have to pay back $21,000.

In doing that:

- ✓ you borrowed $20,000 to collateralize against your reserve
- ✓ the money is still making money inside of there so you are still getting your 4% to 8% on your $20,000 over the six-month term
- ✓ you literally lent out $20,000 to make a difference on the money over the six months - which is going to be $2400 in interest that you made on money that was already sitting there already making money, you just collateralized against it.

We know that at the end of six months you made **$2400** of interest, which is **$2400** plus the **$20,000** that you lent them, you made **$22,400**.

So we do **$22,400** is what you made on lending and you paid this back to the insurance carrier because they allowed you to leverage your money. But what you are going to realize is that you are going to have a positive profit of **$1,400** on top of gaining full access back to the **$20,000** plus the interest that you're going to gain on the **4% to 8%**.

So if we did this for the entire year, twice a for a six-month period, we would have an additional **$2800** on top of let's say **6% of $20,000** for the year, on top of the **6%** that you gained in your policy. That means for the year you made **$4,000** in profit utilizing the same money over and over again eliminating the risks. So if they bail on you and don't pay you back, you know that you are still making money. You just got to recoup what you lost and continue to work and utilize like that. And that's just the basic function of using your insurance reserve to lend money and taking a risk while getting your same interest that you're getting on the money.

So let's see how much interest we actually gained this year on the **$20,000** was a whopping **20%** gain on your money by leveraging your insurance reserve to lend the money out and then you lent the money out and made interest and you made **6%** that year on your insurance reserve.

You take the **$4,000** and divide it by the **$20,000** that you actually used, which will give you **.02** And multiply that times **100** and that's **20%** that you actually gained.

$$\$4,000 / \$20,000 = .02 \quad \text{........} \quad .02 \times 100 = 20\%$$

What do they say the average **stock market** gives you? **10%**

They say the average **real estate** gives you **8% to 15%** - so by you lending your money – you not only beating the stock market, and the real estate market by becoming the lender and taking as less risk as possible utilizing your insurance reserve. If you understand how that functions, you can put yourself in a lot better position.

So what's going to happen in the latest segments, we're going to go over terminology and go over things that you need to know when it comes to the private lending business. Such as setting up your LLC and understanding some of the rules to lending and other things like that. This way you are able to have a legitimate lending business because as you can see there is plenty of money that you can make lending money to put yourself in better situations.

The shorter the terms, the more the return and the more you can actually flip that money and you would have seen a lot better return, so if there are some things that are kind of hazy, review this segment over and over again until you can understand this concept because we got a lot more to go.

I will see you on the next lesson.

NOTES

Unsecured Promissory Notes

Hey Family! This is *Jake Tayler Jacobs, MR BE THE BANK*, and welcome back into the **PRIVATE BANKING BLUEPRINT Business Edition** side. I know that we've been giving you some good sauce inside of this **Master Class**. We've talked about lending and other things, but during this segment, I will be going over with you actually the difference between secured and unsecured loans, and hard money lending versus private money lending, so that you can have an idea of kind of which route that you want to go when it comes to lending. You don't have to complicate it, you literally can just take what I've taught you in this course and you can literally just use your extra money by lending it out to friends, family, or business professionals that you trust by locking up assets and other things that can actually give you more comfort with the lending, and then being able to process that the exact same way.

As my father has done this time and time again, and we will get him on one of our segments for an interview before the end of the **Master Class** so that you can see a real life average normal person who was making from **$2K to $3K** additional revenue stream every single month just lending money to his coworkers. He not only lent money to people he trusted but he had a family and had something to lose. You never want to lend to somebody that doesn't have anything to lose. Like a single person that can literally disappear on the side of the plan, that lives in an apartment complex and they can just literally disappear and go into another complex. You want to lend to people who have more things to lose, whether its assets or their family.

I don't mean that you are going to heist their families but, what I'm saying is you have less risk than somebody whose a parent that goes to work every single day and you see them regularly and they cannot miss you, they have children, you know when and the time they get paid, and that's what my father did. He lent money to people when he knew their schedule, and usually his entire customer base was with his coworkers, the people he was working with every single day. So these are ways for you to be able to do it with - typically single mothers, and single fathers that are trying to make ends meet and get a hold of their finances.

My dad kind of did a very cool thing where he didn't allow people to stay on his lending program, which meant he would literally place them in a system where they would start to live within their means, and they stopped needing the lending services; because they were able to get their finances in order. I thought that was cool of my dad to be teaching these single mothers and fathers how to live a much more frugal financial life, and he didn't allow them to use him as a crutch like Ace Cash Express or like these hard money lenders. As he helped those he wanted to help groom of course he had to make money but my daddy also has a heart. So If you borrowed **$1000** from him, lets say regularly, he will let you know that you have three chances to borrow this max amount, and after that you only have access to borrow $500 no matter if it was paid it back or not. He did not want his customers to become addicted because he knew how that would make them feel.

He actually created another service for people who did not trust having their money with them. So what he did was hold their money for them and literally hold it for two or three weeks, and for some four weeks. He literally became like a little private bank and he used to lend the money at a higher interest rate with unsecured at **25%**, and then he would give them like **4%** on the money that he earned because he was using their money in order to leverage it.

An absolute genius!

I wish somebody would have sat my father down and showed him that it could be a legitimate business. My dad just thought there were more loopholes to jump through to start a private lending business and he did not want the government all in his business. In actuality, all you need to start a private lending business is a sole proprietorship, a free EIN, a DBA, and literally start lending that way. As a lender, you will only get charged taxes on your reported gains when it comes to that.

When it comes to lending – what we have to understand is that there are different types of promissory notes. You have your unsecured and your secured promissory notes and we are going to discuss both of them within this master class.

Let's talk about a promissory note:

- A promissory note is a legal document that obligates the person who signs it to pay a certain amount of money to another person and sets forth the terms of payment. The person who owes the money is called the payor, maker, issuer, or promissor. The person who is owed the money is called the payee, promissee, or noteholder. A promissory note is sometimes called a note payable, or simply a note.

When it comes to the legalities or the terms, you just want to know these things. So if someone owes you money, and you are the person that lent it out, you are the payor, the maker, the issuer, or the promissor. **Why do you need to know this?** In case you have to go to court, you have to go seize property. You want to use legal words so you can assume the authority of utilizing this promissory note:

- The lender (you) are the payee because they paid you

    - The promissee because they promised to pay you

        - The noteholder which means you hold the note

So it's no different than when the bank holds your mortgage note or when the bank holds your title to your car as, these are notes that are held in that regard. And these examples are just to make it simple so you can have a better understanding.

Unsecured VS Secured

- An unsecured promissory note can be used to raise capital to start or expand your business. You also can use a promissory note when you borrow money. Alternatively, if you are the holder of the promissory note, you may be able to raise money by selling it.

The unsecured note has no asset attachment. To be unsecured means all you have to go on is that person's word, credibility, and that person's integrity. You don't have anything of asset to be able to collateralize against them being able to borrow money from you.

- If payment of the promissory note is guaranteed by property called collateral, it is a secured promissory note. If the payor fails to pay, the noteholder can take the collateral as payment for the debt. Collateral can be real estate secured by a mortgage, or personal property secured as a

211

security agreement. If no collateral secures payment, the promissory note is called an unsecured promissory note.

Borrowing with an Unsecured Promissory Note

- An unsecured promissory note can be used in connection with borrowing money for your business from a commercial lender, or from friends and family members. If you borrow from a friend or family member, memorializing the loan with an unsecured promissory note gives them some assurance of repayment of the loan, avoids misunderstanding by clearly setting forth the terms for the repayment, and gives them proof of the debt in case they later need to file a claim against your estate.

- There are various ways to structure repayment. Especially for a relatively small loan, you might use a note that is to be paid back in full, with one payment in a short period of time. Such as an unsecured promissory note lump sum payment can be with or without interest. Either a long-term or short-term promissory note also can be repaid in periodic installments, typically with monthly payments.

That simply means that you have the ability to determine the terms of the agreement.

Selling an Unsecured Promissory Note

- If you are the holder of a promissory note, you may be able to sell the note. However, you will be selling the note for less than the face value. Generally the buyer will discount the note by **10 to 35** percent. For example, if the amount under the promissory note is **$10,000**, and the buyer discounts the note **$2500** – you will receive **$7500**.

- The discount may vary from buyer to buyer, and will take into consideration factors as the note's being unsecured, the amount of the note, the interest rate of the note, and especially the credit rating of the note's promissor. Selling an unsecured promissory note will result in a greater discount than if it were a secured note.

How to Collect on an Unsecured Promissory Note

- If the borrower fails to pay as required by the terms of the promissory note, the first step is to send the borrower a letter giving notice of the default, giving a deadline of the payment, and giving notice that further collection efforts will be pursued if payment is not made.

- If the default continues, the noteholder has two options: Obtain the services of the debt collector, or file suit against the borrower. The Federal Fair Debt Collection Practices Act is a complex set of laws governing debt collection and has significant penalties for violations. Therefore, using the services of a knowledgeable debt collection agency are recommended.

Debt Collection Agencies

- Some debt collection agencies will buy the note that is in default for a discount. This will be a much greater discount than if the note were in default. The agency then keeps whatever it ends up collecting from the borrower. Other agencies will keep a percentage of what they collect and forward the balance to you.

If the promissory note that someone is paying you is not in default which means they are paying you and they haven't missed the debt, you just want out of the deal – then the discount is not going to be no more than 25% typically.

However, if they have defaulted and have not paid you and you are just trying to salvage and get whatever out of the deal that you can, typically when you sell that debt to a collection's agency – you will sell the debt for like 50% to 60% off for what they owe you. The collection agency has to do a lot of work to get that debt back active.

That is something to really think about if you are going to bring the debt collections agency to the table. And that is the unsecured game and if you understand the game, then you know how to play. Just like everything in life, when it comes to building a successful business, some things take time.

- Like my dad always tells me, **"Son if you want to get into lending, it will take about a month to find a trustworthy person that you want to lend to and then six to twelve months for you to become active with consistent customers that are coming in, lending money to you."**

No different than any other business and every business has risks. And this, when it comes to unsecured, your risk is somebody just bailing on you and then you have to sell that debt for pennies on the dollar just to salvage that.

That's the risk of lending money! You have the risk of someone not paying you back. Its just like renting – if you had real estate, the risk of somebody dipping on you and you are responsible for the note. The difference between lending and getting into real estate, most people who lend, the only thing that you lose is some of your capital. But you are not in debt $250K to $300K with the banks in order to do it.

I tell people all the time, if you want to get into real estate, you either build a business, and generate extra income and then start lending to make money on that money and then use the money from your business and your lending business to get into real estate or you can do **wholesaling** – which means you can get into real estate without having to use capital. And then you connect the seller to a buyer or someone who is trying to sell quick to a person who is trying to buy an undervalue asset. You set up a contract as the middle man – you collect ownership as authority of that property, you sell your authority to somebody else and you get paid the difference, and you are making money **wholesaling** in that aspect.

You can put yourself in that position to do that, but guess what family, you have to be ready and understand the risks that come along with it, but also the rewards. My dad had more rewards than lost accounts. **Why?** He told me that about 90% of the people that he lent money – actually paid him back. Out of those people, 10% did not pay him back and one of the people was someone that I sent him, I vouched for the young lady and she bailed on him and I ended up paying him the difference of what she owed.

Family, this concludes our segment on Unsecured Notes. This is **Jake Tayler Jacobs,** *MR BE THE BANK*, I will see you on the next lesson!

NOTES

Secured Promissory Note (How to Guide)

Hey what's going on family? This is *Jake Tayler Jacobs*, welcome back to the Business Edition of PRIVATE BANKING BLUEPRINT Master Class and this is *Mr.BE THE BANK,* and we are in another segment where we will be talking about the actual secured promissory note and locking in those contracts. I know these couple of lessons or segments are not as exciting, but the truth is these are the most important. If you do not lock in these contracts with these promissory notes of these people that owe you – you know what will happen? They will bail on you and then you are going to be really mad. Because you are going to be like, "Man this sucks! I wanted to do this without the promissory note."

The promissory note is what helps with binding that contract and making it legal for you to come after somebody in court. So I think its very important that we understand the value of these quote on quote promissory notes and I want for you to understand that even though these segments are not as illustrious or charismatic, or drawn out with a piece of paper, review this section over and over again until you get it.

So in this segment we will be talking about the secured promissory note and the **"How To Guidelines."**

We got to understand that there are plenty of opportunities out there.

> # PLENTY OF OPPORTUNITY
>
> - Successful businesses are built on big ideas and long-range goals, but without sufficient capital, many believe that those dreams may never be realized. Limited start-up funds can stop a company in its tracks: business owners often underestimate the amount of money they will need to keep their organization running, and close their doors before they've had a chance to get a market foothold. Many owners also expect their companies to turn a profit on Day 1, failing to consider expenses, competition, and the time it takes to build a customer

Because you have a lot of entrepreneurs that are not as vested in learning processes first and they just jump into entrepreneurship and they don't tip toe into it. You're going to have a lot of people who need funding from lenders and need funding from banks and things of that nature,

215

typically to be able to bridge the gap for them not taking into account all the other things that happen wrong in business, which means you will always be the lender, especially if you are dealing with professional career people, especially dealing with entrepreneurs and being able to tie in those things.

So what you got to understand is, you can be the person that stands in the gap.

My dad used to always say, "Son, I'm the gap man. I'm the person that stands in that gap. I'm the person who people lean on or they go to when they need something the most."

And he took it seriously and the biggest reason why he took it seriously was because he understood the gravity that came with standing in the gap from somebody's paycheck to the very next paycheck and you got bills in between and things that are happening if you are living from paycheck to paycheck. And most entrepreneurs are living paycheck to paycheck, deal to deal and they need credit to keep them alive during those deals.

YOU CAN STAND IN THE GAP.

- Whatever the reasons, individuals and companies often turn to borrowing money to keep their businesses afloat. They can turn either to large financial institutions or to friends, colleagues, and relatives for support. Our private banking strategies are extremely useful for those companies looking to borrow money from less formal sources, since commercial lenders may be reluctant to loan money to businesses without defined income streams and, moreover, will usually require businesses to use their standardized forms.

So typically when it comes to borrowing money from these institutions – it takes a lot longer than borrowing money from you or from me. So if somebody comes to me with a great deal and I see the value of it – I'm looking at their income statement and I'm looking at their finances and I'm able to determine that they are somebody that's extremely beneficial or somebody that is extremely successful, they're just feeling gap space or whatever the case may be and I see that my risk isn't that big. They will turn to private lenders because they need that money fast! They need the money quick! They can't wait three months. They got a deal, they're trying to hit the deal, they need the money and they are trying to take advantage of the opportunity! And you're the person who can get them that money within the week.

So they are going to come to you, but you got to understand that you always have the opportunity to truly stand in the gap. So what we have to understand when it comes to standing in the gap and when it comes to the secured promissory note, its not like the unsecured. Remember the unsecured is based on word, secured is based on tying up assets.

216

TYING UP THOSE ASSETS...

- Borrowers who agree to sign secured notes may find loans more readily available to them. Lenders know that if a default occurs, they can sell the property used as collateral under the secured note. This protection may, in turn, make a borrower more comfortable with the loan arrangement. Nobody wants to default on a loan or force others to absorb losses on their behalf. With a secured note, you can be sure you're not leaving lenders – who may be colleagues or other individuals close to you – out in the cold.

When it comes to secured notes and secured loans – I'm a lot more readily available to lend somebody money if I can tie up an asset I mean you can get me quick. If you got an asset and I know I can get at least my money back for the deal, or I can at least become a little bit positive out of the deal – I would definitely sign a contract with you. And not only that – I need to also make sure the effort it will take to get that asset off of you. I got to take that into account too. Those are things you got to kind take into account on a regular basis.

- • • • • • •

- This training will contains everything you'll need to customize and complete your secured promissory note. A written note can minimize confusion, misunderstanding, and error, and clearly set forth the parties' expectations and fulfillment obligations. In every way, this promotes a successful and profitable business arrangement.

So if you don't have promissory notes in place you will fall on your face, because now it's he said, she said. Listen family, I don't borrow money from the bank, but I do borrow money from my father. When I got into a little spoof in the business I borrowed $4,000 from my father and he charged me 25 cents on the dollar, which means he charged me 25% to borrow money from him, and I did it.

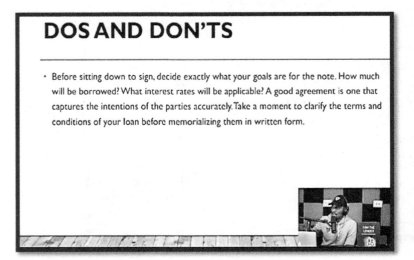

This is going to be the start of the **Do's and Don'ts** segment and we're actually going to pause right here because we are going to start another segment and we want to make these concise so that you can understand. So I am actually going to go back to **Tying Up Those Assets** because it is very important that you understand to make sure that those assets are easily accessible.

So I either take ownership of them now, or I get the title from them now or I invest in trackers I can put on a car, so I can know exactly where the car is. These are things you have to think of when you go into it. So starting off your lending business with people that you care about and they care about you and they have this respect factor. I would start with people that are closer to you versus people that you don't know. My father he made a great business on warm market lending – which meant he never dealt with anybody he did not know. So if he didn't know you for more than six months, you could not borrow money from him because he did not know who you were, he did not know what you stood for. So it's very important that you understand the moral and the integrity of these people that you're lending money to, because guess what? Your capital is at risk.

The beauty of it is that if you're using insurance reserves to lend money to people – you have the protection of your money still gaining money even during a loss so you have time to make up for that capital loss and still have money inside of your reserve, and that's the best part to using your insurance reserves to leverage money. So if somebody literally burns you and you have to make up the costs, as you're saving money to make up that cost, your initial principal is still making money whether you paid it back tomorrow or three years from now. Your principal amount in your insurance reserve is still getting 4% to 8% no matter what. So I think that's very important to understand and I think that if you understand how much safer it is for you to actually put yourself in a great position.

I will see you on the next lesson!

NOTES

Do's and Don'ts

Now family let's talk about the **Do's and the Don'ts** as it pertains to lending and finding people that you want to lend to. As we went over before:

- **Before sitting down to sign, decide exactly what your goals are for the note.**
- **How much will be borrowed?**
- **What interest rates will be applicable?**

A good agreement is one that captures the intentions of both parties accurately. Take a moment to clarify the terms and conditions of your loan before memorializing them in written form. You have to decide what is a best agreement between the two of you. I know that sounds rudimentary and I know that it sounds simple and fundamental but this is something people often forget. You have to sit down and figure out the goals of what this person is trying to accomplish. This is why banks make people bring their business plan. Because they want to understand what's going on so it's very important that you understand that.

- Allow each party to spend some time reviewing the promissory note. This will reduce the likelihood, or at least the efficacy of claims that a party did not understand any terms or know what their obligations were under the document.

So when I give them the terms and agreement, allow them time because you do not want them to be like, **"I did not know this or I did not know that."** Tell them that they need to look at it in full and you have it signed in the contract saying they have read it in full. So you want to let them know to take their time, allow 24 to 48 hours to read over this contract. Advise them to read it thoroughly so they understand the agreements on both sides.

- Both parties should review the note carefully to ensure that all relevant deal points have been included. Do not assume that certain expectations or terms are agreed to if they are not stated expressly in the document.

So you as the lender, sometimes you can just be moving fast trying to make quick money, trying to get that money moving – that you don't ensure all relevant deal points have been included. You want to make sure that you **highlight** how you are going to collect the debt if they don't pay. You want to make sure that you **highlight** the stuff they need to know and the things you are not playing about! These things are important and do not assume that certain expectations or terms are agreed to if they are not stated expressively in the document. So you cannot have a promissory note that doesn't have anything specifically stated in the document and assume that they are going to do it.

Basically, you can't have a promissory note that you want them to pay you *interest only* for the first four months; and then the last two months you want them to pay you interest and principal in full.

You can't expect them to know that if it's not *fully written down* in the promissory note.

The following form is a secured promissory note. This means that the lender takes a secured interest in the borrower's property. If the borrower defaults on the loan, the lender can seize that property almost immediately. By contrast, with an unsecured note, the lender would have to go to court to demand payment if a default occurred.

Secured Promissory Note (Fully Amortized)

0.00

04/15/2020
Dallas, Texas

On or before 08/12/2020, for value received, the undersigned TEST (the "Borrower") promises to pay to the order of TEST COMPANY (the "Holder"), in the manner and at the place provided below, the
principal sum of $0.00.

1. PAYMENT.

All payments of principal and interest under this note will be made in lawful money of the United States,
without offset, deduction, or counterclaim, by wire transfer of immediately available funds to an account designated by the Holder in writing at least 14 days after the effective date of this note or, if this designation is not made, by check mailed to the Holder at 555 Test Drive, Dallas, Texas, 55555, or at
such other place as the Holder may designate in writing.

2. MONTHLY INSTALLMENT PAYMENTS.

Principal and interest will be payable in 35 consecutive monthly installments of $1,000.00, beginning on
or before 04/17/2020 and continuing on the 15 day of each month, until the principal and interest have
been paid in full. Each payment will be credited first to interest and then to principal, and interest will
cease to accrue on any principal paid. Acceptance by the Holder of any payment differing from the
designated installment payment listed above does not relieve the Borrower of the obligation to honor the requirements of this note.

3. INTEREST.

Interest on the unpaid principal balance of this note is payable from the date of this note until this note is paid in full, at the rate of 12% per year, or the maximum amount allowed by applicable law, whichever is less. Accrued interest will be computed on the basis of a 365-day or 366-day year, as the case may be, based on the actual number of days elapsed in the period in which it accrues.

4. PREPAYMENT.

The Borrower may prepay this note, in whole or in part, at any time before maturity without penalty or
premium. Any partial prepayment will be credited first to accrued interest, then to principal. No
prepayment extends or postpones the maturity date of this note.

5. SECURITY FOR PAYMENT.

This note is secured by certain assets of the Borrower in accordance with a separate security agreement
dated 04/15/2020 between the Holder and the Borrower (the "Security Agreement"). If an Event of Default (defined below) occurs, the Holder will have the rights set forth below and in the Security Agreement.

6. EVENTS OF DEFAULT

Each of the following constitutes an "Event of Default" under this note: the Borrower's failure to make any payment when due under the terms of this note, including the final payment due under this note when fully amortized. the filing of any voluntary or involuntary petition in bankruptcy by or regarding the Borrower or the initiation of any proceeding under bankruptcy or insolvency laws against the Borrower.an assignment made by the Borrower for the benefit of creditors the appointment of a receiver, custodian, trustee, or similar party to take possession of the Borrower's assets or property; or the death of the Borrower.

7. ACCELERATION; REMEDIES ON DEFAULT.

If any Event of Default occurs, all principal and other amounts owed under this note will become immediately due without any action by the Holder, the Borrower, or any other person. The Holder, in addition to any rights and remedies available to the Holder under this note, may, in its sole discretion, pursue any legal or equitable remedies available to it under applicable law or in equity, including taking any of the following actions:

(a) personally, or by agents or attorneys (in compliance with applicable law), take immediate possession of the collateral. To that end, the Holder may pursue the collateral where it may be found, and enter the Borrower's remises, with or without notice, demand, process of law, or legal procedure if this can be done without breach of the peace. If the premises on which any part of the collateral is located are not under the Borrower's direct control, the Borrower will exercise its best efforts to ensure that the Holder is promptly provided right of access to those premises. To the extent that the Borrower's consent would otherwise be required before a right of access could be granted, the Borrower hereby irrevocably grants that consent.

(b) require the Borrower to assemble the collateral and make it available to the Holder at a place to be designated

(c) by the Holder that is reasonably convenient to both parties (it being acknowledged that the Borrower's premises are reasonably convenient to the Borrower).
sell, lease, or dispose of the collateral or any part of it in any manner permitted by applicable law or by contract; and

(d) exercise all rights and remedies of a secured party under applicable law.

8. WAIVER OF PRESENTMENT; DEMAND. The Borrower hereby waives presentment, demand, notice of dishonor, notice of default or delinquency, notice of protest and nonpayment, notice of costs, expenses or losses and interest on those, notice of interest on interest and late charges, and diligence in taking any action to collect any sums owing under this note, including (to the extent permitted by law) waiving the pleading of any statute of limitations as a defense to any demand against the undersigned. Acceptance by the Holder or any other holder of this note of any payment differing from the designated payments listed does not relieve the undersigned of the obligation to honor the requirements of this note.

9. GOVERNING LAW.
(a) Choice of Law. The laws of the state of Texas govern this note (without giving effect to its conflicts of law principles).
(b) Choice of Forum. Both parties consent to the personal jurisdiction of the state and federal courts in Dallas County, Texas.

10. COLLECTION COSTS AND ATTORNEYS' FEES.
The Borrower shall pay all expenses of the collection of indebtedness evidenced by this note, including reasonable attorneys' fees and court costs in addition to other amounts due.

11. ASSIGNMENT AND DELEGATION.
(a) No Assignment. The Borrower may not assign any of its rights under this note. All voluntary assignments of rights are limited by this subsection.
(b) No Delegation. The Borrower may not delegate any performance under this note
(c) Enforceability of an Assignment or Delegation. If a purported assignment or purported delegation is made in violation of this section, it is void.

12. SEVERABILITY.
If any one or more of the provisions contained in this note is, for any reason, held to be invalid, illegal, or unenforceable in any respect, that invalidity, illegality, or unenforceability will not affect any other provisions of this note, but this note will be construed as if those invalid, illegal, or unenforceable provisions had never been contained in it, unless the deletion of those provisions would result in such a material change so as to cause completion of the transactions contemplated by this note to be unreasonable.

13. NOTICES.
(a) Writing - Permitted Delivery Methods. Each party giving or making any notice, request, demand, or other communication required or permitted by this note shall give that notice in writing and use one of the following types of delivery, each of which is a writing for purposes of this note: personal delivery, mail (registered or certified mail, postage prepaid, return-receipt requested), nationally recognized overnight courier (fees prepaid), facsimile, or email.
(b) Addresses. A party shall address notices under this section to a party at the following addresses:

If to the Borrower: Test 5555 Test Drive Teest, Texas 555555
teest@gmail.com If to the Holder: Teest Company555 Test Drive Dallas, Texas 55555test@gmail.com

14. WAIVER.

No waiver of a breach, failure of any condition, or any right or remedy contained in or granted by the provisions of this note will be effective unless it is in writing and signed by the party waiving the breach, failure, right, or remedy. No waiver of any breach, failure, right, or remedy will be deemed a waiver of any other breach, failure, right, or remedy, whether or not similar, and no waiver will constitute a continuing waiver unless the writing so specifies.

15. HEADINGS. The descriptive headings of the sections and subsections of this note are for convenience only, and do not affect this note's construction or interpretation.

[SIGNATURE PAGE FOLLOWS]

Each party is signing this agreement on the date stated opposite that party's signature.

Date: _____ By: _____

Name: Teest   Test Company

Date: _____ By: _____

Name: Test Teest Title: Test CEO

- If your agreement is complicated, do not use the enclosed form. Contact an attorney to help you draft a document that will meet your specific needs.

If you have an unsecured note, and take the person to court to get the judge to force to liquidate something to pay you or garnish their wage or something – but when you have a secured promissory note, when they default on that loan, you don't even have to send them a letter, you can literally go seize the property if you want.

223

This is something that you want to do and make sure they understand the ramifications of this so that they can put themselves in position. You can put yourself into position of the wining position. Notice why I do secured lending and not unsecured.

- In general, secured promissory notes are supplemented with and supported by security agreements. Those security agreements are what allow lenders to take property if a default occurs. The enclosed note assumes the existence of a security agreement, but that agreement is not included with this package.

- A security interest in property can (and should) be memorialized with a financing statement (more specifically, a document called a UCC financing statement). Once a financing statement is completed and filed with the correct governmental authority, the lender's interest in the property is considered "perfected."

- This means that if future lenders also seek a security interest in the same asset, the lender with the perfected interest would have top priority and could take the property for itself after a default.

So what this means is priority perfected interest or first lienholder's interest which means, that if you take or seize ownership of the property – when you seize control of the property, that the borrower makes you the preferred lienholder of that property. Which means if they die, you will get paid first before anybody else that they owe.

I would encourage you to make sure that you put yourself in that position. Do your own research to see what a UCC financing statement is to make sure that when you secure assets you become the first lienholder on that asset.

So if they owed anybody before you that don't matter today! You are about to get paid! OK!!

So that's something that we want to make sure that we look at and we pay attention to because with that it will allow for us to be able to put ourselves in **position of authority** and that's what we want.

- The enclosed document is also a **demand note**. This means that the lender can demand repayment of the loan at any time. This is a point that should be emphasized to the borrower – it may be required to pay back that loan on very little notice.

224

Unsecured Demand Promissory Note

$20,000.00   05/08/2020
                                                             Dallas, Texas

For value received, the undersigned TEEST (the "Borrower") promises to pay to the order of Jon ME
Tombo (the "Holder"), in the manner and at the place provided below, the principal sum of $20,000.00
on demand, but in any event no later than 06/20/2020.

1. PAYMENT.

All payments of principal and interest under this note will be made in lawful money of the United States,
without offset, deduction, or counterclaim, by wire transfer of immediately available funds to an account designated by the Holder in
writing at least 15 days after the effective date of this note or, if this designation is not made, by check mailed to the Holder at 5555 Oak,
Oak, Texas, 75555, or at such other place as the Holder may designate in writing.

2. INTEREST.

Interest on the unpaid principal balance of this note is payable from the date of this note until this note is paid in full, at the rate of 20%
per year, or the maximum amount allowed by applicable law, whichever is less. Accrued interest will be computed on the basis of a 365-
day or 366-day year, as the case may be,
based on the actual number of days elapsed in the period in which it accrues.

3. PREPAYMENT.

The Borrower may prepay this note, in whole or in part, at any time before demand, without penalty or
premium. Any partial prepayment will be credited first to accrued interest, then to principal.

4. EVENTS OF DEFAULT.

Each of the following constitutes an "Event of Default" under this note:

(a) the Borrower's failure to make a payment in full to the Holder within 30 business day(s)
following the date of the Holder's demand for payment.

(b) the filing of any voluntary or involuntary petition in bankruptcy by or regarding the Borrower or the initiation of any proceeding under
bankruptcy or insolvency laws against the Borrower.

(c) an assignment made by the Borrower for the benefit of creditors; or
(d) the appointment of a receiver, custodian, trustee, or similar party to take possession of the Borrower's assets or property; or
(e) the death of the Borrower.

5. ACCELERATION; REMEDIES ON DEFAULT.
If any Event of Default occurs, all principal and other amounts owed under this note will become
immediately due without any action by the Holder, the Borrower, or any other person. The Holder, in
addition to any rights and remedies available to the Holder under this note, may, in its sole discretion,
pursue any legal or equitable remedies available to it under applicable law or in equity.

6. WAIVER OF PRESENTMENT; DEMAND.
The Borrower hereby waives presentment, demand, notice of dishonor, notice of default or delinquency, notice of protest and
nonpayment, notice of costs, expenses or losses and interest on those, notice of interest on interest and late charges, and diligence in
taking any action to collect any sums owing under this note, including (to the extent permitted by law) waiving the pleading of any statute
of limitations as a defense to any demand against the undersigned. Acceptance by the Holder or any other holder of this note of any
payment differing from the designated lump-sum payment listed above does not relieve the undersigned of the obligation to honor the
requirements of this not

7. GOVERNING LAW.

(a) Choice of Law. The laws of the state of Texas govern this agreement (without giving effect to its conflicts of law principles).

(b) Choice of Forum. Both parties consent to the personal jurisdiction of the state and federal courts in Dallas County, Texas.

8. COLLECTION COSTS AND ATTORNEYS' FEES.

The Borrower shall pay all expenses of the collection of indebtedness evidenced by this note, including reasonable attorneys' fees and court costs in addition to other amounts due.

9. ASSIGNMENT AND DELEGATION.

(a) No Assignment. The Borrower may not assign any of its rights under this note. All voluntary assignments of rights are limited by this subsection.
(b) No Delegation. The Borrower may not delegate any performance under this note.
(c) Enforceability of an Assignment or Delegation. If a purported assignment or purported delegation is made in violation of this section, it is void.

10. SEVERABILITY.

If any one or more of the provisions contained in this note is, for any reason, held to be invalid, illegal, or unenforceable in any respect, that invalidity, illegality, or unenforceability will not affect any other provisions of this note, but this note will be construed as if those invalid, illegal, or unenforceable provisions had never been contained in it, unless the deletion of those provisions would result in such a material change so as to cause completion of the transactions contemplated by this note to be unreasonable.

11. NOTICES.

(a) Writing; Permitted Delivery Methods. Each party giving or making any notice, request, demand, or other communication required or permitted by this note shall give that notice in writing and use one of the following types of delivery, each of which is a writing for purposes of this note: personal delivery, mail (registered or certified mail, postage prepaid, return-receipt requested), nationally recognized overnight courier (fees prepaid), or email.

(b) Addresses. A party shall address notices under this section to a party at the following addresses:
If to the Borrower:

Teest
5555 you owe
me money, Texas 55555
youoweme@money.com

If to the Holder:
Jon ME Tombo
5555 Oak
Oak, Texas 75555
jonmetombo@gmail.com
(c) Effectiveness. A notice is effective only if the party giving notice complies with subsections (a) and (b) and if the recipient receives the notice.

12. WAIVER.\No waiver of a breach, failure of any condition, or any right or remedy contained in or granted by the provisions of this note will be effective unless it is in writing and signed by the party waiving the breach, failure, right, or remedy. No waiver of any breach, failure, right, or remedy will be deemed a waiver of any other breach, failure, right, or remedy, whether or not similar, and no waiver will constitute a continuing waiver unless the writing so specifies.

13. HEADINGS.

The descriptive headings of the sections and subsections of this note are for convenience only, and do not affect this note's construction or interpretation.

[SIGNATURE PAGE FOLLOWS]

Each party is signing this note on the date stated opposite that party's signature.

Date:_____ By:_____
                                    Name: Teest Jon ME Tombo

Date:_____ By:_____
                                    Name: 'Jon Me Tombo Title: CEO

If you have a six-month term and you have a demand note, you can say within three months, I want all my money back, all my interest and the money – and if you don't have it, I will seize the property. So this is a much more aggressive way to ensure you have everything that you need.

Choose a fair interest rate. Although the enclosed note will "rewrite" any illegal interest rate to make it legal, it's a good idea to select a more reasonable number. This will decrease the chances of default and make for a less strained relationship between the parties.

- Make sure that you're fair. If it's a secured – create a fair interest rate anywhere between 6% and 12%. If there is somebody that is a regular and that has paid all the time, you can create your own preferred interest rates because you know they are going to borrow more money and give you that.

- So somebody that borrows more money typically with a secured asset – you can literally lower the interest rate because you are going to be making more money passively because they are borrowing more money. So make sure that you choose a fair interest rate that doesn't just benefit you.

- The parties should sign only the original document, and that original should be given to the lender. Make at least one photocopy, make sure that the document says **"COPY"** in bold letters, and give the copy to the borrower. After the note has been paid in full, the lender should return the original document to the borrower.

You keep the original and you give the copy to the borrower. Make sure that they have the copy and on their copy it says **"COPY"** because if not – they can go doctor up that original and say these were the term agreements – they're lying and then it's he say she say!

Once they pay the note, you give them the original document, which is them pretty much taking ownership of that debt.

- Depending on the nature of its terms, you may decide to have your note witnessed or notarized. This will limit later challenges to the validity of a party's signature.

- It's important to have a notary. Getting someone who is not a relative to you to get their notary to help you in this business, so that when you're creating these copies and these promissory notes, someone who is either there to witness it and notarize it, and sign their name as an official public notary and prove that this is a valid document, will help you with your things.

Now my dad, he didn't do all that. My dad literally went off friendship and character. But I'm talking about to eliminate a lot of the risk, my dad had a little bit more aggressive tactics too.
But that is just something to pay attention to.

I think it is very important so that we can understand and be able to place ourselves in the driver's seat of our lives and the driver's seat of success. You guys have to realize that lending is a real business and it is something that you have to learn how to do. Start off with a warm market, people that you know, as well as people that you are comfortable with, not people that don't have jobs. You want people that are
business or have assets that you want or that you want to tie up and you make money just like that.

It's very simple and very easy. What I would suggest is that you find someone who wants to start off with borrowing $200 and make them a promissory note – start off small and then work their way up as you get more comfortable with your process and procedures. That's how you do things and you will find that passive income, better than the stock market, better than the real estate, and the person is actually funding the deals.

With that being said, this is **Jake Tayler Jacobs, *Mr. BE THE BANK.*.** this ends this segment and we will see you in the next lesson!

NOTES

Promissory Note Breakdown

Hey Family welcome back! This is **Jake Tayler Jacobs**, *Mr.BE THE BANK*, and again this is the last segment of things dealing with legal or legalities or stuff that's important. During the next segment of Becoming a Private Lender, I'm going to be breaking down some things with that and sooner or later in one of our segments I will do an interview with my dad, Big Jake, and he will break down his process of how and what he did. And when you realize how simple and normal my dad is, it will literally give you confidence – **"like, I can do this too!"**

The biggest thing that I want you to understand is to get out there and try! Get out there and do it. Use money that you are not afraid to lose, like **$200**, **$500** and begin to start lending that money. Use the same money over and over again. So what my dad would do, he took **$1000** that he was ok with losing if he lost it, and he lent that money and he never spent the interest. So he put that interest back into the pot, and when he replaced his **$1000** – he removed his **$1000** and only lent money on the interest that was gained from his **$1000**. So his initial principal is out the way and he was literally making money on the interest that was gained and the interest that was earned. And that is your way to build up to that.

So in this segment we are going to be talking about the **"Promissory Note Breakdown"** and I am going to walk you through the terminology, and what they say. So this is definitely going to be something that you need to go over and over again. Review this section so that you can understand what you are looking at and understand each section fully.

Also be able to understand what you're looking at when you create your templated version so that you get an understanding. **Know your business!**

Don't allow a legal person, don't allow an attorney, don't allow somebody to out know something in your business when it comes to the basic function of your business. Promissory notes and contracts are literally just verbiage on paper which protects your interests. Very simple!

Secured Promissory Note (Demand Instructions)

The following provision-by-provision instructions will help you understand the terms of your secured promissory note.

INTRODUCTION.

- Identifies the document as a note. Write in the date on which the note becomes effective. Identify the parties and, if applicable, what type of organization(s) they are. Note that one party is called the "Payee" and the other the "Borrower." As you may have guessed, the Borrower is the party that is borrowing money and will pay it to the "Payee." The Payee may or may not be the same entity as the lender. Under some loan agreements, the lender requires the borrower make payments to a third party.

The numbers below (e.g., Section 1, and Section 2, etc.) correspond to the provisions in the note. Please review the document in its entirety before starting the step-by-step process.

SECTION 1: PROMISE OF PAYMENT.

- This is the "meat" of the note, where the total principal amount and interest rate are stated. This is also where the Payee designates where exactly it should be paid (usually the Payee's business address). The other language ensures that the interest rates set by the parties aren't illegal. In other words, if an agreed-to interest rate is above what the law allows, this section "rewrites" that provision to make it legal.

Remember you are the payee and you are the person who's going to designate when you get paid, and how you get paid. I like to do ACH drafts, quick books, I like to use where I have their credit card information, and it literally drafts every month, you can use square invoicing – and those are strategies that you can use to literally be able to extract the money out of their account on a weekly basis or you can have them send you money through checks, or to your business address or whatever is best for you – you can definitely do that.

If an agreed interest rate is above what the law allows, this section re-writes that provision to make it legal. So if you are charging like in your state you have to figure out what the maximum amount you can charge somebody for interest.

SECTION 2: PAYMENT.

- The parties' agreement that the borrowed amount will be repaid immediately, whenever the Payee demands it.

And you want to stay relatively as low and safe under that max amount as you can. You want to have a viable business that has fair interest rates that you charge for lending your money out.

You can say the borrowed amount will be paid immediately, or the next pay cycle, or we will give you two months before you pay.

Or you can pay me the full amount in two weeks or you can pay me interest. This is the payment segment on how you will be paid back, and you can also place it in the clause that you can demand it anytime.

Sometimes when you deal with people that borrow money from financial institutions, they will penalize you for paying it early.

Why? Because they wanted that to be passive income. They don't want you to pay it off early because that means you are paying them less interest.

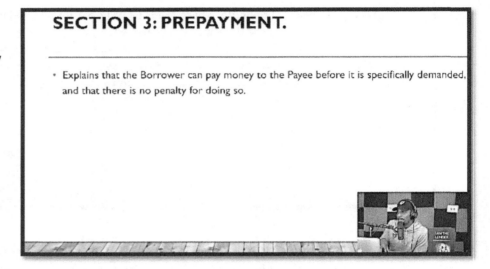

This is you saying in the pre-payment clause of **Section 3** – that you're not going to penalize them for paying it early. Typically private lenders, they get mad at this piece because if they didn't plan for that person to pay them back so soon, they weren't finding somebody that they can lend the money to and keep it in circulation. So if they were depending on that money for passive income and then that person just comes up and pays it – it kind of messes up their flow of things.

*** A security agreement should provide more details about the collateral pledged. Which means the type of collateral, the serial number of the collateral, the year the collateral was created, what the collateral looks like, and pictures of the collateral – every single thing that you can imagine about this collateral, all the way down to its value!

Every single detail - you want to make sure it is enclosed in that section.

In **section 5** it is basically saying – "after you default the first time, I'm going to leave you one letter and leave you one voicemail and if you do not answer back with a payment, I'm going to collateralize the property."

You can create whatever arrangement in this section. You can say – two tries or say once you contact me back – you have 15 days to pay the payment that is due. So these are all things that you can create in the events of a default. You can create late payments, late fee charges, and this is the section to do it.

SECTION 5: EVENTS OF DEFAULT.

- Lists the occasions on which the Payee can declare that a default has occurred under the loan. The first blank allows the parties to determine the amount of time the Borrower has to make its payment after the demand has been made. If you and the other party want to include additional events of default, you can do that in this section.

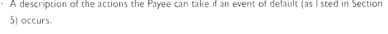

SECTION 6: ACCELERATION; REMEDIES ON DEFAULT.

- A description of the actions the Payee can take if an event of default (as listed in Section 5) occurs.

You can lift this in **section 5** but in **section 6** you can say these are accelerations and remedies on the default and the steps that you are going to take after the default.

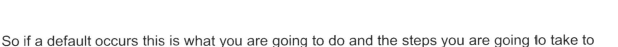

So if a default occurs this is what you are going to do and the steps you are going to take to remedy the situation and begin the collection process.

If the person that owes you does not pay up, you don't have to explain to the borrower that this is going to take action. The payee can simply take action without further notice. Which means if you send that demand letter out and if they do not do anything you can go and do the same thing with the collateral. It's just like the bank does when they foreclose a home or repo your car without letting you know. You can do the same thing – it's very important that you understand that.

When it comes to stressing the terms of the note, if you say six months then you mean six months, there is no extra. Or you can say six months with the option to keep the policy open. Or after six months we will give you the option to renew, and you can pay me back and the deal is done. I would keep **section 8**, as a reference as it allows for you to dictate the time If you are going to allow them fluidity at the end of the note.

For instance, if 50% of the payment has been paid by the sixth month, and it is not paid in full by the sixth month, you are going to give them six months of leeway but you are going to increase the interest by 6%. This will be where you will kind of go back and forth to make sure that you are in good hands.

SECTION 9: SUCCESSORS AND ASSIGNS.

- States that the parties' rights and obligations will be passed on to heirs or, in the case of companies, to successor organizations.

The rights and obligations will be passed down to the heirs. So if somebody owes you in their business and they die, you're going to collect from that business by whomever inherited that business and vice versa for you if you die. Your heirs are going to assume the responsibility of the lender.

SECTION 10: NOTICE.

- Lists the addresses to which all official or legal correspondence should be delivered.
  Write in a mailing address for both the Borrower and the Payee

This is where you advise you are going to write mailing addresses for both parties (**borrower and payee**) to be used as communication and a way to send notices and correspondence to each other.

So If I am in Dallas Texas and I am lending to someone in Austin Texas, this is where I put in the language, that all county laws and state laws are based upon Dallas Texas!
Not Austin – Dallas Texas. If I am lending to someone in Arizona, this is where you put in the terms that Dallas Texas is where this law I'm holding -it is based upon laws of Dallas Texas, not Arizona, because in different states they have different rules.

Some people can say, "Well in my state we don't do that." You need to tell them that this agreement is not based upon your states laws. It's based on my states laws, which dictates that we can do such and such. I would carefully study what your governing laws are when it comes to lending in your state and decide which county or state best suits you as the lender.

SECTION 11: GOVERNING LAW.

- Allows the parties to choose the state and county laws that will be used to interpret the note. This is not a venue provision: the included language will not impact where a potential claim can be brought. Please write the applicable state and county in the blanks provided.

SECTION 12: ENTIRE AGREEMENT.

- The parties' agreement that the note they're signing is "the agreement" about the issues involved. Unfortunately, the inclusion of this provision will not prevent a party from arguing that other enforceable promises exist, but it will provide you some protection from these claims.

Section 12 shows when the borrower signs this, they are saying they have read the entire agreement – but even though they sign it, some people will try and say this, or that.

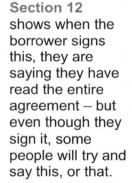

So it is very important that you go over it with them. If I were you I would record yourself going over the promissory note and them agreeing with it. This will give you a lot stronger reason for taking over their assets or taking them to court because you have the recorded proof of that.

SECTION 13: NO IMPLIED WAIVER.

- Explains that even if the Payee ignores or allows the Borrower to break an obligation under the note, it does not mean the Payee waives future rights to require the Borrower to fulfill those obligations.

If you (**payee**) allows the borrower to break some of the obligations that are under the note, it does not mean that you are waiving future rights to assume back authority under the obligations that you allowed them to break.

Say for instance, you let them skip three payments, that is not the standard! You can go back and reinforce anything that you want because you are in control of it.

SECTION 14: COLLECTION COSTS AND ATTORNEY'S FEES.

- Places the responsibility for paying any costs of collecting money under the note on the Borrower's shoulders.

If you have to bring the law in play, the borrower is going to have to pay for all attorney fees and applicable laws.

SECTION 15: SEVERABILITY.

- Protects the terms of the note as a whole, even if one part is later invalidated.
- A **severability clause** in a contract states that its terms are independent of one another so that the rest of the contract will remain in force should a court declare one or more of its provisions void or unenforceable.

If one term that's in the entire contract is no longer legal, it does not void the entire contract – just that piece of the contract is voided. You want to make sure you have the Severability clause, which is Section15, that's going to say not one clause or obligation is not dependent upon another. If one gets voided or one gets eliminated because of law, you can no longer do it, that doesn't mean that the other obligations cannot be taken care of. That allows for you to stop people from trying to take advantage of you by saying, "that is not legal anymore so the entire contract is forfeited." No that is not true because of what we have in place.

So family we are now past the boring parts. You now have the opportunity to be able to put yourself in position and take advantage of becoming the lender.

Yes, the paperwork process is crazy, all you have to do is go to www.legalzoom.com and create an LLC. Or you can go create a DBA – do your sole proprietorship and test it out a little bit, use a little bit of your insurance reserve money $200, $500 or a $1000 and lend that money out and start that process of paying and repaying yourself back. What you are going to realize is you will get yourself in a little groove that is going to allow for you to really take advantage of making this passive income in this world that we call lending.

Remember you are the lender and God wants you to be the bank!

This is **Mr. Jake Tayler Jacobs**, and I am *MR BE THE BANK*, and I will I see you on the next lesson!

NOTES

Becoming A Private Lender

What's going on family? Welcome back, this is **Jake Tayler Jacobs,** *MR BE THE BANK.* We are close to finalizing this course, and we are now in this segment where will be discussing **private money lending,** *which is* when a private individual or small business loans another investor or company money from its own personal funds to use for investment purposes. So in real estate the alternative option for financing investment properties outside of a traditional bank or lending institution is because of what we call, regular financial institutions. They want to use hard money lenders or private money lenders, which are what we are. A lot of things can contest if somebody you don't know and you are lending money to – but they got a good deal, you may ask them to put 5% upfront like a down payment.

You can set up whatever terms that you want for them to give you your down payment upfront, and then to pay you out on the back end. Whatever you decide to do, you can set it up that way. You can also set it up as a private lender. You may give them a much more preferred interest rate, but you want to participate in **equity splits**. If someone says, "Hey Jake, I want to borrow money. I got an asset that I want to take a look into." I will say, ok, well you can borrow the money at 4% - but I also want 10% on your equity split. So instead of charging you 12% to 18%, and I don't really know you or whatever the case may be, or I want to get in on the deal but I want to be an equity partner and a lending partner. You can participate in both the combinations to get both returns, of being the lending partner at the premium rate and then also being able to take participations in the equity splits at the end.

Since private money lending is private, it is up to the lender and the borrower, to establish its terms for the loan. As long as the property is being used for investment purposes, it falls outside of the Dodd-Frank Act which it allows the investor to determine the interest rate or loan terms that are agreed upon by both parties. The interest rates for these loans are often several percentage points higher than what the interest rates on a traditional mortgage would be. So when it comes to you actually lending money to people, what you need to understand is that we cannot lend money to people without having a lender's license or a banking license and we cannot legally lend money to actual homes, like somebody wants to buy a home for themselves and they're paying you a mortgage. Now you would be considered under the Dodd-Frank ruling which means, you are under the ruling of banking and now you have to have your lender's license, or a bankers license, and that's something that you do not want to get into. When it comes to actual investment deals, and business deals, you can kind of create whatever rules that you want in regards to that. One of the main questions that people ask is, **"Can anyone be a private lender?"**

The answer is, **"absolutely!"** Because private money loans are typically created by people the investors or borrowers know personally, such as family members, friends, neighbors, or colleagues. However, anyone who has idle money that would like to receive a better return on their savings account interests, on their yields, on their private money, on their insurance reserves, 401K's, IRA's, those are the people who are typically more prone to become lenders. So my dad, he had idle money in his savings account. And he didn't want to keep his money in his savings account, because he knew the banks were making money on him but he couldn't make money on the banks. So he literally kept his money in a safe and lent his money out. But we teach to place your money in **insurance reserves** and you are getting your guaranteed 4% to 8% a year, and then you can leverage that money to go get greater returns if you feel like you can get greater interests on your money than 4%, or better than giving your money to somebody else.

240

Pros to Private Money Lending:

✓ Your ability to be able to participate in the real estate market passively, while receiving a return on your investment without actually having to be in the real estate.

✓ You do not have to do all the digging.

✓ You do not have to do all the finding and all the research; you can just be the person who's lending.

✓ So when people say you can make money in real estate, there are plenty of ways to make money in real estate without having to put yourself in debt. You can become a part of these deals and be able to make passive income by becoming a lender to these people that want to make the deals.

✓ Another added benefit of being a private lender is that you typically receive a higher rate of return than most saving accounts offer. Typically you can get from 6% to 15% by lending money than you could have in a savings account. So if you're getting 4% guaranteed in your insurance reserve, and then you can lend money at 5% minus the difference of you using the insurance company's money – you are literally going to make a 10% to 15% growth on top of the 4% you got! So its like you are making 19% to 24% on your money by leveraging insurance reserves to be able to do that.

✓ Private money lending – if done correctly can be a great way to grow a retirement account.

Cons to Private Money Lending:

The largest con in private lending is the risk of the borrower defaulting – you have the authority of checking that person out, you have due diligence, and you still will have the risks of someone defaulting. Which is the process of you getting collateral, getting the land, selling the land, and that will be the biggest con you will face. As the lender, you are typically securing that asset with some type of real estate or some type of other asset, it is just taking the legal action of having to get the asset, and sell the asset. The hassle of doing all that is the biggest con when it comes to private money lending.

Additionally you as the lender should be confidant and educated in the investment strategies and understand how to conduct your own due diligence on the investment that the borrower is trying to bring to the table.

I would suggest participating with another lender before you go into real estate. Invest with industries that you already know. My dad was in the working industry working for the Dallas Morning News, and he knew the industry very well. He knew the days they received payroll, he knew the payout schedule, the bonus payouts, and he was so indoctrinated while working there that he knew the schedule of the Dallas Morning News, and it was a safer bet for him to lend money to people he worked with.

I know the Insurance Industry, so if people need money for leads, I am lending money so they can be able to get access to capital fast, I know how the industry works, so I am taking as little risk as possible.

But when it comes to the real estate world, you want to research the market:

- Do you understand how to evaluate plans?
- Do you know how to purchase wholesale courses so you can understand property evaluations?
- Do you understand how to look at the deal?
- Do you understand if you're in a good deal or not?
- Do you understand and how to know if you're in a good position or not?
- Are you able to make sure you're eliminating all possible risks?

More Pros of being a Private Lender:

- Earn a higher interest rate to help you grow your retirement or savings account.
- You earn passive income by securing your real estate or somebody taking a long-term position in paying you on the interest and principal over a certain period of time
- A passive investment – we call it our little black box where you take the piece of paper and put it in a black box and you literally just make money on that black box. Just that simple.

More Cons of being a Private Lender:

- The risk of borrowing money

- People having to foreclose on property

- Not property vetting out the borrower – you're being lazy, trying to skip steps

- Because you do not have your proper vetting process, you're taking more of a risk when it comes to actually lending your money to these folks

When it comes to becoming a private lender there are **six things** that you want to put in place. We talked about the contracts and those things but I want to review a few things with you again so you can have a better understanding of what we have discussed.

1. **Decide where the funds are going to come from?**
   - Is it going to come from a savings account?
   - Is it going to come from your 401K?
   - Are you going to raise the money with your family and friends so you all can lend together?
   - Are you going to use your insurance reserve to lend money?
   - Where is the money going to come from?

2. **Find the opportunities in the industry that best fit your mentality or your understanding**
   - If you do not understand any industry, find one that you will be more prone to
   - If you are feeling like the real estate market peaks your interest, take time to study and do your research on the real estate market. Take three, six to twelve months to understand that market. Invest in education of that market so you can gain a better understanding to become an investor.
   - Certain banks will only lend to certain industries because that is what they specialize in. Find a niche' or something that you specialize in and become a primary lender for that specific niche'. This way you are someone that completely understands and you can adapt and place you and your market in the best position to gain a win, win.

3. **Conduct your due diligence on the investment and the borrower**
   - Due diligence means you look at the investment and when you collateralize an asset you see that they can pay you and you also see that if they do not pay you – you are going to still be good. You know if and you have done your due diligence – you are in a win, win, which takes some time.
   - Do your due diligence on the borrower. Are they a sleazeball? Go look at their social media, literally judge them – you're the banker! You're the boss! You're the master!
   - You can do whatever you want to do in order to perform the best due diligence that you can on somebody to make sure that you are in a win, win situation.

4. **Determine the loan terms**
   - If it is somebody that you do not trust, give shorter loan terms
   - If you trust them wholly – provide longer loan terms
   - If it is someone that you trust completely – provide bigger money with longer loan terms

5. **Finalize the paperwork**
   - Best practice to have a licensed attorney draft or review any paperwork relating to private money loans.
   - This ensures both parties are adequately protected and the proper legal terms were included in the event of default foreclosure action is pursued, the original note and mortgage must be produced in court in order to foreclose.

6. **Begin Collecting**
   - Now the lender can start collecting!
   - Keep good records of the payments the borrower has made, including copies of checks or bank statements or an Excel spreadsheet, to confirm the proper principal and interest was accounted for with each payment.
   - This reduces your risk if the borrower does default while also making the loan marketable if you ever want or need to sell on the secondary market.

Welcome to becoming the LENDER! Take $500 and go lend it to your very first person!

I want you to go inside the **PRIVATE BANKING BLUEPRINT Master Class** when you finally lent money to your first person and you got the principal plus your interest back and your first agreement is complete. Let us know that you've made money lending and you have actually become the lender for your family, you have a guaranteed bank, and have money in your insurance reserve. Borrow money from your insurance reserve – go lend it to somebody, pay it back and then keep the rest for yourself. Let us know that you are actually out there making money becoming lenders!

What I want to do: Our goal is for us to literally become the largest network of independent private lenders so that we can become the funding source and replace these banks and begin to fill our pockets, and our households by becoming the master and not the servant! God told us that we can be the lender and not the borrower and it is up to you to believe it!

This is *Jake Tayler Jacobs - MR BE THE BANK* – I love you and we are out! PEACE!!!!

NOTES

Interview with My Dad:

How He Made $3K - $5K A Month Lending

What's going on Family? This is **Jake Tayler Jacobs** and of course I told guys you I was going to bring the man that started it all my father, my daddy, **this is the original Jake**, he calls me the *imposter Jake,* he literally text my wife, this is **The Real Jake, Big Jake**. I was like Ok, dad. But its true.

I know you guys have received a lot and gotten a lot from this course and I know I have been teaching you guys how to completely eliminate the bank but I am going to do this interview with my daddy because I want you guys to see where my mentality of **F – The Bank** came from. It is not something that I literally just decided to do. It is not something that I just said, **"Oh! One day I decided to say** F- The Bank." I literally saw my father create passive income. He always had money and he did things to be able to just put food on the table out of survival. So it will be good to hear a little bit of his story, so that you guys cannot only see my origin and where I came from but literally standing on my dad's shoulders but to see the mentality of becoming the lender and what it takes to actually get there. **Let's get started….**

Lil Jake: Ok, so Dad, everybody this is Jake Jr and the original Jake and I'm blessed because I can carry on my dad's first (his nickname used to be Jake) and I am branding the Jake and the Jacobs. So I'm a true big flag carrier for that last name like I always tell you guys about.

But before we even get into the lending, Dad just kind of tell us how you grew up, where you grew up and what made you take your finances into your own hands?

Big Jake: Well I grew up in Oak Cliff Texas, as kid I had a couple of uncles who actually used to go by and collect funds that people owed them. Both uncles had their own way about doing things – both uncles kind of did it opposite of each other; of how to go by and basically collect money they lent out to different people.

Lil Jake: At the time Dad, did you realize that they had a lending business or was it something like as you got older, you kind of, think back to like, "man that's where I got it from, the whole lending and getting the money back?"

246

Big Jake: As I got older, I kind of thought back to exactly what was taking place, and at the given time there were things that were happening that I really did not have a clue. But once I got a little bit older, I started to understand things that were taking place at that time.

Lil Jake: Ok. His uncles were very good at managing what they lent out. They had a notepad. My dad even has like a notepad for everyone at one point in time that owed him. It's kind of crazy how I talk to you guys about subconsciously we pick up certain habits and certain things that you don't realize where you got it from until you kind of just sit down and think about all the people that you've been exposed to and realize, **"Dang I kind of picked up that habit from him."** I was actually reading – my dad is working on an autobiography – a story about himself and just to see some of the mannerisms and the sayings that I grew up with him saying to me – you realize that person said this to my dad and it stuck with them.

So, Dad you grew up in a way of hustling, any means necessary, to be able to provide for yourself, and to get cash flow for yourself. I am most proud of this, like the transition that you went from like hustling to trying to find cleaner way to be able to make that income that you needed. So was that the transition of you hustling and wanting to stop hustling and then you started lending or was it blended until you just started to lean more into the lending side?

Big Jake: You're always trying to find a clean way. As I was growing up, you see a lot of your friends going to jail by hustling and a lot of those things. So you try to do it the right way so you don't find yourself being up in jail.

Lil Jake: My dad is a man of few words, so I am going to try to pull out as much as I can. (lol) I think I got my talking from my momma because my daddy barely ever talk. Before we go into lending, let's talk about how you feel about banks. At what point did you say, I am not keeping my money in a bank?

Big Jake: Well usually when you are dealing with banks, they charge you a large amount of fees to just pay back the money. And the hardest part about the banks is you have to have all this criteria to get a loan, especially when you really need it. They make a lot of excuses to not give you a loan or they charge you extra amounts of interest just for you to have a loan for a period of time.

Lil Jake: Tell us that story Dad, you had money in your savings account and you went to the bank to borrow money, and you told them that if you didn't pay to just take it out of your savings and they told you no. And at that moment you just took your money out?

Big Jake: Yes.

Lil Jake: So tell us about that story.

Big Jake: Well my thing is this. A lot of times the bank won't lend you anything, so my thing is – why will I let you guys make money off my money and you guys can't help me out when I really need it for a loan? So at that point and time I decided to take all of my money out the bank and I just use the bank as a – like a lot of people do direct deposit. So I do it and soon as my money, I take my money out

Lil Jake: And its crazy because when I teach this stuff, y'all think I be crazy when I'm telling y'all the exact thing that my dad does when it comes to the bank and how when it comes to the trust with the bank and realizing how much money they make on our money. As soon as we put that money in that savings account, they are lending that money out. They're moving that money. They're lending it out for 6% to 28% and they are giving us like .08% not even 1%. And then when you want to go and leverage their money like they are leveraging your money, now they got all these criteria, but you don't have those criteria for them. My wife and I we actually don't keep money in the savings or checking account – we only keep money in the checking account for the business, just because of how many transactions that we do.

But the overall reserves, I teach y'all to put those in guaranteed reserves for 4% every year but allow us to use that money so that we can go ahead and make use of that. One thing I want to point out is that my dad, even though he has a safe and he kept his money out of the bank and he kept the money everywhere he was or in his safe, he always had the money moving. What I mean by always moving is – always lending the money out. Dad talk to us about when it clicked for you to say, I got a little extra money, this person needs some money. Let me make some extra money lending to them.

Big Jake: Well usually at the beginning of the loaning business, you knew people who needed money and at that time they had the 401K and even though you had money in the 401K you usually had to wait a month in order to get your money but at the time people needed help right then. Not a month later, but right then. I got myself in trouble at a young age going to Ace Check Cashing and these other loan places and found myself getting deeper and deeper in a hole. So at that time I said why not make me some extra money? I had the money, and I was just sitting on it anyway, so let me loan out a few dollars and see how it turns out.

Lil Jake: And you didn't start with crazy amounts, you started with an amount that if I lost it – ok cool?

Big Jake: You don't start off with a crazy amount. You always make sure of that – this is a high-risk business, so you start off with a low amount. At that given time when I started out, I started with $200. And at that given time we got paid bi-weekly, so my money was at that time turned every two weeks. So if you think about the mathematics of it, you're going to make a profit – way more than your money that is sitting in the bank. The bank was giving a low interest rate and I was doubling and tripling that before the bank even processed.

Lil Jake: Doubling and tripling before the bank even processed! I'm like my dad. I feel like I'm a better manager of my money than giving it to somebody else. Dad, talk about why you didn't trust the 401K? Because I actually look and talk about that, and I break down how the 401K is not made for us. Everybody eats on our money, but when you need your money, you got to wait for forever, and then you get penalized. So what made you look at that 401K and be like … naw I'm not rocking with that?

Big Jake: A lot of people I was around at the time, 401K was the ideal thing to get into. At that time like I said, you had people who needed it and they couldn't go get their own money. And like I said, they are charging you interest, and penalizing you for getting your money early. Actually they were charging them quite a bit of money to come get their money early, which is a penalty. The whole catch was they had put your money in stocks and bonds, so basically they were making money off your money regardless. So I did my research. You always got to do your research to kind of find out how things operate.

Lil Jake: And that's crazy because my auntie was pushing my dad. Aunt Barbara got you on with the job didn't she?

Big Jake: Yes

Lil Jake: And she was pushing you like **401K ….401K ……401K**
To have the temperament to take advice from someone who you admire, and love and come up with your own decision after you do your own research – Family that's something that I want to make sure that you guys always remember. Now your family and friends, your mom, and the people that you care about, it's their job to try to protect you. Its their job to try to give you advice from making mistakes, but you have to do your own due diligence too.

You have to do your own research to decide if something is best for you. Me and my dad were kind of playing with numbers and we will talk a little more about that later in the interview, but seeing the money that he was making, lending that money out and seeing that money kind of move, it was a no brainer when he said – why would I put my money in a 401K and give money to people I don't know who is managing money where I don't know where it's going? You trap my money; I need my money and I get penalized if I withdraw it too soon or I get charged interest on my money for accessing it too soon. So that's just something that he saw. But notice what he said family?

When I said how did you start your lending business the first thing that he didn't say was –"Dang let me see how much money I can make?" He said, "Man, I began to see people were in need, and it took them a while to be able to get their own money and I felt like I could fill that gap and I started off with a little bit of money to do that." Dad, what was your market that you started off? Like what type of person or characteristic did somebody have to have in order for you to be like ok, I can help you out?

Big Jake: Usually I started with families, like husband and wife, and a lot of single moms. At that time it was just a gut feeling that I had and I try to follow my heart on a lot of people, and at that given time back then, your word was your bond. It wasn't so much as having a contract at that time but at the beginning your word was your bond. So as I looked at these people I knew the history of the family and I knew the background of the family and made sure that most of the people that worked with me that was usually who I lent to. So I knew exactly when you would get paid and I got paid – because we all got paid on the same day.

Lil Jake: These of course weren't people that you met on the side of the street. These were people that you were around enough to be able to know if they were solid people right?

Big Jake: Right

Lil Jake: And so, talking about you lending money, when it came to lending you typically only lent your money out to people who were in the building or at your work place, people that you could see regularly right?

Big Jake: Yes

Lil Jake: What made you not extend that lending business out to areas where you weren't regularly like another state or to another city nearby?

Big Jake: Well like I told you earlier, with the lending business it's a high-risk business. And by people that's close to you – you kind of keep track of a lot things going on around you. It's a lifestyle that I wasn't trying to go back to. And that's why I didn't lend out to a lot of different places.

Lil Jake: When he is talking about a lifestyle that he did not want to go back to – just to keep it brief, he didn't want to have to muscle up people for not doing right or keeping their word because at that time he didn't have this contract that we will talk about in second. So since he had no contract, it was your word. So if you broke your word, my daddy always told me all the time your word is your bond. If you say you are going to do something do it, if you can't do it, just don't say you are going to do it. Just that simple. That's his code. If somebody that he felt he trusted and gave their word at a specific time, that was the only contract that he needed – a handshake. Some people may say why were you targeting single mothers? Talk about how you were not targeting single mothers but those were typically the people you helped the most and had more to lose than to do you wrong? Talk about why your business catered to single mothers, now he had married couples too but why did it tailor to helping single mothers more?

Big Jake: Most of the time the single mothers were really in need. Like I said I was at the point of my life that you know going through all these other financial institutions they were getting themselves deeper in the hole. And my way out was a whole lot less interesting than you know finding themselves deeper in the hole than what they were. It wasn't so much of me picking them out. My method came by word of mouth.

Lil Jake: So talk about that dad. Talk about that word of mouth piece. How did it grow by word of mouth and typically what did you do to vet this was a good person that was introduced?

Big Jake: Usually most of the people when I first got started were people that I already knew. And word of mouth was that you lend to one and they go tell somebody else and that person go tell someone else and that person go tells somebody else, and that person go tells somebody else. And it just goes like a chain reaction.

Lil Jake: And he did this not only at one work place, but he did it at other work places. And it typically takes you a while before you start telling people that you will lend money to them. Why does it kind of take you a while before you start telling people?

Big Jake: I never did tell anyone. Like I said, word of mouth came out you know and by that time somebody said they heard Susie was interested in getting a loan and mentioned it to me, so by that time I have done my background check on Susie and her history of payments. I do my research on that person. And if I feel the need or see it in my heart to give it to her, I will give it. I don't have rules and regulations to follow. So it is not like I am mandated to give anybody a loan. Its based on how I feel and if I feel like you are going to pay me back my money.

Lil Jake: Right. And just to let you guys know, in the private lending business, I know in Texas but for the most part, or all across the country – it typically tells you that there are no lending rules or banking rules that you are under, especially if you are not lending to people like if you have someone with a bunch of money and as long as you are not building a house and they are not paying their mortgage back to you – that's the only thing. So as long as you are a private lender and you are a small-time lender – you can lend to friends and extended friends without having to follow the tax laws or tax codes that come with actual lending. How did you come up with your contract dad? You went from word of mouth to creating a contract, how did you create that?

Big Jake: Some of the people that I was lending to they gave me pointers and ideas of what to come up with and have it in writing. So basically I took their opinion and started coming up with things from their ideas and things to writing it down and after a while you of course you know you have to change things up or basically tweak it to make it whole. And me as a business minded person I decided – let me tweak this enough so I can put this in front of a lawyer and see if it will hold up in court. And that's what I did over the years but the ups and downs sometimes the rules changed - you know a lot of things change as time goes by.

Lil Jake: It's crazy looking at my Dad's contract because the contract that I have put inside of the Master Class, in one of the lessons, Unsecured and Secured Lending – it is legitimately just like the one you will have access to through Legal Zoom. But to say that he created this on his own and the verbiage that he has in here, I am going to try and convince him to let us have a copy of it so we can give you all access to it so you can see how to do it for yourselves.

My dad did what we call unsecured lending which means you do not attach your contract to an asset. You are literally going off word of bond and it's no different than having a credit score. No different than your reputation with a credit score when banks lend to you based on your reputation of paying things back, that's what this contract was – unsecured. So when he is talking about high risk when it comes to lending this is what he is talking about, going off somebody's word. I actually have an experience, there was a young lady who was in need of money and she seemed like a legit person, and she was going to come work for the firm.

I asked my dad if he could lend to her, and originally he didn't want to lend to her because she was single with no kids, lived in an apartment by herself, like isolation so she could literally disappear and I didn't understand why my dad felt that way until it happened and then I understood why he doesn't lend to people with nothing to lose. So Dad, talk about what you mean when you say people don't have anything to lose and why you don't lend to people who don't have anything to lose?

Big Jake: Usually it's like a single person who like to borrow a whole lot of money, never had any intentions to pay you back and they just up and leave. Usually if you got like a single parent you have big things to lose because you got your children. You can't mess around and have yourself in jail behind some debt and you still got to raise your child because your child will be basically be going into the system.

Lil Jake: So this young lady, I almost became like a co-signer on the loan because my dad didn't go off of her, he went off of me. So I said, Dad, whatever she doesn't pay, I will make sure I cover it, because I wanted her to get help and I know at the time we didn't have any extra reserves to lend. So my dad lent to her and she made like one payment. What was it like one or two payments?

Big Jake: Yes, something like that.

Lil Jake: She made like one or two payments and then she disappeared. So of course with the contract and just like any other contract, they put their address because as the lender you have the rights to knowing where they are because they have your money. He went by, trying to check he reached out to me, and then I reached out to her and called him maybe one time and said, "My check was this." You know how we do when you borrow money and you don't to pay it back the lender.

This is a prime example of why you don't want to lend to: (1) people that you really don't know like that, (2) there is no real background on them and (3) they have nothing to lose. These are people that you don't want to put your reserves and your money with because you have more of a high risk of losing that money then you do in actually getting that money back. Dad, at your peak, how many clients do you think you had when you were actually lending and making the money move?

Big Jake: Probably about 50

Lil Jake: He had about 50 people. And we kind of did the numbers, he was doing like $3K -$4K passively lending. This is without debt. Some people literally get real estate properties and they say the only way you can make passive income is by getting real estate properties, getting into debt to get these big ole houses and you're trying to trust somebody else to rent. Then you got to pay the mortgage, then you got to pay for maintenance.

My grandfather did that and it was a headache. In order to make what my dad was making passively you would have to have between eight to ten rent houses. That's talking about having at least $750K to $2.5M worth of debt with the bank just to make that type of passive income. My dad was able to make that type of passive income by moving his money just like the banks were.

Dad let's talk about the program you put in place where you saw people began to get addicted. What program did you put in place to get them off of needing your services?

Big Jake: Well like said before, I had myself in debt with the loan business and I saw how long it took me to get out and I know how addictive it is to keep borrowing money. So the plan I put in after a certain period of time, I started decreasing the amount of income that you could borrow from me.

Lil Jake: Even if they paid on time all the time?

Big Jake: Even if they paid on time all the time. It didn't matter. I know how addictive this loaning business is so I decreased the amount of money that you could get. To give you an example, if you were always coming to get $300 from me for a loan and it seemed like it was every week or every other week, after a while what I would do is, I would cut that $300 down to maybe $250.

And after that, you would come for that amount for a certain period of time then I would cut it down to $200. Like I said, I would keep cutting it, all the way down and at that point if it's under $100 then you really don't need to get a loan from me. You need to learn how to manage that lil $100 that you have.

Lil Jake: Right

Big Jake: At that point, you do not need any money from me, just better management.

Lil Jake: This is something that my dad did out of thinking about other people and remembering his experiences because the truth is we do get in binds in life, and you need to be bailed out. Like my dad helped bail me out for my company the end of last year. Is that right, you came through in the clutch for me like towards the end of last year dad?

Big Jake: Probably something like that.

Lil Jake: And you will always need people because I had some trouble with my license and I didn't even think to go to the bank. I literally went had a conversation with my dad

because of this process so when we talk about becoming the lender and building your own banking system for your family – just imagine if you were a lot more resourceful with your money. And you can have money to be able to lend to your family so that you can build like a family reserve and you all can borrow and lend from it. You can make your own banking system rich. The research that I did dad, it say that the average African American makes $1.5M over their working career. And the average African American takes $1,082,577 of the $1.5M paying debt and finance charges to the bank. That sound about right?

Big Jake: That sounds about right. I can agree with that.

Lil Jake: Just imagine family if we didn't have to do that. Just imagine if that $1,082,577 that we paid in finance charges and debt charges and bank finance charges, imagine if you were able to keep that money and put that in your own family banking system? So you had this program dad where you weeded people off the system of needing you, but talk about the other program where people were just not good at saving. What did you establish for them?

Big Jake: I had a few families that had struggles saving money period. What I did for them was I made an agreement that I would hold their money for three months. So every time they get paid I would save money up for three months. At the end of the third month, I always gave the full amount back. If they wanted to invest it again then we would go another three months, but – just like the bank, if you decided that you needed all your money in two or three weeks, then just like the bank, I charge them a penalty to actually come and get their money like the banks would. I didn't charge as much as the bank, but I did charge you a percentage of coming back to get your funds.

Lil Jake: Dad talk about what you did when you were holding their money like the banks. Did you just let it sit or did you make money along the way?

Big Jake: Typically what I would do is when I was basically saving their money, I actually lent their money out to different people, and charged them the same percentage that I was charging at that time, so if I lent their money out and they wanted their money at that time, I still had money in the reserve to pay them back. Basically I made money off of their money.

Lil Jake: For some of you that think you need thousands of dollars to start off your lending business. How much did you start your lending business with Dad?

Big Jake: $200

Lil Jake: $200 – you find someone that is in need and you get that money back. What you do as my dad taught me, that interest, you don't spend it. You just allow that interest to grow your stock pile so that you begin to lend more. That $200 that you had initially – now you have that in interest, now you got $400. You take your $200 out the pot and now you have interest. Talk about the strategy of doing that and why it's important to not mix personal and business?

Big Jake: Well like I said you start off with **$200** and at that given time when you make that **$200** back you put that **$200** to the side, so that is basically money that you start off with so that means if anything goes wrong, you're basically even. So anything else is basically like profit. It depends on how big you want your business to grow and how long you want to keep turning your **$200** its entirely up to you – because like I said this is a high-risk business and it is a chance you are taking to lose all of it if you keep putting all of it in. See once you get to a certain status, see I was at that status before, you never mix your business money with personal. A lot of times, personal stuff will go on in your life and its going to be real hard. And you see all this money you have made in your business and you go and use some of your business money to catch up on your personal money and that is the biggest mistake that you can make. A lot of time, if you are mixing business with personal, at that point it's time to start over from scratch. Now you have built yourself with all these different clients that you have and you do not have enough revenue to match the clients that you have. And at that point they can't depend on you anymore and they are going to start seeking other areas to go and try to find money, and you lose your clients.

Lil Jake: What were some of the mistakes that you made?

Big Jake: That was it, mixing business with personal.

Lil Jake: What can people do to keep themselves disciplined and not mixing business with personal?

Big Jake: It's about yourself on that one, to not mix business with personal. Sometimes your personal gets so distraught that you are looking at that business money like .. hmm yeah…let me go ahead and use this so I get out of trouble, but you need to get yourself a game plan to not use your business money and for your personal try to find some type of bridgeway to come up out of it. It's just going to be a slow process. At the end of the day, you still got all this over here because this is your money. But it depends on how you want to go about doing things.

Lil Jake: I was talking to my dad, talking about being in his bag and his zone, his money was being lent out and he was dealing with personal issues, and he was really disciplined – he would go to a friend who was lending too and borrow from the friend. Is that what you said Dad?

Big Jake: Yes.

Lil Jake: And borrow from that friend and leverage that money – guys we know that term to be arbitrage right? The money that you are making from the interest from what you are borrowing – the money in between that's the profit that you make. So if he was borrowing from his friend at **10%** and he was making **25%** lending money out – the difference was he had a **15%** profit. We talk about that in the course. So I know some of y'all will say Jake, if Big Jake was lending like that as you say, how come the lending business didn't grow or how come it didn't grow or expand like that? I'm going to tell you guys, my dad is nothing like me, my dad was literally doing it for survival. I'm doing what I am doing to stand on my dad's shoulders. I wouldn't be where I am right now without my dad planting that business seed inside of me.

Dad tell your purpose on why you did it and why you wanted to stay low?

Big Jake: The bigger you grow, the more eyes you will have on you. Basically you find more problems. Like I said, I like to stay up under the radar.

Lil Jake: You told me, son – I didn't do it to get rich.

Big Jake: Oh no, I didn't do it to get rich. I did enough just to keep me like easy and laid back.

Lil Jake: Like I tell you guys all the time. Do not allow me or anyone to make you feel bad that you have to have the nicest stuff. My dad saw me make crazy decisions when I came out of college making good money. I can't say I am the kid that complained that my dad wasn't around, he didn't teach me about finances. **No!** My dad preached to us all the time about finances, make sure you got enough cushion and always prepare for a rainy day and when you are thriving make sure you have your money saved. So these are things that my dad taught me. These are some of the biggest things and why I am trying to teach you guys about passive income and being able to do for self. You want to start reserving money just in case your job lays you off! It can happen. Dad talk about your experience.

Big Jake: A lot of times we have in our mindset that we are going to be at this company for ever and ever, but in reality you have to say my time came up and I got laid off. A lot of times for a lot of people, like I said I am very outspoken

Lil Jake: Yeah he may not talk a lot but he will tell you how he feels **(LOL)**

Big Jake: I was telling people all the time that if you want to keep working where you are working you cant take the route I took by being outspoken.

Lil Jake: So that means you got to be quiet. Be quiet and work, if something make you mad, just go to your car, cuss in your car and come back smiling.

Big Jake: Yeah

Lil Jake: I mean think about your company … you would fire somebody if they were always outspoken – like confidence, but if you are somebody who is a confidence CEO or a company with confidence, you would appreciate someone who is outspoken that can help you fill the holes of your business versus being upset for some of you that are business owners just think about it. If somebody is willing to work there and they have been there for years, and they need to speak out about certain problems that your company is having – Listen!

Big Jake: Listen to them.

Lil Jake: Listen! Because they are coming from a place because they want to keep working there. You want these holes to be filled and they are probably good managers trying to look out for your business. Because if they are willing to speak to you and speak out against you with certain things that are going on with your business, they probably would speak up for you if you put them in positions. I just think it was crazy how they let my dad go and I think he was **18 years and 3 months** away from getting his pension. At **20 years** you would've had a lifetime pension?

Big Jake: Right

Lil Jake: I just thought it was really weird of how close he was to his lifetime pension, as everyone else was opting out and taking their 401K packages. He was literally right there at the cusp of being taken care of with a pension with all the years that he put in at this specific company. The reason why we are teaching you these strategies is so that you can generate passive income. You guys know me and I am never talking about getting rich, but what I am talking about is to find the best version of yourself and the best version of yourself is not in cars. I tried that. It is not in nice places, I tried that. It is not in the clothes that you purchased, I tried that too. The best version of yourself is understanding what makes you happy and staying in your zone.

And that is one thing that my dad taught me – he made that passive income, he had a little bit of a habit, but if you understand finances and you understand money, you can take these passive strategies that we are teaching you and start to stack and save your reserve. You can use this money to save and buy your house, without using a bank. All of these strategies are important for you to understand so that you do not have to use the bank and that is the KEY! We want you to become the lender, we want you to be the banking system for your family and for your life. But in order for you to do that – you have to put yourself in position to be able to stop becoming so dependent on the banking system and decide to do the very same thing that the banking system is doing for you. The lending business – you don't have to do it forever, you can do it just to get enough of what you need. And when you get what you need you can stop. Dad is there anything that you want to leave people with in their lending business?

Big Jake: No

Lil Jake: Any strategies? Any advice?

Big Jake: Nope (with a huge smile)

Lil Jake: You don't have no advice?

Big Jake: Nope (continues to smile)

Lil Jake: Somebody out there is a young Jake – wants to be just like you, and you have no advice to tell him?

Big Jake: Be patient and do it correctly.

Lil Jake: OK be patient and do it correctly because it doesn't happen overnight, right dad?

Big Jake: No it doesn't happen overnight. Like I said it is different if you are advertising your business out there and basically you are creating problems. But if you are going by word of mouth, it is a slow process. I always believe with word of mouth you get loyal people that will actually try to do the right thing. A lot of times you going off someone else word and they are trusting you off that and I recommend it then, so you know I always thought word of mouth was the best thing.

Lil Jake: So you would advise people to stick with word of mouth if you want to stay good?

Big Jake: Yes

Lil Jake: Stick with the word of mouth from **OG Lending Big Jake** to the **Imposter Jake** – he told you to stick with the word of mouth and stay under the radar and learn how to stay within your legal rights. We are not a legal team but get with somebody that is in your legal world and make sure that your contracts are good. We are not tax professionals so make sure that you get with your tax person to make sure that you are good because we do not want you to be facing jail and say that **OG Jake and Imposter Jake** told you anything. We want to make sure that you at least have strategies that can teach you how to be as independent as you can so that you do not have to use the bank. Let me tell you family – you can be the lender, you just got to decide to do it Peace!

Made in the USA
Middletown, DE
28 May 2023